MW00583922

Know the cycles of Moor
**Understand your past, your prese**
**create your future and gr**

*With this powerful book....unlock doors to perception and increase self-awareness...Tapping into the magical power of the Moon and its cycles can bring great comfort adn connect us to an ancient unifying force, something everyone, everywhere has shared for all time.*
—Jim Barnes, *Independent Publisher Highlighted Title Review*, June '05

*Throughout this captivating book, Maria provides an insightful depth of detail...This book is a "must have" for your personal library, as you will find yourself referring to it again and again.*
—Kathryn Fuller for Covenant of the Goddess, *Midsummer '05*

*If you use astrology at any level, regardless of your current expertise, I will just about guarantee you'll use this book and CD. Consider this a must-have!*
—Donna Van Toen, *NCGR Memberletter*, June '05

*Maria's inner awareness flows through the pages, drawing you ever deeper into lunar consciousness. Even as an experienced astrologer, I was led to new revelations about this subject as old as time. I highly recommend it for any reader who wants to know more about their hidden nature, even if you know nothing of astrology. You will be richly rewarded.*
—Terry Lamb, author of *Born to Be Together*

*A lyrical guide to weaving the rhythms of the Moon into the daily fabric of your life by attuning yourself to the flow of the Moon Goddess' cycles of ever-renewing.* —Demetra George, *Author of Asteroid Goddesses and Mysteries of the Dark Moon*

*Psychology has taught us that people have cycles and rhythms in their lives. Astrology helps us to identify some of those cycles. Maria Kay Simms has created a clear guide to lunar cycles ...The Moon is a key to our emotional life and each of its phases represents different spiritual tasks. This book will show you how to correlate the cycles of the Moon with events, feelings and interactions in your life. For people who want to "walk the talk" (live their values fully), Moon Tides, Soul Passages is a very helpful tool.*

—Maritha Pottenger, author of *Easy Astrology Guide* and *Unveiling the Future*

# Other Books by Maria Kay Simms

*Fashion Kit,* Troubador Press, 1972 (as Maria Sullivan)

*Twelve Wings of the Eagle,* ACS Publications, 1989

*Search for the Christmas Star* (with Neil F. Michelsen),
ACS Publications,1989

*Dial Detective,* ACS Publications, 1989

*Dial Detective, Revised Second Edition,*
Cosmic Muse Publications, 2001

*Your Magical Child,* ACS Publications, 1994, 1996

*The Witch's Circle* (formerly *Circle of the Cosmic Muse*),
Llewellyn Publications, 1994 and 1996

*Future Signs: How to Make Astrological Predictions,*
ACS Publications, 1996

*Millenium: Fears, Fantasies and Facts* (with others),
ACS Publications, 1998

*A Time for Magick,* Llewellyn Publications, 2001

# Moon Tides,
# Soul Passages

## Maria Kay Simms

**2006**
**Starcrafts Publishing**
Exeter, New Hampshire

# Moon Tides, Soul Passages

SECOND EDITION, Revised
Second printing 2006

FIRST EDITION
First printing 2004

Cover: Maria Kay Simms
Paintings by Maria Kay Simms and Molly A. Sullivan
Graphic Illustrations: Maria Kay Simms
Book Design: Maria Kay Simms

*Moon Tides* software, © 2004, 2006 by Maria Kay Simms and Rique Pottenger.
Programming of *Moon Tides* software by Rique Pottenger

**System requirements for the *Moon Tides* CD:**
Windows 95 and above
Disk space required for install: 10MB if JPL ephemeris is run from the CD
260 MB for full installation including JPL ephemeris
(For Power Macintosh requirements, see Appendix I)

Library of Congress Control Number: 2006903632


ISBN 978-0-9762422-1-5
ISBN 0-9762422-1-4


Published by **Starcrafts Publishing**, Starcrafts LLC
PO Box 446, Exeter, NH 03833-0446
http://www.starcraftspublishing.com

Printed in the United States of America

**Dedicated**

in loving and grateful memory

to


**Zipporah Pottenger Dobyns, Ph.D.**

(1921-2003)


whose inspiration

led me to a deeper understanding

of the

evolutionary process of living

through the

phases of my Moon

# Acknowledgments

At the top of my list of those to whom I am grateful for the influence and assistance that led toward my writing of this book is the late, great astrologer, Zipporah Dobyns, Ph.D, who first inspired me with the great significance of the lunar phase cycle. A close second on my list is her son, Rique Pottenger, whose programming of *Moon Tides* software has made my preparatory research for this book infinitely easier and will also contribute greatly to its value for readers.

Many others have helped with both my process and the production of this book. With deep gratitude, I especially acknowledge: Deane Driscoll, Zita Christian, Tom Canfield, Judi Vitali and Stephanie Clement for reviewing my manuscript in process and providing both encouragement and useful editorial suggestions; Joanne O'Brien and Susan Lacey for their assistance in testing and their suggestions for improvement during the early stages of software design; Jason Bennington for production design on my First Edition and assistance with files for this edition; the late Lois Rodden and programmer Mark McDonough of AstroDatabank for providing their superior research tool that has become indispensable for this astrological writer, Astro Communications Services for permission to utilize calculation routines in the ACS system for software design, my daughter Molly Sullivan for permission to print images of her paintings, David Mosley for permission to print lyrics to his song in Chapter 9, and authors Maritha Pottenger, Terry Lamb, and Demetra George for graciously agreeing to provide pre-publication reviews. Thank you to Lisa Vasher and Stephanie Reedy of McNaughton & Gunn for helpfulness and patience with my preparation of this Second Edition. I'm grateful to all the many unnamed people whose sharing of their personal charts and anecdotes with me over the years enabled me to provide a dimension to this book's interpretive material that could never have been achieved from public figure examples alone. Thank you to the readers of my First Edition, especially those who were totally new to astrology. Their feedback has guided a few clarifying additions to this new edition. Last, but certainly not least, I am thankful to my husband Jim Jossick and my next-door neighbor Jessie York for all the times they listened to me and provided encouragement during the sometimes frustrating process of birthing this book from my initial manuscript to what you now hold in your hands.

# Table of Contents

## Paintings and Illustrations

# About the Programmer
# of *Moon Tides* Software

**Rique Pottenger** was born September 16, 1949 in Tucson, Arizona at 6:18 am. He has a B.Sc. in Math and Astronomy from the University of Arizona and an M.S. in Computer Science from UCLA. Though never formally trained in astrology, he has absorbed quite a bit of it from his mother, Zipporah Dobyns, Ph.D, and his sister, Maritha Pottenger. Rique, who has has been a programmer for more than 30 years, worked for Astro Computing Services/ACS Publications from 1984 to 2004. Following the 1990 passing of Neil F. Michelsen, founder of ACS, Rique assumed responsibility for the maintenance and improvements in Astro's production systems, programmed the *Electronic Astrologer* software series, maintained and improved the ACS Atlas data base, and programmed updates and revisions to Michelsen's highly popular *American Ephemeris* series.

Now semi-retired, Rique continues to do astrological programming for a small list of clients. He lives in Opelika, Alabama, with his beloved wife, Zowie Wharton and their two cats. In their spare time they work at home-improvement projects (both have lots of Virgo), play computer games on their home network, and do puzzles together.

# About the Author

**Maria Kay Simms** has led a varied career life as artist, astrologer, author and businesswoman. Born November 18, 1940, 8:01am, Princeton, IL, she began her career as an artist (B.F.A., Illinois Wesleyan U.), at first teaching and later as a gallery painter and commercial illustrator, one assignment of which became her first book, an art kit for young girls. She began studying astrology in the '70s and for a time combined her interests in Mystic Arts, a metaphysical book, art and crafts shop. In the late '80s, while she was Art Director of ACS Publications in San Diego, her first astrology books
were published. After the 1990 death of her husband, ACS founder Neil F. Michelsen, Maria became president of ACS, serving until 1998, when she sold the company, moved to New Hampshire and remarried. From 1999-2004 she served as Chair of National Council for Geocosmic Research, Inc. (NCGR). Maria is certified as a professional consulting astrologer by NCGR and by American Federation of Astrologers, and she is a member of Asssociation of Professional Astrologers International (APAI).

With this book, her eighth as solo author, Maria combines the most powerful of astrological cycles for understanding one's innermost soul passages—the lunar phase cycle—with the Goddess spirituality of her experience as a Wiccan High Priestess. Maria's Circle of the Cosmic Muse is affiliated with Covenant of the Goddess, through which she has a legal ministry. She is also an ordained minister through Los Angeles Community Church of Religious Science.

At home in New Hampshire, Maria enjoys the full flow of the seasons with her large family, loves having time to paint in oils once again, and is collaborating with daughter, Molly Sullivan, in publishing art products from their paintings—some of which you'll see reproduced in this book.

*Yes, Eve would surely eat from the Tree of Knowledge...*
*and why not, after all?*

*She a Tree,* pen & ink drawing by Maria Kay Simms

# Introduction

## A Look at the Sky...

Astrologers really ought to put aside their charts, turn off their computers and go outside much more often to look at the sky. Ought to? It's more than that. We **need** to! I remember a night when that thought "came home" to me especially. Thanks to the astronomy column I'd happened to read in my local paper, rather more than my own foresight as an astrologer, I was aware that this night would be the first visit of the Moon to one of five of the planets visible to the naked eye, and that during the rest of this month, she would visit each of the others in turn.

Early evening that night, from the front deck of our home in seacoast New Hampshire, my husband and I looked up at the slender crescent Moon just above the trees to the west. Venus, with her bright white light, was easy to spot quite close to Moon. So very beautiful they were! Looking back along the southern sky to our left, we could make out what was surely the reddish light of Mars not far away. Jupiter was also easy to spot—he'd been a standout among most other lights in the night sky for months. We are fairly sure that another light, not quite so bright, but at what looked to be the likely place in between Mars and Jupiter where I knew it ought to be was Saturn.[1]

As I gazed at Moon and Venus, so closely conjunct in the sky, and then went outside again each night in the days after that to watch the Moon both gradually wax in light and then conjoin each of the other planets, I reflected on the beauty, the majesty and the order of it all, and how much more intimately connected I felt to Cosmos and Earth out here in Nature. These feelings had grown enormously since I'd moved beyond using books, charts and computers to apply the techniques of astrology to correspondences within my own life and the lives of others, toward an ever-increasing emphasis upon living my astrology through my spiritual path.

Looking at the sky was a soul experience. Learning to look at and understand astrological glyphs arranged on a chart is another matter entirely. Both, I believe, are essential to becoming an astrologer, for when we apply planetary positions to people, we are interacting with souls, a responsibility that cannot be taken lightly.

Though I've intensely studied technical astrology, I know that my core reason for studying it has always been mostly about my quest for spiritual understanding. Over the years I've found myself taking an ever simpler approach and finding deeper insights in the process. A major reason for my transfer of emphasis from complex technique to a profound appreciation of the most basic astrological concepts has emerged through experiencing astrology by working in ritual celebration of natural cycles, especially of the Moon.

## About this Book and the *Moon Tides* Software

This book is about the Moon and her phases—natal, progressed and transiting—plus her role in eclipse phenomena. Other than references to Sun and Earth, quite necessary to lunar phenomena, you'll find very little mention of any other planet. I intend this work to have the simplicity and the clarity to be of benefit to a reader who has never before worked with astrology, but also to offer sufficient depth about its subject to be of use to serious students and to my professional colleagues. With each interpretive section I have referred to various  public figures as examples of how the interpretations have worked within their lives. My source for verification of the accuracy of birth data for all public figures used as examples, and also for many of the dates I've cited for events in their lives, is the software and/or the website of *AstroDatabank*. (See Appendix III.) Biographical information derived from sources other than *AstroDatabank* or my own memory  are cited within the text or in footnotes.

Inside the back cover is a CD containing a Windows software program, designed for me by Rique Pottenger. It is very easy to install and use. You can also run it on a Macintosh computer (I do) if you have *Virtual PC* (from Microsoft) installed. *Moon Tides* enables you to enter your date, time and place of birth and then print simple one-page reports listing everything you need to know to apply the interpretations in this book to your own natal and progressed horoscope or that of anyone else whose birth information you have. You can also print two pages listing current lunar phases and eclipses for one year, plus the Sabbat dates for the eight solar holidays. Instructions for getting started with the software are in Appendix I. See pages 190 and 219, with Chapters 7 and 8, for examples of using the report.

**Your Birth Time—What if you don't know it?**

If you are a beginner and don't yet know your precise birth time, I urge you to obtain it. Though most of this book's technique works well even if birth time is not known, some sections will be unreliable, particularly House of Moon and to a lesser extent Moon Sign. The phase cycle will work quite well in terms of evolutionary pattern and approximate times of change, but the exact dates for phase change will be off. Since the 1930s all birth records in the United States should have included time of birth. If you don't know yours, contact the office in your city or county seat where you'd go if you needed a birth certificate. Make sure to specify that you want the time, because some offices may complete only the short birth certificate form rather just photocopying the birth record and won't note the time because it isn't required for such things as passports. The time is almost surely in their records, though. I found that out years ago when I marched into my birthplace's county seat office and insisted on seeing their big book of records. The time of my birth was only four minutes off from my mother's memory, but to an astrologer, that makes a difference! Alternatively, try an Internet search. I tried Google, typed in "how to find birth records," and found services that will search for you, plus state web sites that offer their own search capacities.

**Natural Astrology and Neopagan Spirituality**

Beyond providing Moon theory and examples illustrating it, I want to tell you a little about where I'm "coming from," something I think that any reader of astrological interpretation ought to know about who wrote it. Every author writes to some degree from personal perspective no matter how objective they may think they are.

In my own personal map of the sky at the moment and from the place of my birth, Moon is in Cancer, the sign she rules, a water sign. Sun is in Scorpio—more water. I was born on the final day of a Full Moon phase. The dry seas of the Moon above, visible as the depressions that cause us to imagine a face on the Moon, are called "marias," as the root word for water in so many languages is "mar." Maria, Mari, del Mar, the sea…her tides ebb and flow, pulled by the Moon. Some say we are given our names for a reason, or that whatever name we are given, we grow into it. I wonder.

Looking back, I can ruefully reflect on how truly my life has reflected the interpretations I've read about my own Full Moon phase. Learn from relationships? Oh, yes, and still learning. I've now passed through two progressed Full Moon phases, with major complex turning points each time. This book is primarily written near the end of my progressed Disseminating Phase, a time to teach what you have learned, so says traditional wisdom, and so I shall attempt to do just that.

This book, while based on over 25 years of observing how Moon and her phases are reflected in life, also flows from my own continuing soul passages, inextricably entwined with an instinctively developing world view that has become my spiritual path. I hope to share with you my sense of an inherently natural astrology, its connection with spirituality, the sacred feminine and a concept of Wholeness encompassing that which is above and that which is below. Most of all, I seek to inspire you with the magical tides of the Moon in your own life, from her sign at the time of your birth through her cyclically changing phases as they are reflected in your own personal and spiritual journey.

"Nature," so says the dictionary on my desk, "is the material world and its phenomena, the forces that control that phenomena…the world of living things." Though we tend to think of "Mother Earth" as Nature, sometimes it seems we are all too prone to think of the cosmos as something beyond, and somehow in control. I speculate that this is an outgrowth of the still dominant paradigm of patriarchal religion that God and heaven are "above," transcendent to Nature and superior to it. The "stars" appear to be "above" from our perspective, but they are only part of Nature, the material universe, just as Earth and earthlings are. Though some causal effects of the Moon on the tides have been established, it is a far and completely unproven stretch to pose that the planets cause or control the details of human behavior and thought that common astrological chatter often tends to imply.

The concept of deity as being within Nature, rather than "above" it, is basic to Pagan spirituality. "Pagan" is a word that has morphed through history and cultural changes. To newly Christianized Rome *paganus* meant country folk, the hicks who were too unsophisticated to understand the new urban religion. Later *paganus* gained a new connotation of "civilian" as opposed to *miles*, the "soldiers of Christ."[2] Eventually, Christian dominance led to dictionary definitions of "pagan" as "one who has no religion." More recently, my new dictionary has modified the definition to merely "one who is not a Christian, Muslim or Jew."[3] Oh, so anyone who does not adhere to a religion derived from the patriarch Abraham is a Pagan? Interesting, but I suspect that many would dispute that definition.

The "country bumpkins" of ancient Rome lived close to the land and respected it. They knew the herbs of healing and the lore of folk magic handed down through generations. Living by the cycles of seasons, they observed the celestial changes that corresponded with earth changes and marked the times for planting, for harvest, for the hunt. Spirits lived within Nature, elfin and fairie folk. The Goddess was Mother Earth, and she was seen in every plant and creature. So pervasive was the mother concept of the divine that the Christian hierarchy had little choice but to create a veneration of Mary the Mother in hopes she might suffice as substitute, just as they co-opted the popular Pagan festivals and reimaged them as Christian holy days. Various Pagan deities were also reimaged as saints.

The legacy and lore of paganus came from much older times, in stories and myths of oral tradition. Evidence that divine Spirit was seen within Nature has been found in cave paintings of great antiquity, and ancient carvings of the female form seem inescapably suggestive of a veneration of the feminine as divine. All the way back to the stone age notched bones correspond to the lunar cycle, providing evidence that ancient people looked to the sky, and in particular the Moon, for the timing of their lives. Yes, perhaps they saw the Moon and stars as divine, but no more so than the spirits of Nature all around them. All above and below are part of our natural world. Pagan spirituality sees God—Goddess, by any name called—not as a transcendent entity set apart from Nature, but rather as immanent within the life force. That force is an interconnected energy in which all entities within Nature are both individual and also aspects of the whole. We all have the ability to access this energy, for we are part of it and it is within us. The energy, or power, is neither inherently "good" nor "bad"—how can it be when it is All? How one feels, draws upon and uses energy is largely a matter of choice. Though an ancient Pagan may not have explained it in quite those terms, this Neopagan can.[4]

## Cosmos to Earth: Mirror or Reflection?

Astrology is at the ancient roots of both science and religion—it may be the oldest, or nearly the oldest, of both. Astrology, so essential for timing, was studied for omens and portents, and as ancient humanity saw deity in the plants and animals of Earth, they also saw deity in the Sun, the Moon and the stars. Increasingly sophisticated methods of observing and predicting celestial movement over the ages became science, but in some cases, it was a science that first existed to serve the needs of religion. Certainly the science of astronomy evolved to serve the needs of astrology.

Astrology studies the correspondences and cycles of Nature, earth and cosmos, and all entities within, seeing in them a living spirituality— purpose, guidance, past, present, future, eternal cycles. In a Neopagan view of astrology, all Gods are respected, including the Gods of a science that studies the natural world while denying the existence of spirituality within it simply because Spirit cannot be proved by mechanistic and statistical methodology. The Neopagan view of astrology even respects the Gods of religions whose adherents deem astrology evil because of tenets that deny all concepts of God save one.

Astrology sees within the cosmos a vast macrocosm. From our perspective on Earth, we can see in it a Divine Order of dependable cycles that with scientific study are predictable into the far distant future. Do we understand it all? Of course not. The Whole is so vast, so complex that always something new can be discovered. Still, each discovery continues to fit a pattern of

Order, and then becomes part of that which we can study and predict when it will again repeat and what theme is likely to correspond with it. Here on Earth, in our physical bodies and with our minds, we see correspondence with the cosmic order, and our understanding of our mundane and spiritual world develops.

In the words attributed to the ancient Hermes Trismegistus,

*As above, so below...*

Each microcosm, each living entity, reflects the macrocosm. In the signs of the sky we see corresponding signs on Earth. But that is not all. The Hermes observation continues...

*...as within, so without.*
*As the Universe, so the Soul*

I see the Hermetic concept as that of deity within. Each One reflects the Whole, just as the Whole is the essence of each One, and all are eternal living aspects of each other, forming and reforming, dying and being born again, in an ever-changing cycle that is of the Whole. One breathes in the Whole and breathes out to the Whole, and the Whole breathes back. Which is the mirror, and which is the reflection? Does it matter? Each of us is a little Universe onto self. We perceive the Universe, the Whole... God...as a reflection of our own eternal souls, in whatever our focus is at a given moment. So, if we change our perception, if we smile into the cosmic mirror instead of frowning, will it reflect that change upon us? Think about that. Has the Universe/Whole/God caused our change? Or has it simply reflected it? Or have WE changed it?

## The Power is Within!

Certainly things happen outside our personal control—external events affecting the masses, personal events in the lives of others close to us, weather conditions, economic cycles—many things that happen to which we must respond. How one responds is a matter of one's personal choice and personal ability to control that choice. Individuals may be predisposed to respond in certain ways by upbringing, heredity, environment and birth chart, but none of those factors are absolutes through which a given individual is fated to a predetermined response. Even the birth chart itself, as well as the hereditary and environmental factors that can be read within the chart, may be a choice. The incoming soul chooses the moment of birth and a place of birth, knowing that the personality tendencies, hereditary and environmental conditions, as well as the future cycles revealed by the resulting astrological chart, provide the very best pattern needed for continued spiritual growth. Why not? I can't prove this is so, but I choose to believe it to be so. It's a plausible idea, and in my opinion, much more plausible than others offered by linear religions that preach one soul for one body in one short life from birth to death, followed by an eternity in heaven or hell.

Everything we see in Nature is cyclical. Why should we be linear? Why should God (whatever he, she or it is perceived to be) create a soul and then give it only the infinitesimal speck of time and space of one human life span in the vast Universe to learn enough to warrant heaven or hell for eternity?  Grace alone, or lack of it? Sounds like a pretty capricious and unfeeling God to me. Let's replay that down-grading of Eve for wanting to eat of the Tree of Knowledge. The lady was both spunky and wise. The God of Genesis may have been scripted to disapprove of Eve, but the Neopagan Goddess and God would love her!

Heaven and hell are spoken of as if they are places outside of physical reality where a soul goes to be rewarded or punished. This is a convenient belief for religious leaders who seek power and control, but it denies Wholeness by creating a reality where the soul is forever separate. Despite teachings of an omnipresent deity, it implies a primary concept of transcendent deity, always "out there" and never fully knowable. The Neopagan concept I prefer is one of immanence, of deity not separate from the physical universe, but inherent with it. In this, it can be said that the divine is truly within.

Reincarnation  (body recycling by eternal soul!) in some form seems a far more believable idea to me than the one body-one soul idea that dominates the main established religions of our culture. I won't presume to describe exactly what form it takes merely because I just don't know. I have had a few personal experiences that have strongly suggested to me that somehow soul consciousness or spirit (call it what you will) lives beyond the death of the physical body—a feeling of presence of a loved one who had passed on, the shock of recognition of one well known to me whom I'd just met in this life, vivid dreams that seemed like lives lived before. Many of you, I'm sure, could relate similar experiences. Skeptics, citing science, may call this wishful thinking. So be it. Let them. Many things science has at one time deemed impossible have become common. I don't need to know the details of what lies beyond—that time will come soon enough.

Meanwhile, in this present moment in which I live, I have choices to make...and so do you. What about destiny? Fate? How much choice do we have? I don't know that either, so I won't pretend I do. One thing I do know, though, is this: regardless of how much of our destiny may have been determined for us, or chosen by us before entering this life, we cannot be sure what it is. No matter how highly developed one's skills at prediction may be, have you ever heard of a forecaster of any type who was accurate each and every time? I certainly haven't.

I enjoy looking ahead and trying to speculate on the future as much as any astrologer. It's one very significant reason for why we study this stuff! I've done pretty well with it, too, on everything from world events to my less-than-objective attempts to look ahead for myself. Sometimes my attempts at personal forecasting have been useful for decisions that later proved to be for the best. At other times, what actually happened (though admittedly, when I looked back on it, may have fit the general theme of the astrological phenomena of the time) took an unexpected twist—quite different than what I'd anticipated.

The way I see it is this: what we think will happen in the future is but a facet of the present moment. We can't live in the future moment until we get there. So, in this present moment we can choose...what? To anticipate, plan, plot, take action to avoid or take other actions to encourage. We can be elated, fearful, morose, excited, worry, worry, worry...but we are still in the present, are we not? And we don't yet know whether what we anticipate will, in fact, be our future. No matter what we do, or don't do, about it, the choice must be made now. Choosing to spend our time and energy worrying is one option. Choosing to ignore and disregard the signs and signals is another. A third option is the one that I've personally found to be the most effective: pay attention to the basic themes of the current patterns of the planets, and then choose to express them according to your preferred potential outcome. It is important to understand that all astrological factors have multiple options, every one of them.None have only one meaning, and none have only a "good" or a "bad" potential. Within a generalized theme, many manifestations are possible.

When you accept and own the power with you, your knowledge and use of astrology can become an important tool of personal and spiritual growth. Rather than regarding the problem areas that show in your chart as reasons or excuses for how you behave, you'll think about how you can avoid their pitfalls, and even find that often what appeared to be weaknesses can be transmuted into strengths. Rather than dreading a "bad" cycle you see in your future, you'll project how that same cycle could be "good" for you, and frame your plans for it according to that choice. You learn that your sense of inner well being is not dependent upon any other person or circumstance, and that no person or thing outside yourself has the power to force you to feel sad or worried or afraid unless you, personally, permit it. I won't tell you that staying on this path is always easy, because it isn't. We all slip, at times, into patterns of thinking and behaving that we'd sworn to leave behind. But when we accept the responsibility for all that within, as well as our power to change, it becomes much easier to get back on the track we've chosen.

I've found that when I deliberately act according to what I consider to be the most favorable interpretation of my current astrological indicators, what actually "happens" more often than not turns out for the best. Once in a while, one of the more unfavorable options "happens," too. External events and the choices of others around us are often beyond our personal control, but they still affect us.Then, too, with the best of intent, we can still make mistakes. In such cases, what we can control is how we respond. Response is very often the key to making the best of any situation. In crisis situations, it is that which distinguishes the heroes and helpers from the hand wringers who are of no help to anybody, not even themselves.

## Moon and the Tides of Soul

Astrological symbolism associates the Moon with the element water, water being one of the four elements of the ancients (fire, earth, air, water). As the Moon pulls the tides of Earth's oceans, so is astrological Moon said to pull the tides of our emotions—our moods and feelings that ebb and flow. Astrology also sees the Moon as ruling memory. In this physical life memories both conscious and buried deep within our subconscious exert tidal pulls on our feelings often without our ability to identify the source. Those who believe, as I do, that consciousness in some form lived before this physical life and will live beyond it, also consider memory to include deep soul memories from wherever or whoever we may have been before. Soul is that which defines, for believers, the aspect of consciousness, of being, that transcends the physical body and connects with something far more vast, the mysterious power that we think of as divine.

The air element is most commonly associated with the mind and intellect: consciousness, logic, and rational thought. But, the Moon's watery realm is also that of the mind. I've often laughed to myself at the words "subconscious" and "unconscious," two terms often associated with the Moon. Both "sub" and "un" indicate something somehow inferior to just plain "conscious," and so it was believed for many centuries. This type of thinking was true enough in the generation in which I grew up, to the point that I, whose astrological chart is drenched with water symbolism and sparse in air, was driven to focus on what would today be termed as "left-brain" thinking, for that was the only way to succeed. Fortunately, current thinking recognizes and respects the importance and the value of the "right brain," home of the mysterious subconscious. The right brain is Moon territory, and in my experience and observation, its power is far from inferior. Think about it: how much of your thinking, or that of anyone else you know, is wholly objective logic, with no influence from past programming (memories, experiences, forgotten impressions) carried around inside unrecognized, but nevertheless directing what comes out as "logic?" One person's logical and objective observation is all too often another's prejudice or "attitude," and which is which (to you) depends on which one you are. Scientific advances often begin with a hunch—purely intuitive, realm of the Moon— and only later become the logical step-by-step process that tests and proves the hunch. Moon rules a very vital part of mind—the part least understood, mysterious, intangible, intuitive and very, very powerful. Soul is generally defined in dictionaries as the central or vital part of something, in the case of humanity, the vital animating principle.

In *Moon Tides, Soul Passages* I bring you my experience of the Moon in her ever-changing cycles through which we can see the ebb and flow of that deep vital inner evolutionary process of soul. In the vast complexity of astrology, this is only one symbol seen in one cycle of phases, but it is one that I've come to know as especially vital to understand and assimilate. As astrological techniques go, those covered in this book are among the simplest to learn—Moon by sign, house and phase, eight phases that you can see in the sky as each month goes by, and recognize in the longer-term process that unfolds as your life progresses. But technique alone is a left-brain thing and only the bare framework for what I hope to share with you. To know the tides of your Moon and corresponding soul passages is an inner process that unfolds through experience. I hope to motivate you, too, to experience living with the Moon, as you become more aware of her phases in the flow of your life through each month of current time and through 29-year repeating cycles of your life. May your reading of this book, while referring to your *Moon Tides* computer report, trigger personal memories and deep reflections on life patterns and soul passages of your past. Then, as you think about how the past flows to the present, you'll receive insights into how you might best direct your future. Most of all, it is my hope that what I offer you within this book will assist your inner process, the soul process that serves your personal and spiritual growth.

## Endnotes

[1]My reference for knowing where Saturn "ought to be" is an ephemeris, specifically *The American Ephemeris for the 21st Century* programmed by Neil F. Michelsen with revisions by Rique Pottenger. (see bibliography).

[2]Evolution of "Pagan" from Hines, Welch and Bacon, *Our Latin Heritage, Fourth Edition*, New York: Harcourt, Brace, Jovanovich, 1966.

[3]*The American Heritage Dictionary, Fourth Edition,* New York: Houghton-Mifflin, 2001

[4]Neopagan simply means "new" Pagan, referring to a revival of spirituality based on the immanence of divine spirit with the living Earth and all of Nature (the Universe). It is a general term encompassing a number of alternative spiritualities sharing similar core concepts, such as Wicca, feminist spirituality, various" new age" practices, eco-spiritualities, family craft traditions, and some Native American rites.

# Chapter One

# Moon and the Constancy of Change

In writing ritual, I've often included within the Charge of the Goddess— "the only constant is change." Where did I first hear that? I have no idea— it's said so often that it has become a cliché. It's such a simple statement, but so very, very true. The only thing that can absolutely be counted on in life is that sooner or later, things will change. Even rock is eventually worn down by the waves of the sea and changed in form.

My father often said, when anything seemed challenging or stuck, "Things can only get so bad, and then they get better. The wheel always turns." My father never called himself Pagan—though I've often thought that, at heart, he was, if Pagan can be defined as being attuned to and perceiving deity within Nature. He often said he felt closer to God in the forest than in church. He always had a large garden and often hunted. Nothing was wasted; the family ate everything he grew or caught. I remember standing at a window and observing him, elderly and retired, hold out birdseed in the palm of his hand, and the birds—a robin, a wren—flew to him, perched on his fingers and ate. His adage of the wheel was to him, as it became for me, nothing more than plain common sense.

Change is inevitable, all around us and within us, noticeable in one thing or another in every year, every day, every moment. Since we obviously can't change the fact of change, why do we humans so often seem to resist and even fear it? What do we fear? Deep down, when we really observe what goes on around us and reflect back on our lives, we can see the truth of that simple common sense: "things can only get so bad and then they get better." The thing that we don't like to look at is the reverse, also true: things can only get so good before something else we don't like will happen. We can climb to the top of a mountain, but sooner or later (lacking wings), we'll have to begin the trek downward.

The scary part is not the fact of change—we all know that is inevitable—but is, instead, our lack of control over it. We seek control by fiercely trying to hold onto what we have, and by trying to predict what may lurk ahead. Determination to hold on, no matter how firmly we plant our roots and remain stuck in one place, will be foiled (if nothing else) by the natural aging process. Prediction is, to say the least, an inexact science. Whether we speak of predicting the weather, financial or political trends, or any other form of mundane forecasting or of using astrology or psychic flash, sometimes a prediction is right (or partially right) and sometimes it is all wrong. Absolutely, totally right is rare, and even then, can best be called an educated guess or sheer luck. Still, we keep trying to outguess the future. But, much more often than not, what actually happens involves many more factors and nuances that we did not expect over and above those we did.

The effectiveness of astrology in making those "educated guesses" and then being able to use them to help ourselves or others is what drives most of us, maybe all of us, to study it. Psychological and/or spiritual astrologers may feel uncomfortable with that statement, but even if they claim not to use "prediction" they still do—and I'll bet they all look ahead with their own charts to see what might be expected, even if they take care never to forecast for clients. The sheer fact of using a chart of the moment a person is born to extrapolate anything about how that person's personality might develop or life unfold is an act of prediction.

Though a lot of astrological energy does and will continue to be put toward trying to improve methods of prediction, most modern astrologers (even those who specialize in forecasting methods) will agree that prediction, alone, is not helpful and may even be damaging, if understood in a fatalistic manner. In order to learn to manage our mundane lives effectively, each of us has to accept responsibility for our own decisions and the consequences of them. The only true security in life is that which we build within, enabling us to both initiate action and respond to what is initiated from outside ourselves, as well as to handle the aftermath of either in a manner that serves our ability to continue on, having grown through the experience.

Some of this is an expansion of the section within my Introduction under the heading "The Power is Within." If you skipped that, please re-read it because the whole issue of personal responsibility, choice and empowerment is at the core of everything I have to share with you. Prediction is only helpful if it is personally empowering and thereby serves one's inner strength and security to deal with the inevitability of change—initiate it when appropriate, flow with it when that is appropriate, cope effectively with it even when we didn't choose it, and sometimes, just gracefully accept it.

## The Moon, Signs and Seasons

One way the Moon constantly changes is by her movement through the signs of the zodiac, all twelve of them every month of the year. In fact, she makes nearly 13 passages through the zodiac every year, traveling through each sign faster than the Sun or any of the planets. At the beginning of each lunar month she catches up with the Sun and becomes the New Moon, conjunction of Sun and Moon. The New Moon, of course, is in the sign of the Sun, and the double emphasis on that sign is said to have meaning in terms of what we all experience that month. The Sun's sign, now given extra emphasis by the addition of the Moon, is a seasonal theme.

The signs of the tropical (western) zodiac derive the larger part of their interpretive themes from seasonal mythology of the parts of the world where the system was developed, that is, northern hemisphere locales where there are significantly noticeable seasonal changes. Though this may not have been entirely true in the beginning, I think it evolved that way over time. Once archetypes are projected onto the sky, they are elaborated over the years through observations that are again projected until both projections and the observations become predictably "true" even if the archetypes originally based on seasonal themes don't really fit the season where one lives.

Astrology is, for the most part, an interpretation of how our solar system, as archetypes projected onto the bodies within it, can be applied to life on Earth. In truth, astrology is an Earth-centered system, though of course we now know (as the ancients did not) that Earth and all other bodies in this system are orbiting the Sun, rather than the Sun orbiting us. Still, from our vantage point on Earth, it looks like the Sun and other planets are moving around us. Astronomy calls this "apparent" motion. It seems apparent that we, on Earth, are the center of the Universe. In a way, it's quite true. Perception is relative to one's point of view. Each of us, in our own perception, sees the entire cosmos and everything in it from the vantage point of who and where we are.

Chapter Two will be all about the signs of the Moon. Probably everyone reading this knows about Sun signs, but some may not be so familiar with the sign of Moon in their birth chart. Then, because there is some controversy about the signs, I've occasionally heard students speculate that since the signs don't fit the constellations any longer, maybe we should be using the sidereal signs associated with eastern systems such as Vedic astrology. That is, of course, a valid choice, but know that this book is based on the signs of western astrology. I prefer the western system in part because I began with it, but Goddess knows I've changed many things in my life, so why not this? It's because western (properly called "tropical") astrology is defined by the seasons, its zodiac measured from 0° Aries at Spring Equinox. My spiritual path is thoroughly meshed with the seasons and with rituals based on seasonal mythology. Personally, I find the seasonal symbolism to be deeply entrenched within how the sign personalities are described. The spiritual rituals that I celebrate, and design with astrological themes as their basis, are highly seasonal, so the tropical system with its emphasis on seasons just feels right to me.

Of course each sign description comes from more than seasonal themes alone, but I think it is fair to say that at least as much, if not considerably more, derives from seasonal ideas than from the creatures of the constellational zodiac for which the signs are named. Each sign also derives meaning from the elemental and modal families that are also seasonally derived. Each quarter begins with a sign of initiative, called Cardinal, followed by one that is stable and firmly established, Fixed, followed by one that is clearly

Mutable or changeable, blending the season that is passing with the one that is emerging.

Aries, the first Cardinal sign, is of the element Fire, appropriate for the season in which waxing sunlight "springs" forward, active and bright. Cancer, the Cardinal sign of the summer solstice, is of the element Water, symbolizing the feeling and flow of emotion. At the height of summer, with sunlight culminating and warming Mother Earth who bursts with life from her womb, Water as the initiator fits nicely. Libra, the Cardinal sign of the autumnal equinox, expresses the element Air. This one isn't so obvious, but of the four it could be thought ("thought," mental function is Air) that since just ahead lies increasing darkness, plans must be made to prepare for winter. Finally, Capricorn, the sign of winter solstice, the longest and darkest night of the year, is of the element Earth, the most dense and dark of all the elements. Earth signs demand resourceful, practical determination, all of which are needed to pass successfully through the dark to the light once again. Each of the modal triads that make up a quarter has a different element, all progressing in order with the fourth one the lead sign of the next quadrant. These elemental and modal groupings will be handled more dramatically with stories from Goddess mythology within the next chapter on the signs of the Moon.

Some sign interpretations derive from the zodiac creature for which the sign was named, but others clearly derive from the season so much that one has to wonder if the seasonal theme was imposed upon the archetype of the creature, rather than the other way around.

The following interpretations are derived more from seasons than from constellational creatures. I'll take each sign in order, identify it by element and mode and offer a few key words or ideas associated with it that relate to the season in which the Sun occupies that sign.

Sun, Moon and each of the planets in astrology has a specific function, and that function is described by the signs in a similar way that a noun or verb (the planet) is defined by adjectives and adverbs (the signs). Another way to put it is that Moon represents the function of emotion and the sign is the style with which that function is expressed. Simplistically, here's an example of contrast in style between our two first signs:

**Moon:** function—emotion
**Style:** Aries—emotionally impulsive; Taurus–emotionally calm
**Mars:** function—action
**Style:** Aries—acts assertively; Taurus—acts slowly

### Aries the Ram—Cardinal Fire, March 20-April 19
0° Aries marks the official beginning of spring and the first sign of the zodiac. From a point of equilibrium (equal days and nights), the Arian light "springs" forward: surging, instinctive, impulsive, risk-taking. Aries wants to be first, and is adventurous, courageous, pioneering, direct, energetic and assertive. (The Ram, if threatened, can point those horns down and "ram" forward, so certainly that image fits…but most sheep I've seen, be they ram or ewe, seem pretty placid more often than not.)

### Taurus the Bull—Fixed Earth, April 20-May 20
Spring season is now firmly and fully established. Steady, stubborn, patient, persistent and calm, Taurus holds on, Taurus wants comfort and security, is practical, stable and does not like to be rushed. A cow peacefully chewing her cud is more evocative of Taurus than a bull, though we do say that Taureans, if finally at long last provoked to anger, can rage like a bull. A "bull market" can certainly contribute to security needs, evoking an image of economic increase. Taurus is likely do well financially, but more likely through prudence and saving than through speculation. This is the time to plant crops with an eye toward abundant future harvest.

### Gemini the Twins—Mutable Air, May 21-June 20
Spring blends into summer. Adaptable, versatile, quick, flexible, restless, communicative, curious, spontaneous, indecisive, the Twins can be taken to mean a dual-sided or multi-faceted personality, but that alone doesn't say as much for the description of the sign as the fact of mutability. The first sign in the zodiac within each of the modes expresses that mode most emphatically (Aries is considered the most obviously Cardinal of the Cardinals, Taurus the most obviously Fixed of the Fixed). Indeed, some Gemini keywords are also used to define Mutability, itself. Here we have a reflection of change, not only in the weather, but also in the upbeat anticipation of major changes of activities that happen with the shift into summer.

**Cancer the Crab—Cardinal Water, June 21-July 22**
0° Cancer marks the beginning of summer. Emotional, sensitive, protective, moody, nurturing, sentimental, maternal and domestic, the Cancerian initiative supports life in all its forms, creating from the womb of deep feeling. Water feeds and nurtures, the source of life. From the crab's shell that protects its soft inside we can derive the vulnerability of Cancer, but it is from this season of life-giving power that we most fully see the Mother.

**Leo the Lion—Fixed Fire, July 23-August 22**
The height of summer's hot season, with crops maturing to early harvest. Bright fire of the Sun that sustains—generous, energizing and grand. Charismatic, fun-loving, magnanimous and proud and very much in the [spot] light, our bright hot sun of full summer calls for a regal symbol like the tawny Lion (or Lioness).

**Virgo the Virgin—Mutable Earth, August 23-September 22**
The signs of impending full harvest approach daily, and with them, change. Efficient, pragmatic, attentive to detail, service-oriented and conscious of health requirements, Virgo sees ahead to earthly changes to which she must attend, and takes responsibility seriously. Modesty, an imposition of patriarchal interpretations of the meaning of Virgin may or may not fit the earthy Goddess imaged in the stars with her grains of harvest's bounty.

**Libra the Balance—Cardinal Air, September 23-October 22**
0° Libra marks the beginning of autumn. The days and nights are again equal, but this time with knowledge that ahead lies increasing darkness. Cooperation and compromise, with fairness to all will be necessary in the season to come, when harvest must be brought in and shared. Diplomacy, charm, peacefulness and the ability to relate are all advantageous. Equilibrium and harmony must prevail and the tone is set through the initiative of Air, the mind.

**Scorpio the Scorpion—Fixed Water, October 23-November 21**
Water, like 'tis said of hell, may freeze over, but there's determination to survive.Darkness builds, intense, penetrating, secretive, mysterious and inscrutable. The veil to the beyond thins, and deep, watery emotional power seeks through inner sight to see beyond. Winter and darkness cannot be avoided, but can they be controlled? Perhaps. Shall the Scorpion sting,

or shall the spirit of Eagle (the higher symbol of Scorpio) soar above the watery depths? That is the mystery.

### Sagittarius the Archer—Mutable Fire, November 22-December 21
The change to winter approaches with acceptance but also with the will and spirit to light the way through. Around bright hearth fires the people gather, as with stories and festivity they seek to cheer. Optimistic, enthusiastic, idealistic and inspired, Sagittarius has utter faith and confidence that somehow goals will be reached. The archer's arrow shoots for the stars, energetic and always free in spirit.

### Capricorn the Goat—Cardinal Earth, December 22-January 19
0° Capricorn marks the beginning of winter. It is the longest night, and the waxing light is reborn, but is not yet visible and won't be for quite a while. No longer are expectations met with the cock-eyed optimism of the fiery spirit that saw winter ahead, but was not quite there. Reality has fully set in. The initiative of earthy practicality must now be realized in order to assure success in the seasons to come. Serious, disciplined, organized and authoritative with a "let's get down to business" attitude, Capricorn looks ahead, determines goals and works toward them diligently.

### Aquarius the Waterbearer—Fixed Air, January 20-February 17
Winter seems longest now, even toward the later days of the sign when days are noticeably lengthening and other hints raise hope of early spring…only to be dashed again with another blast of cold. Still, with knowledge gained through the sustaining power of Air, the mind, one can use this time to learn, to invent and to plan ahead. The bonds of winter can never chain our ability to think. Through thought, alone, all boundaries vanish. Though the Waterbearer is pictured pouring water, I think that what is truly being poured forth should be depicted as light-waves, the power of mind.

### Pisces the Fishes—Mutable Water, February 18-March 19
Ice melts and waters flow again with the changes that will lead to spring. We feel the change in every fiber of being, though not without the uncertainty of warmth one day and cold the next—warmth and light, then rain or perhaps another snow. Dreamy, confused, imaginative, impressionable and sensitive, an elusively mystical and ideal beauty is sought through vision or through escape. Soon it will be spring, but for now, the energy to push ahead is just not quite there. Beauty found within heals.

## The Moon in Cycles of Relationship and Change

In astrology, our Moon pulls on the tides of the seas, and on the fluids and soul within each of us. She is said to "rule" change, and this stems from observation of her constantly changing faces, observed by humanity since at least the Stone Age, as evidenced by lunar phases notched on ancient bones. It is rather ironic, then, that the constancy of her change became sufficiently predictable that people found security in learning to time their lives by her changes. They decided when to hunt, when to plant and when to do (or not do) all manner of other things necessary to daily life, all according to the Moon. And so the Moon also came to be associated with domesticity.

Though there have been Moon gods in the past—the "man in the Moon" is a vestige of that—and also Sun goddesses, astrology has defined Moon as feminine and Sun as masculine for at least 2000+ years, so in keeping with that, as well as the more common Wiccan tradition, I am associating Moon throughout this book with Goddess; Sun as God. Actually, the primary Mother Goddess image is our planet Earth, source of life, and by extension, Moon, the satellite of Earth.

There is always some difficulty in considering one astrological factor in isolation from the others, for each individual's personality and life reflect a complex blend of all of them that can best be seen in synthesis. Especially with the Moon, we can say little about her without also considering her relationship to Sun, for that is how we see her changing faces, by her reflection of Sun's light. The Moon is about relationship. The relationship of Sun and Moon is seen from the perspective of the third factor, Earth. So, all together, we have a triad of relationship, and most of what can be said about Moon interpretively involves all three, whether Earth and Sun are specifically mentioned or not. From our vantage point on Earth, we view the Moon as she reflects the light of the Sun in changing phases formed as Earth's shadow falls upon her.

We say in astrology that the Sun is consciousness, and Mercury, the planet most closely associated with mind and the intellect, is his messenger. Moon is deemed emotional, subconscious, unconscious—but this, too, is part of mind. Moon's traits are usually considered to be subjective, rather than objective, but in reflecting Sun's light back to Earth, we could say that she makes it objective, showing it in phases and in smaller, more palatable doses. Mercury may be a messenger, but Moon is the mediator, much in the same way as Mary, Mother of God, is seen as the gentle mediator whose appearances around the world then become sacred shrines. From widespread veneration and constant pleas for her to pray for us, Mary is apparently thought more compassionately approachable than the man-God she bore.

Sun is so very bright we can't look directly at him without permanent damage to our eyes. He is pure vibrant energy, generating the heat and light that is necessary for life on Earth. Earth is form, equally necessary for life. Without form, energy has no purpose. Without energy, form is inert and lifeless. The Moon may have once been part of Earth, it is said. Though in reality no longer a source of life, she is an extension of Earth Mother, a mediator conveying the message of Sun by reflecting his light and rendering it to Earth objectively and compassionately to the view of Earth's people. We might imagine Sun proclaiming, "I am light and vitality. Receive my energy so together we can create life and purpose for being." Earthlings respond, "Too much! To look right at you hurts. All that energy at once will burn me out. I need rest!" Sun sets, night falls and the Moon rises, saying, "Let me serve you. I will mediate by reflecting Sun's brightness in softer hues that you can look upon in comfort. I am approachable and I will show you his light in progressive stages so you will understand the flow of energy within you. Let me show you the seasons of your life."

## The Changing Lunar Phases and the Changing Seasons of Life

Sun, Moon and Earth together show you the seasons of your life, and the archetypical spirit, soul and body of all three live within you. Many phases of the changing faces of the Moon have been defined. You will find posters and calendars showing one slight change of the Moon pictured for every day, for the Moon's face is constantly changing. The word for month is moon-th, derived from the cycles of Moon from New Moon until New Moon, called a synodic month, and lasting 29.540589 mean (average) solar days. Various systems have been devised using lunar changes. The one I like best and find to be the most powerful in my life is a cycle of eight phases.

I find that any cycle of experience I could describe for you can be seen within an eight-fold cycle of transformation. We can see them in the phases of the Moon, in the cycles of Earth's seasons and in both short-term and long-term changes in our lives.

The Moon may be our Queen of Time within the great cosmic clock in the sky above us, but all around us the natural cycles of Mother Earth show us the same constancy and predictability of change. Seasons may vary from one climate to another, extreme in some, subtle in others, but no matter where you may be, cycles can be observed to follow a pattern of change along these lines:

1. initiation
2. emergence
3. growth
4. development
5. peak
6. demonstration
7. reorientation
8. completion

and then something new is initiated once again. This can perhaps be more clearly depicted in a cycle of plant life:

1. germination of seed beneath the ground
2. seed sprouts, becoming visible above ground
3. roots and stems develop
4. buds form
5. buds open into flowers
6. plant bears fruit
7. fruit ripens and falls
8. plant withers and dies, dropping seeds to earth
   and then the seeds germinate once again.

This book will deal primarily with the eight lunar phases as defined by the late and great astrological philosopher, Dane Rudhyar, in his 1967 book, *The Lunation Cycle.*[1] Since then countless astrologers have used the eight lunar phases in their work and a number of books have been written to include them. I first wrote about them for publication back in 1990 in an article called "The Lunar Cycle: an 8-Fold Cycle of Transformation" to precede calculated tables of "The Eight Phases of the Moon 1900-2020" in *Tables of Planetary Phenomena*,[2] the last work of my late husband, Neil F. Michelsen.

Back in 1994, I already knew that I would correlate the eight lunar phases with the eight-fold cycle of Sun and Earth that forms the seasonal basis for the Wiccan Wheel of the Year—I did so within the article in Neil's book and later expanded on the idea in *The Witch's Circle*.[3] The eight seasonal holidays are apparently a blend of two ancient traditions that had four festivals each, and at some point became eight, probably through the influx of Norse tribes into Celtic areas. In the north the big annual sacred days were the equinoxes and the solstices. For the Celts, the major festivals came at the cross-quarters in between. Each set of the four had its sequence of birth, culmination, harvest and death, and then somewhere along the line, the four became eight, and the blended mythologies became a bit confusing. I was confused when I first began to study Wicca and was confronted with rites that celebrated the birth of the divine child (Sun) to the Mother Goddess at Yule (Winter Solstice) only to find the Goddess pregnant at Imbolc (translated as "in the belly"). Then a battle between Bright Lord and Dark Lord or Oak King and Holly King at Midsummer resulted in the death of the god of the waxing year thus beginning the reign of the god of the waning year…but then at Lammas, and again at Fall Equinox, and again at Samhain, the poor God (by whatever name he was called) was often portrayed as meeting his death again. It didn't make much sense until it dawned on me that the Rudhyar lunar phases had symbolic meanings that fit the seasonal agricultural cycle, as well as all cycles of human experience, quite admirably. Since much of the Wheel of the Year mythology is derived from the life cycle of Nature (plant, agricultural and animal—the "Circle of Life," as the song in *Lion King* goes), an overlay of the Rudhyar phases sorted out those confused mythologies into what became, for me, a neat and satisfying sequence. I designed, led and later wrote full rituals for each of the eight Wiccan Sabbats in *The Witch's Circle*. Since then I've developed the idea with many variations through years of celebrating the Sabbats, and have on several occasions also used the rituals as the basis for experiential astrology presentations.

Just as the eight lunar phases help to define the Wheel of the Year, the Wheel of the Year contributes to our understanding the lunar phases. In later chapters the eight phases are defined in much more detail as they specifically apply to lunar phases, natal, progressed and in transit. Here I will introduce them in correlation with the Wheel of the Year.

## Timing of the Eight Wheel of the Year Sabbats

The dates of equinoxes and solstices, acknowledged as seasonal beginnings, appear on nearly every calendar and they are generally announced on every T.V. news show as the beginning of the four seasons. The four cross-quarter Sabbats, however, were apparently not considered important by astronomers and calendar makers and remain somewhat in dispute as a result. Due to calendar changes the dates when these four were celebrated in ancient times no longer place them at the half-way points between the equinoxes and solstices where they should be, in order to make a true eight-spoked symbolic wheel. Because the ancient dates have held in memory, many still celebrate them then. Astrologically savvy Neopagan groups or Wiccan circles are more likely to celebrate them on the exact cross-quarter days, specifically when the Sun reaches the 15th degree of each fixed sign: Aquarius, Taurus, Leo, and Scorpio.

Rudhyar said that the cross-quarters of the lunar phase cycle are the points of greatest momentum and the most critical release of energy. This jibes with the Wiccan designation of the cross-quarters as the Greater Sabbats, while the Sabbats of the cardinal cross are considered the Lesser Sabbats. I'd think that ought to be enough to make anyone who stops to think about it decide to do their Greater Sabbat rituals as close as possible to the actual cross-quarters, for these are the times of power. Your *Moon Tides* transit pages show the exact dates and times of each of the eight Sabbats mixed in where they occur in sequence with the transiting lunar phases.

# The Eight Lunar Phases in Symbolic Correlation with the Eight Sabbats

## New Moon Phase and Winter Solstice (also called Yule), Sun at 0° Capricorn

Winter Solstice is the longest night of the year. Where winter means snow, seeds germinate in the ground. Since ancient times Winter Solstice has been heralded as the birth of the Sun that will steadily wax (increase in light) from this point forward until the longest day of Summer Solstice. Christianity changed the birth of the Sun to the birth of the Son, the Christ, in order to "Christianize" what was a popular festival time for Pagans, but even before that, other celebrations at or near this time included the idea of a divine child's birth. Wiccan rituals of this season often include birth—the Mother gives birth to the baby Bright Lord of the waxing year, the Crone serves as midwife, the Maiden heralds the new light. The last saved remnant of last year's Yule Log is used to ignite the Yule Fire on which the new Yule Log will be burned. This symbolizes the passing away of the old year, and the igniting of hopes and plans for the new.

The symbolic impact of **New Moon** is much the same. The sky is completely dark; no Moon can be seen, for conjunct the Sun she is "up" by day, invisible when so near his blinding light. In either cycle what is experienced is a dark moment before anticipated light when the future is as yet unknown. Something new is beginning, but is not yet clearly visible or defined. This can be compared to the newborn baby who's just entered the world, but we have little idea just what kind of individual he or she will become, what personality will be expressed. The baby sleeps most of the time at first, looking pretty much like any other baby, except perhaps to his mother.

Like the year ahead at Yule, the month ahead at New Moon or the 30 years ahead at progressed New Moon, all is potential, but without definition. Action moves forward on impulse and pure instinct, just like a newborn babe. Another symbolic analogy is the seed that protected by winter's blanket and invisible to our human eyes, is very much alive, germinating and waiting to emerge.

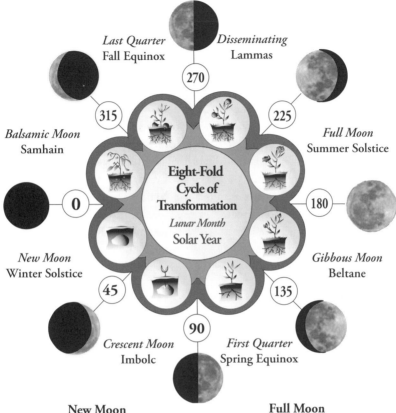

*Last Quarter*
Fall Equinox

*Disseminating*
Lammas

*Balsamic Moon*
Samhain

*Full Moon*
Summer Solstice

**Eight-Fold
Cycle of
Transformation**
*Lunar Month*
**Solar Year**

*New Moon*
Winter Solstice

*Gibbous Moon*
Beltane

*Crescent Moon*
Imbolc

*First Quarter*
Spring Equinox

**New Moon**
*New Beginnings
Rebirth, Instinctive
Seed germinates underground.*

**Full Moon**
*Fulfillment, Consumation
Illumination
Plants in full bloom.*

**Crescent Moon**
*Challenge—The New in
Struggle with the Old
Seed spouts; becomes visible.*

**Disseminating Moon**
*Teaching, Reaping, Wisdom
Abundance
Plant bears fruit.*

**First Quarter Moon**
*Crisis of Action
Break with Past; Decisions
Roots and Stems develop.*

**Last Quarter Moon**
*Crisis of Consciousness
Reorientation
Fruit ripens and falls.*

**Gibbous Moon**
*Development, Growth,
Evaluation
Flower buds form.*

**Balsamic Moon**
*Death and Seeds of Rebirth
Plant withers and dies;
seeds lie dormant.*

## Crescent Phase and Candlemas
## (also called Brighid, Imbolc or Oimelc), Sun at 15° Aquarius

At Crescent phase the waxing light becomes visible, the days of the waxing year noticeably longer. The hope for spring wells up inside but the weather is uncertain. Ask the groundhog! Or the little crocus trying to push its way into the light only to get dumped on with new snow. This first of the four annual Celtic holidays called the Greater Sabbats was a festival of fire, sacred to the goddess Brighid (later called St. Bridget in the Catholic Church). She is a goddess of creativity, inspiration, fertility and healing. Other traditions called the Maiden Goddess of the season the Corn Maiden. Imbolc meant "in the belly" but in 8-fold sequence the Child of Promise has been born, so the alternative Oimelc, meaning "in the milk" fits better. This referred to the milk of the lambs, for this was the lambing season that told the people spring was coming.

Imagine the Mother now nursing her toddler Bright Lord, who begins to show his individuality. The promise has become visible potential. The concept of emerging, visible light has made this a preferred season for initiation in many Pagan traditions. Like **Crescent Moon,** a sliver of light appears, but there is still much to do. Like the seed that has now sprouted through the brown earth, the initiative of New Moon has come to light, but like the uncertain weather, is challenged in moving forward.

## First Quarter Phase and Spring Equinox
## (also called Ostara or Eostar), Sun at 0° Aries

The days and nights are now of equal length, equal light and dark. From this point the light will "spring forward." The bonds of winter must now be decisively broken, for spring is fully in sight and like the "crisis of action" label with which Rudhyar defined this phase, will not be denied. The eggs of spring symbolize new life. Decorated gaily, they are offered to the goddess Ostara or Eostar (east dawning), for whom the name of Easter derived. She appears as the white moonhare, forerunner of the Easter bunny. This festival often honors the inner child, as the young Bright Lord is now a growing youth at play with the young Maiden.

The **First Quarter Moon** is half light and half dark, briefly at a point of equilibrium before she increases in light. This, too, is a time poised for decisive action, when with a goal now clearly defined, it is time to do what we must to make it happen. Imagine the seeds that sprouted at Candlemas (Crescent phase) now at Eostar (First Quarter) developing stems and leaves, growing ever stronger.

## Gibbous Phase and Beltane
## (also called May Day or May Eve), Sun at 15° Taurus

The Maiden Goddess and the Bright Lord meet in sacred marriage at this festival of fertility honoring the "marriage" of Earth and Sun, as Sun's increasing warmth energizes the Earth Mother so her womb may bring forth abundant life. Our seed has now become a full fledged plant budding with promise and determined to bloom. Like the maturing young couple celebrated as Maiden and Bright Lord, hormones are racing and the chase is on, building toward fulfillment that can be anticipated just ahead, but is not yet quite realized. A favorite part of Beltane ritual is the dance to weave the Maypole. Dancers circle the tall phallic pole festooned with ribbons the ends of which are held in each hand. The dancers alternate with one group dancing in one direction, the other opposite, bobbing first under an oncoming ribbon and then lifting one's own ribbon for the next dancer so that ribbons become woven down the pole. The dance is more than just fun, for it is a fertility rite that magically weaves personal creative intents toward the culmination to come.

The **Gibbous Moon** is similar, swelling in light but not yet quite full, budding but not yet in full flower, anticipating and full of hope, but with culmination still just out of reach. We chase the dream, but like the young Lord, we may experience some frustrations along the way. That Maiden can be a tease!

## Full Moon Phase and Summer Solstice
## (also called Midsummer or Litha), Sun at 0° Cancer

This is the longest day of the year, the shortest night. The Sun has reached the culmination of waxing light; the Bright Lord is at the height of his power. In meeting with him in fulfillment of their love, the Maiden becomes Mother, the Queen of Summer. The Bright Lord…well, he is struck with a very sobering realization that he hadn't considered before, so intent was he in consummating his desire. Mother? That means…Oh! Is there something beyond being on top of my world and getting what I wanted—something that might involve a bit of responsibility? Maybe even sacrifice? In his illumination, the Bright Lord becomes the Dark Lord, accepting his responsibility as Father and Protector.

At Midsummer and at **Full Moon**, the light culminates, but nothing can remain the same, change is constant. Once having achieved full light there is nowhere to go except toward the dark once again. From the vantage point of one extreme, the opposite must be illuminated, confronted and balance sought. From this point forward the light will wane. That opposing force of darkness cannot be denied and must be integrated. But still, the plant has flowered, and the light is full, so the celebration goes on.

## Disseminating Phase and Lammas (also called Lughnasad),
## Sun at 15° Leo

In early August the days are still long, but beginning to noticeably shorten. Corn is ripe for the picking, and the Mother is Corn Mother. The plants that flowered at Midsummer begin to bear fruit. It is the time of early harvest, celebrated by the baking and eating of cornbread, and perhaps the making of solar crosses of cornhusks or wheat sheaves to bless the home. The Dark Lord now fully realizing his role as Father, recognizes the sacrifice that will be required of him, but for now he and the Mother share their wisdom and the bounty from her body that his warm light has energized. This is a time to share.

**Disseminating Moon** is, like Gibbous Moon, a little less than round, but now gradually losing light. The name of this phase ties it neatly to the early harvest themes of sharing. The light wanes but not drastically. It is time to make use of what culminated at Full Moon, to disseminate what was learned by sharing it with others.

## Last Quarter Phase and Fall Equinox (also called Harvest or Mabon), Sun at 0° Libra

At Fall Equinox full Harvest is at hand, a cause for celebration, and rituals of the season may involve a feast. This Sabbat is sometimes called the Witch's Thanksgiving. It is a time of equilibrium, equal days and equal nights. Libra's Scales of Balance weigh light and dark, but this time they tip toward the dark. The Dark Lord, whose energy has gone into the grain and animates the Great Stag of the forest, confronts the sacrifice that must be made. The Mother, in full realization of that, too, becomes the Crone, accepting her necessary role as Destroyer. The grain must be reaped and the stag must fall, so that the people might survive through the darkness and cold of the winter that will soon come. The plant whose life we have followed from its germination has born its fruit, but the fruit is heavy and must be picked or it will spoil. Harvest work proceeds, harvest abundance is enjoyed, but within the thoughts of fall is the knowledge that change must come.

**Last Quarter Moon** was defined by Dane Rudhyar as the "crisis of consciousness," and that, in itself, needs no elaboration to explain its correspondence with the mythology of Fall Equinox. The Moon in the sky is half light, half dark, but we know the dark will soon overtake the light, and so as we go on with our daily routine, we think, reflect and deal with both the internal and external changes and we begin to let go of the cycle now nearing completion.

## Balsamic Phase and Samhain
## (also called Halloween), Sun at 15° Scorpio

On Samhain, or All Hallows Eve, it is said that the veil between the visible and invisible worlds grows thin and the shades of those who have passed beyond walk among us. In the mythology of the season, the Dark Lord has passed beyond the veil, traveling to the Underworld, also called in Wicca the Summerland. (This name may be derived from his home in the South, as Sun's declination has moved to its southern extreme.) At Midsummer, in the northern hemisphere, he is seen at extreme northern declination, where he comes to warm the Earth Mother). Other mythologies of both God and Goddess depict the descent into the Underworld at the onset of winter and the return to herald the spring. This is the time of descent, and rituals of the season honor those who have passed, and celebrate the passing as a necessary part of the endless cycle, knowing that as the plant's fruit is harvested, seeds have also fallen to the Earth, where in time, they will germinate and return to life. The Dark Lord assists the passing of souls leaving physical life, and also those who are seeking reentry. The Crone, Queen of Night and winter, reigns on Earth.

When the waning crescent sliver of Moon appears in the early morning sky just before dawn, we know that the **Balsamic Moon**, also in Wiccan lore called the Crone's Moon, has come, and in just a few nights she'll wane to the point of vanishing from our sight. It is time to let go, to dream and to be open to the new that may be elusive now, but will surely come. We can be certain in the knowledge that it will come. The Wheel never stops turning. Death, like birth and each of the other phases, is only change. And change is constant.

### Endnotes

[1] Rudhyar, Dane, *The Lunation Cycle*, Santa Fe, NM: Aurora Press, 1967.

[2] Michelsen, Neil F., *Tables of Planetary Phenomena,* San Diego, ACS Publications, 1990.

[3] Simms, Maria Kay, *The Witch's Circle*, St. Paul, MN: Llewellyn, 1996 (first published in 1994 with the title, *Circle of the Cosmic Muse*).

# Chapter Two

# *Your Moon through Sign, Element and Mode*

Your Moon sign is listed near the top of your Moon Tides report under the heading At Time of Birth. The exact sign position in degrees and minutes is listed on the report line headed Birth Phase, found right under the column header Moon Position. In that column you'll also find the signs into which your Moon progresses at the onset of your progressed lunar phases. "Progression" is a symbolic method that astrologers use to move a horoscope forward in time. You'll find a more detailed explanation of how that works within the beginning of Chapter Four. For now, in reading this chapter, let it be enough to say this: please don't read only your birth Moon sign and skip over the others. Though your birth Moon will always be a part of you, the sign of your progressed Moon may provoke significant memories, and perhaps even revelations, about how you were responding to events of your life during the time of its passage. The dates Moon enters each sign can be found in a separate section in the lower part of the page.

The sign of your birth Moon, and for temporal periods, the sign of your progressed Moon, show your emotional needs and how you express and handle feelings. Through the Moon we see memory and perhaps insight into what inner programming may stem from the past and influence the present. We can probe for subconscious memories deep inside the behaviors, feelings and fears that formed in early childhood or even before that, perhaps in another lifetime. Such things, whether or not we remember or understand them, influence the present. Moon shows the capacity to nurture and the need to be nurtured, so she may offer insight into how we perceive the person who is normally expected to be our earliest nurturer, Mother. Our Moon sign can be interpreted for information about our roots, our ancestry and our home, both of origin and in the present.

I first began this chapter during a transiting[1] Moon in Gemini, writing each sign interpretation in zodiacal order like most books do, with the extra little touch of a Moon Goddess ritual idea based on a typical theme of each sign, I was going along fine until I got to my own Moon sign, Cancer, and realized two things: #1: I was rather bored with reworking the same old typically basic astrology sign interpretations, even though I'd included the more enjoyable task of creating little rituals, and #2: I realized that even though what I had written for my own sign, Cancer, read well enough and certainly fit the expected mold, I didn't like it. Maybe it fit at one stage of my life and I guess still does, in part, but what I had written was just too mundane. "There must be a better way of doing this," I thought.

A horoscope, just as the entity it represents, is a complex blend, often even beyond what attempts full synthesis of all factors can reveal. What could I say about each Moon sign that would provoke insight beyond the usual zodiacal sign characteristics such that, in keeping with the title of this book, I might speak to the soul? Then, as I sat perplexed, the transiting Moon went into Cancer and I left my computer to go into my ritual space to meditate, first asking the elemental guardians of the four directions for their assistance…then I took a long look at the paintings of dancers in each element I'd recently finished and thought, yes! The elements! And, within that, the transformative process…I had my answer, but first I must explain the basis.

## The Four Elements of the Ancients

The ancients saw the material world in terms of four elements: air, fire, water and earth. So pervasive are the symbolic meanings of these elements as they refer to human life that they permeate our language with idiomatic expressions to this day. You've all heard them used in describing people, and everyone "gets" what they mean. Here are a few examples:

**Water:** You're all wet! She expresses such a deep well of feeling. What a wet blanket! He's drowning in self-pity. Don't dowse my plans with cold water! Go with the flow.

**Fire:** What a fiery temper! Light a fire under him! Hothead! He burns with intensity. She's burning up the track! He was really burned up by that slight. She's simmering.

**Earth:** Don't be a stick-in-the-mud. He's a regular down-to-earth guy. That clinging vine—she's strangling him.  He's stone cold. I'll bury you! He's rooted to that place.

**Air:** She's just an airhead. Isn't she a breath of fresh air? What a breezy style of speaking she has! This is a stifling relationship. His head is in the clouds.

Of the twelve signs of the zodiac, three each have similarities in temperament according to their affinity with one of the four elements. Here they are, with four of the most typical keywords commonly used to describe each elemental family.

**Keywords for the elements:**
**Fire:** Aries, Leo, Sagittarius—vital, passionate, enthusiastic, spirited
**Earth**: Taurus, Virgo, Capricorn—solid, grounded, sensual, pragmatic
**Air:** Gemini, Libra, Aquarius—logical, rational, reasonable, analytical
**Water:** Cancer, Scorpio, Pisces—fluid, deep, intuitive, emotional

### The Three-in-One:  Modes and the Triple Goddess

Astrological tradition also divides the twelve signs into three basic modes or qualities of being: cardinal, fixed and mutable. Within each elemental group of three signs, one will express in each of the three modes. Here they are, with the most typical keywords for each mode:

**Keywords for the Modes:**
**Cardinal:** Aries, Cancer, Libra, Capricorn—initiating, action-oriented
**Fixed:** Taurus, Leo, Scorpio, Aquarius—sustaining, resists change
**Mutable:** Gemini, Virgo, Sagittarius, Pisces—changeable, versatile

The Great Goddess has long been seen as *triformis*—three-in-one— since long before Christianity conceived of the Holy Trinity. By all the thousands of names she has been called throughout the world, she has been imaged in three stages of the life of woman: Maiden, Mother and Crone. A similarity in process can be seen by comparing the astrological modes with the Triple Goddess. It's not about age, but instead, a quality of being.

**Maiden** is Creator, the creative force who dances out of chaos to bring forth the new. Like the first of the three Fates, she gathers the stuff of life but may not stay to weave it. She is virgin, but not at all in the chaste image of having "known" no man, but instead in the ancient understanding of being owned by no man. She is independent and free. Though usually envisioned as the young aspect of Triple Goddess, she is but part of an ageless whole. She sets the tone or introduces the basic idea we have of a larger total image. As Creator, she is like the Cardinal quality of being.

**Mother** is Preserver, the sustaining force of life and the Lady of the Dance. The whole of her nature is life perpetuating, no matter what challenge she faces. She gives birth to life and then feeds it, ever protecting and nurturing. She is the ultimate fullness of sensual, sexual womanhood, fertile, strong and powerful. As Preserver, she fits well the Fixed quality of being,

**Crone** has been called Destroyer, but that fails to describe her true nature adequately. Yes, she faces death and may bring it, but she sees far beyond the last notes of the dance. I prefer to think of her as Wise Woman. In that, she is the recognition that death is only change, and beyond death is life in a new form, one more turn in an eternal cycle. In keeping with the Mutable quality of being, the Crone is transformative. She is change. She completes the elemental soul process and sees beyond it, to continued development through cycles to come.

With the elemental Goddess theme as guidance, I will not describe the signs of the Moon in zodiacal order, but instead by one element at a time.

For each I will use the mythologies of a well-known Triple Goddess closely associated with each elemental theme. I have chosen from the pantheon of a different culture for each element. In working with the three signs of each elemental Goddess as a transformational process, I hope to lead you to a more satisfying intuitive understanding of your natal Moon and her signs by progression, just as I hope this process may lead me to even more satisfying insights into my own.

A note about gender: the astrological Moon is feminine, and among the other planets, only Venus is distinctly feminine, named for a Goddess. All the others are named for Gods. Whether you are female or male, the essence of both Goddess and God live within you. In Spirit I believe that all Gods and Goddesses are One. In the physical body we express one gender overtly, but carry the spiritual energy of the other within. The great psychological thinker, Carl Jung, called the feminine within the male the anima, and the male within the female, animus.

The Moon was not always seen as female. Some ancient cultures saw Moon as a God, and some saw Sun as a Goddess. The "man in the moon" image still persists in folklore. A popular Moon God of ancient times was named Sin, a fact that makes me wonder about the roots of that word and how it seems to have changed from a name of deity to a word of shame that became attached in religious tradition to Eve and her daughters. Sin, the Moon God, was prominent during the Middle Eastern part of the world that eventually birthed the three religions of Abraham: Judaism, Christianity and Islam. Abraham came from Ur of the Chaldees. By the time ancient Chaldean astrology had influenced the development of our western astrological tradition in classical Greece, well over 2000 years ago, the Middle Eastern Moon God had become Goddess. This change may have also played a role when biblical scripture was created. The Greeks cast Moon as feminine and domestic, with the nurturing qualities of motherhood. So, somehow, in those ancient times, "Sin" became feminine? Food for thought.

In this book about the Moon, in keeping with astrological tradition and with my own preferences, she is unabashedly feminine, her spiritual energy the Goddess. Whether you are male or female, your first Goddess-type image was quite likely your mother, and so you may perceive her according to the sign, house and phase of the Moon in your birth chart. If you are female, discover your own personal Goddess energy within your Moon. Invoke her! If you are male, the Goddess is also within you. She is, as Jung would say, the anima. She is an image of the feminine toward which you are in some way irresistibly drawn. Invoke her! Female or male, she teaches you about yourself. May your astrological Moon and the Goddess guide you all to a deeper, more intuitive and spiritual understanding of the Moon and how she pulls on the tides of your soul. (See the paintings that inspired the elemental Goddess theme on pages 116-119).

# Goddess of the Sea

*Arise, O Goddess of the Sea*
*Speak to me of mystery*
*As tides of passion, depths of truth,*
*Flow now through me.*
*Open up your soul to me*
*Mystic waves will help me see*
*My strength within, my power of love*
*Serenity!*

*Live within me, I will serve you*
*I feel your tides within my soul*
*May it grow now, ever stronger*
*As I live in peace and joy and love.*[2]

## Ishtar and the Water Moons

There are many images of the Goddess of the Sea, and I was tempted to choose Mari, my personal Goddess, whose name derives from mar, the sea in many languages, and who as the forerunner of Mary, brought in the age of Pisces. She is a Triple Goddess: Mary the Virgin, Mary the Mother, and Mary the Pieta, Mother of sorrows. But I did that explanation within *The Witch's Circle*,[3] so I have decided that in sharing this lunar process with you, I will take you back to an even more ancient time to look for deeper understanding of the primordial Goddess, old before time, who is the watery womb from which all life on Earth emerged. We'll go to ancient Sumeria for Inanna, who in Babylonia and Assyria circa 3000 BC became Ishtar. She, the greatest of the Middle Eastern Goddesses, was later known to the Phoenicians as Astarte or Asherah, and her continued cultural evolution eventually took her to Greece, where she was born of the sea as Aphrodite. Though her name may have varied, throughout the Middle East she reigned as Queen of Heaven. For the convenience of using one name, I will focus on Ishtar, but I have two reasons more important than that. For one, Babylonia is a culture that was important in the development of astrology (the zodiacal belt was known as Ishtar's girdle), and for the other, Ishtar is the very oldest of Moon Goddesses. She was daughter of Sin the Moon God, and traveled with him in the sky, smaller than the Moon but still brightly shining as the morning and evening star we now call Venus. (Ishtar means, "star.") As Ishtar's popularity grew, she eventually eclipsed her father and became the Moon herself. Ishtar was always associated with water in both its life-giving and destructive aspects. We'll explore how her myths of the great flood and of her descent into the underworld can offer depth to our understanding of the water signs.

**Cancer—the Cardinal Water Moon**

Ishtar was seen as both a Goddess of love and a warrior Goddess who led her people into battle, and as such expresses the initiative of the Maiden. Virgin in the most independent sense, she had many lovers. It has been said that it was the priestesses of Ishtar who each year in the temple of Jerusalem, took on the role of Goddess for the rites of sacred marriage, hieiros gamos, and there her virgin aspect was called Mari or Miriam.[4] But while all this fits the image of Ishtar in cardinal mode, it says little about her watery nature as specifically applies to Cancer Moon.

As fertility Goddess, Ishtar had a water jar that never emptied[5] from which she nourished plant and animal life. That fits the typical image of Cancer's nurturing qualities, but let's explore a little further. Multiple sources told me that Ishtar inherited the great flood myth from an earlier Babylonian Goddess called Nuah, which in later scriptural writing became Noah. In the Ishtar version of the flood tale, related in the Gilgamesh epic, the disaster is prophesied by Ishtar who weeps, but then most definitely takes both cardinal initiative and Cancerian care in seeing that all species of her children are protected and saved. In one version of the tale, she actually makes and sails the ark (its "horns' pointed upward, as the Maiden crescent Moon often appears). On the seventh day she sends forth the dove to look for land. After the flood subsided, *"Then at last Ishtar also came, she lifted her necklace with the jewels of heaven… by the lapis lazuli round my neck I shall remember these days as I remember the jewels of my throat; these last days I shall not forget."*[6]

With Moon in Cancer, you are strong on empathy and perhaps even psychic. You are a natural nurturer who will do most anything to protect your home and loved ones, and you have a very long memory.

Let's probe a little further, into the best known of Ishtar myths, that of her descent into the underworld, the commemoration of which was an important annual Middle Eastern ritual. It begins when Ishtar's lover Tammuz is killed and taken to the underworld, ruled by Ishtar's dark sister Ereshkigal. Ishtar is desolate and weeping, but not for long. No way will she allow Tammuz to get away from her! She storms to the gates of the underworld and demands to be let in, to break in by force, if necessary.[7]

Like you, Ishtar does not hesitate to take the initiative if one of her own is threatened, even to the point of warrior maiden battle gear. Is this the independent freedom of the Maiden archetype, though? Yes, in part, but not exactly. There is a more complex undertone. After all, Tammuz needs her, doesn't he? Of course, he does! How can anyone you love truly get along without you?

A part of the lunar challenge of Cancer is to know when to let go, recognizing that nurturing the dependency of others can be a co-dependency. Who really needs whom? How much support for others is help and at what point does it become stifling to their own progress? Ask yourself that question in any relationship (with child, spouse, relative, friend, organization, business) in which you perceive problems and seek to solve them. Too much help can seek to hold others within a strong emotional need for security that is really your own.

That said, you are caring, compassionate and devoted. Your emotions flow, but when you understand them, you usually handle them better than most. Calm in a crisis, you'll do what you can to make sure others are safe and cared for.

Hold in your mind an image of Ishtar as active, independent, protective and nurturing Cancerian Maiden as we progress to...

**Scorpio—the Fixed Water Moon**

Visualize Ishtar in her full-fledged Mother persona, for that she was, typically imaged in ancient statuary with her hands under massive breasts, offering them as symbol of her benevolence. Sensual, sexual and very strong, she is both Bright Mother and Dark Mother. Scorpio, a complex sign for Moon (or any planet) symbolizes the challenge to meet and confront one's dark side, and through that passage, acquire self-mastery.

Think of Ishtar, indignantly demanding to be let in, while her dark sister Ereshkigal (who is really another aspect of Ishtar, herself) stands firm and unrelenting. Finally, Ereshkigal agrees to let Ishtar in, but only on condition that she shed one of her jewels or garments at each of the underworld's seven gates.[8] Determined to get in (to probe within), Ishtar complies, first giving up her crown of sovereignty, then each of her ornaments and finally her garment, until she stands naked and vulnerable before Ereshkigal. But still, the dark sister will not surrender Tammuz. She imprisons Ishtar, hanging her on a hook to die.

Here we see the intensity, passion, strength and determination of Moon in Scorpio. Deep attachments are formed such that you may be willing to go to hell and back for them. Or, fearful of loss of control—or perhaps fearful of true closeness—you might take on your shadow self. Like Ereshkigal, you are capable of being obstinate, jealous and unforgiving.

Think of the emotional flow of water like the waters of the sea, crashing against the rocks and flowing into every crack and crevice of the land, nourishing and life giving. Tides of emotion can pull the sands from under your feet, throwing you off balance. Over time, water wears down the rocks and the land, changing their form—or can suddenly overwhelm in tidal wave and flood. Even the nourishing rain can become a storm that overwhelms and turns destructive. Water, like the mythical cauldron of Cerridwen, has the capacity to create or consecrate, to cleanse or destroy. Your Scorpionic emotions flow with great intensity. Lacking self-awareness and self-control, those emotions can work destructively against you and those you love. When you are willing to confront your dark side and truly understand and master yourself emotionally, you can emerge strong and charismatic, able to heal yourself and others with transformative power.

To return to the myth, Ishtar's brother, a God of water and wisdom, intervenes and persuades Ereshkigal to relent and allow Ishtar to be sprinkled with the waters of life. She revives and returns to Earth, passing once again through the seven gates where at each one she recovers that which she had relinquished on her descent.

From the crown that was her pride and sovereignty through all of the six other things that Ishtar relinquished and then reclaimed, there is a lesson: after confronting your own emotional vulnerabilities, you must own them in order to express them more wisely as you move forward. Your shadow-self is a threat when denied, but when acknowledged, it supports and increases your sense of self-mastery. You learn that there can be great power in letting go of those veils to reveal the secrets they only partially obscured.

Nothing had grown on Earth while Ishtar was gone, nor did animals or humans mate, but with her return, it was spring again. Ishtar had survived, and grown stronger in the process. This, too, is the strength of Scorpio and of you. You are a survivor.

**Pisces—the Mutable Water Moon**

The sea that churned with Scorpio calms in Pisces to gentler waves that ebb and flow. Let's return for a moment to Ishtar's version of the great flood. The lapis lazuli necklace she lifted up to the sky in memory was the rainbow, with its arc of seven heavenly colors glowing over land and sea. Here is the more passive water Moon of imagination, vision, and the eternal quest for beauty. You are the most secure when you are feeling spiritually connected.

Imagine the priestesses of Ishtar dancing with seven veils,[9] whirling in trance with beautiful veils in all the colors of the rainbow, as they depict the death of Tammuz, returned to life only after Ishtar descended to retrieve him, shedding one of her seven garments at each of the gates of hell. For three days each year this sacred drama was repeated with penitence and sacrifice, ending in the joyous return of Tammuz and Ishtar, celebrated as the onset of the new year. The initiative, the fury, the trials, and the humiliation of Ishtar stripped bare and then redeemed have now become, in this final Piscean water Moon, rites of beauty and healing.

You may feel you were born a very old soul, and perhaps you were. With wisdom and compassion for self, you feel great compassion for others, for all living things. This is not with the urgency of Maiden or the intensity of Mother, but with the deep, passive acceptance of Crone, for whom no veil may hide the secrets of soul. You are highly intuitive and sensitive to the emotions that swirl around you from others. Your challenge is to know when to say no, both to others who take advantage of your empathy, and also to yourself, when your own wish to avoid the harsher realities of life may lead you to unhealthy and addictive forms of escape. If escape you must, then express yourself in the quest for beauty through art, poetry, music, dance, meditation or ritual. Regardless that other factors in your horoscope cast you in roles of strength and command, there is a soft spot in your soul for those in need, and a pure idealism that seeks the highest truth.

There is another story of Ishtar's forerunner, who was called Inanna, but whose dark sister had the same name, Ereshkigal. Translated from an ancient cuneiform inscription, it offers further insight for Pisces Moon. Ereshkigal's husband has died, so Inanna travels to the underworld to comfort her. Wary of the danger of traveling to her sister's realm, Inanna prepares by giving her servant special instructions to follow if she is not back within three days. Inanna descends, relinquishing her garments at the seven gates to hell, at last standing naked in the darkness. Even though Inanna seeks only to grieve with her sister, Ereshkigal turns her own fierce grief against Inanna and kills her. Above ground the third day passes and the faithful servant, as instructed, goes for help. Enki, God of the ocean, creates two small creatures, giving to one the breath of life, and the other the water of life, and he instructs them on how to behave in the presence of Ereshkigal.

They do just that. Finding Ereshkigal alone and wailing, they do nothing but mourn with her. They do not give advice, nor tell her everything will be all right, nor ask her to look on the bright side or to try not to think about her loss. They simply honor her grief, crying when she cries. When she finally notices them, she rewards them as being the first to truly mourn with her. Offered the gift of anything they want, they ask for Inanna, and restore her with the breath and water of life.[10]

Passive? Yes, but also intuitive and truly empathic. With divine compassion and love, you can allow others—and yourself—to simply be, and that, in itself, can be healing.

### Public Figures with Moon in Water signs:[10]

**Cancer:** former First Lady **Nancy Reagan**, operatic composer **Giaccamo Puccini**, researcher on death and dying, **Elizabeth Kubler-Ross**, one of history's greatest artists, **Michelangelo**; astrologer and data queen, **Lois Rodden**, famed comedian **Bob Hope**.

**Scorpio:** movie star, **Elizabeth Taylor**; astrologer **Rob Hand**, TV evangelist/singer **Tammy Faye Bakker**; author and Witch, **Margot Adler**; author, *Sex and the Single Girl, Cosmopolitan* editor, **Helen Gurley Brown**; innovative dancer and author, **Isadora Duncan**; actress **Shannen Doherty**; innovative educator **Maria Montessori**

**Pisces:** Olympic figure skater, **Dorothy Hamill**; rock 'n roll idol **Elvis Presley**; famed designer **Coco Chanel**, actress **Catherine Zeta-Jones**; Vice-President **Dick Cheney**

# Goddess of the Fire

*Oh, bright Goddess of the Fire*
*Light the flame of my desire*
*Live within my heart and soul*
*With spirit glow*
*Let your spark within me be*
*A shining flame for all to see*
*Energy, the joy of life*
*The flame of love!*

*Live within me, I will serve you*
*I feel your fire within my soul*
*May it grow now, ever brighter*
*As I live in peace and joy and love.*

**Brighid and the Fire Moons**

To the British Isles we go for inspiration from the Goddess of Fire who is known as St. Bridget of Ireland in modern times, but of old as Triple Goddess of the great Celtic empire that was Brigantia. Also called Brigantia, Bride, Brigit or Brigandu in various dialects of the time, her name (according to Celtic Wiccan traditions) is pronounced "Breed." So firmly set was devotion to Brighid within the Irish people, as the onset of Catholicism moved into her territory, that the Church saw no alternative other than to "Christianize" her. So, circa AD 450, they made her a saint, attributing to her much the same lore as the Goddess she still is, only thinly veiled in the garb of the holy nuns, priestesses of Kildare, who keep her sacred fires burning. Brighid's fires burn to this day, and with them the legends of Brighid live on as an archetypal Goddess of Fire in the modern revival of Goddess worship. So, there, oh Church fathers who think you claim the only right of succession from deity. Your time is waning, and the fires of the eternal Goddess burn ever more brightly!

I'd read or heard somewhere that the flames of Kildare were closed down by the monarchy in the 18th century but had been relit by nuns in recent years. By searching the internet, I found two organizations devoted to keeping the holy flame of Brighid burning, and within their websites, the information I needed. According to ancient tradition of having nineteen priestess to tend the flame, the groups or cills of *Ord Brighideach* and Daughters of the Flame are made up of nineteen members each. Nineteen, a number sacred to Brighid, refers to the Celtic Great Year, the number of years it takes from one New Moon to the next one that coincides with Winter Solstice, the birth of waxing light after the longest night. The flamekeepers work in 19 shifts in 20-day cycles and in keeping with ancient legend, on the twentieth day it is believed that Brighid, herself, tends the flame. A Catholic Brigidine nun of Kildare, Sister Mary Minehan,[12] relit St. Bridget's flame in 1993 at Imbolc, one of the 8-fold holy days of the Wheel of the Year that is often popularly called Brighid's Day. Sister Mary is one of two Brigidine nuns who have formed *Solas Bhride*, a Christian Community Centre for Celtic spirituality.

Though modern Neopagan lore primarily sees Brighid in her Maiden aspect, in Celtic lore she was most definitely Triple Goddess, a mother Goddess seen as interchangeable with Dana, great mother Goddess of Ireland. Brighid was worshipped as warrior and protector, for her healing powers and as the guardian of children. Indeed, lore of the Christianized version has her as the foster mother of Christ. She is a Goddess of creative inspiration, divination, poetry and craft, and she was the comforter of those in mourning. Let's see what inspiration she can bring to our understanding of the fire Moons.

### Aries—the Cardinal Fire Moon

Brighid's name means "fiery arrow." An arrow tipped in flame is a good image to begin our comparison with Aries, the archetypical sign of action and initiative. The Celts were a people of fighting spirit, and Brighid, their warrior Goddess, inspired soldiers who were called brigands, though the Christians called them outlaws. Think of the legends of Robin Hood, Maid Marion and their Merry Men and you have a taste of the spirit of your fiery Maiden Moon. Courageous and not afraid to take a chance, you'll look for adventure and most likely find it, perhaps more than you expected. Independent of spirit, you'll fight with great courage for what you feel is right.

Brighid is said to have once been accused of being wicked, rather than holy. Not to shun a dare, she proved her holiness by putting a burning coal into her bosom and walking with it a great distance without being burned at all. It is a tale of the miracles of St. Bridget that from the spot she dropped the coal, a well sprang up. This became one of her sacred wells through which countless cures are attributed.[13] But fire inspires far more than courage and fighting. Brighid is the fire of creativity that illuminates the poet and bard, and spurs on the maker of crafts to new designs of beauty.

Legend has it that the Cailleach, as the Crone was called among the Celts, imprisoned the maiden Bride through the winter, but the Crone's own son fell in love with Bride. At winter's end he eloped with her. The hag chased them fiercely, causing storms as she went, but in the end Bride was free. Brighid, who is Bride, is a Goddess of springtime. In ancient times and still, she is celebrated at Imbolc as the bringer of fertility. A doll created from sheaves of grain or cornhusks is dressed in bridal white and placed in a basket-bed with a phallic wand. Brighid is invoked and welcomed in with the hope that she will assure strong growth of plant life in the coming season.

You have the courage and drive to flee from the hag to get what you want, and the charisma to attract, as well. Do you have the staying power to stay and till the soil? Probably not, unless you're reflecting it from other parts of your horoscope. Your Moon energy is like that of a burning arrow—you release it quickly, instinctively and spontaneously. Your anger, your newest passion or your best intentions may flare brightly for a while, but will it last? Well, it depends. It could be that the arrow ignites a mighty flame that may hold your attention longer. But if not, and the flame subsides on impact, that's another story.

Your moods can shift rapidly. Anger, passion or intent may ebb as quickly as they flowed, while you light and draw another arrow to shoot. You like action, want to be where the action is, and have a need to get there first and do things your way. When you feel free to express your high-spirited independence, you express natural warmth that can inspire and lead. It's not just about winning, though. It's about creating. When you understand the flow of energy within your soul, then like your Maiden Goddess of Fire, you'll channel that energy to feel and to inspire her bright spiritual power.

## Leo—the Fixed Fire Moon

Beyond her Maiden persona, Brighid was a great Mother Goddess of Brigantia, and a Goddess of sovereignty. From *The Witches Goddess*:

> *As Proinsias MacCanna puts it (Celtic Mythology, p. 95): "The criterion of a rightful King is that the land should be prosperous and inviolate under his rule—and this can only be achieved if he is accepted as her legitimate spouse by the Goddess who personifies his kingdom."[14]*

Brighid was regal, older than Celtic Ireland, and has been said to be the same as Rome's Juno Regina, Queen of Heaven. A royal daughter, she was married for dynastic reasons and bore children. Sadly, her husband, Bres, who was High King, failed to meet the standards of generosity required of his station, imposing excessive taxes on his subjects. As retribution, the bard Caire satirized him causing boils to appear on his face, and so he had to abdicate, since Celtic Kings were expected to be physically perfect. This leads to a Crone story, so enough of that for now, except to say that you, of the Leo Moon, are naturally regal. You feel most secure when you are the center of attention, receiving approval and admiration. This spurs you on to accomplish even more. Most likely you are warmly generous, as well. As Queen or King you may be inclined to extravagance, and some approval you elicit may be mere flattery, rather than sincerity. It would be well to have a trusted friend or two who'll tell you the truth when you're pushing things too far. You are capable of being too self-absorbed, so sometimes need a gentle nudge to look at what is really happening around you.

On the other hand, negative attention can be hard to take, causing you to sulk or even withdraw behind the scenes.  My mother, a Leo Moon, withdrew after an embarrassing attack of childhood stage fright and would never speak in public again. But, Leo Moon can find other ways to regain the spotlight.  Mom redirected her energy toward craftwork, and throughout her life received admiration and awards for her skill and artistic ability. She put her crafts"out front" rather than herself.

The fact that Brighid has prevailed for so many centuries and through so many cultural changes is a model for the fixed quality of your steady fire. You are passionate, but also persistent, able to turn creative inspiration into true craftsmanship, honing your fiery and dramatic expression into lasting pursuits.

As Brighid, a Goddess of the hearth and protector of children, kept the home fires burning, so do you. You can, in fact, be a sort of "Pied Piper" for children, yours and their friends, when your lively sense of the dramatic keeps your inner child alive and ready for fun.  By inspiring and encouraging in this way, you nurture, contributing to the self-esteem and emotional stability of your children.

One more tale of Brighid's fixed power: One day, after she had done some laundry, she hung her newly washed clothes on a beam of light, which remained absolutely solid until her clothes were dry! So much for limiting this lady to unreliable Imbolc weather. This is a Goddess of Fire whose will shines with magical power. With that and the light of Brighid's perpetual flame to guide you, share the magic and emotional power of your Moon with humility and generosity, and your spirit will soar with beauty.

**Sagittarius—the Mutable Fire Moon**

Let's return to the story of Brighid and her hapless husband, Bres, who was forced to abdicate. This led to one of the many Celtic battles (the Celtics were a fiery people!), in which Brighid's son, Ruadan, was killed.  It was then that Brighid created the Irish mourning wail known as keening. With that, she became the comforter of all mourners, a function of the Crone aspect of the Triple Goddess, a transformative figure that fits the mutable mode of any sign.

So, what does that have to do with Sagittarian fire? A Sagittarian need is to express feelings outwardly, and when fire has something to express, it is done with great energy. Your bright and flaming arrows are intended to hit the mark and cause a raging fire that will be unmistakably convincing. Keening, though not as gentle an assist to mourning as the little creatures of the Pisces-Water Ishtar tale, has nevertheless an effective healing power. What it provides is emotional release. Brighid was a Goddess of healing and medicine. Often the best medicine will not work without a spiritual healing, as well. Through your expression of feeling, whether in joy or in sorrow, or in the expression of any idea that is very important to you, you can heal yourself and perhaps also inspire others.

It is not at all within your nature to keep things pent up inside. You express what you are feeling and thinking with energy, as you seek your highest truth. It reminds me of the tale of Brighid's birth, when a magical fire formed around her head and extended up into the heavens, such that some thought the house was afire.

Ever optimistic and out for adventure, you reach out for the transformation that can come from seeking, learning, traveling, but this is not without its possible setbacks. Take the tale of a certain archer who was determined to trespass within the hedge circling Brighid's sacred fire at Kildare, the hedge through which no man is allowed to enter. He leapt over the hedge and blew on Brighid's fire. Jumping back immediately, he went quite mad until he was finally captured and bound. Then, he asked for water and drank so much his belly ruptured. Not to scare you, of course, but this little tale is a fun way to mention that a possible challenge of your Moon is not to completely overestimate yourself in your zeal to reach your goal. That said, you have a gift of persuasion that can sell or teach, convincing others of the fire of your convictions.

A final legend of Brighid I'll relate to you is that when she was born, at sunrise, her mother was standing over the threshold of their home, one foot in and one foot out. This is symbolic of Brighid's destiny as a Goddess of the threshold, who transcends the gateway between the worlds of earth and spirit. When you reach beyond the physical to seek spiritual truth, you'll find the ultimate fulfillment for the heart and soul of your fiery Moon sign.

**Public Figures with Moon in the Fire signs:**

**Aries:** former First Lady **Jacqueline Kennedy Onassis**; opera star **Luciano Pavarotti,** Microsoft founder and humanitarian, **Bill Gates**; movie star **Marlon Brando**

**Leo: Queen Elizabeth II**; astrologer **Marc Edmund Jones**; abstract expressionist painter **Willem de Kooning**; actor **Clint Eastwood**; leading feminist **Gloria Steinem**

**Sagittarius:** genius **Albert Einstein**; famed and highly influential artists **Vincent Van Gogh** and **Pablo Picasso**; TV talk show hostess **Oprah Winfrey**, astrologer/author **Marion D. March**

## Goddess of the Earth

*O great Mother of the Earth,*
*You give to all who live our birth.*
*All who come from you return*
*Then are reborn.*
*I worship you in seeds I sow*
*And nurture as they bloom and grow,*
*That harvest of my life have worth*
*For this I know...*

*You'll live within me and I will serve you*
*I feel your strength within my soul*
*May it grow now, ever stronger*
*As I live in peace and joy and love.*

**Demeter and the Earth Moons**

Demeter, Greek Goddess of the Olympians, is one of the most familiar of Earth Mother archetypes. The most widely known of her myths involves her daughter who is Kore and/or Persephone. Kore is a widespread Goddess name that seems to be perhaps more of a titular designation for a Goddess who is Maiden or Virgin than an actual persona. Persephone is the more commonly used name for Demeter's daughter in both Maiden and Crone aspects, for Persephone reigned as Queen of the Underworld. Most references I have checked, though, either suggest or outright say that the daughter names depict aspects of Demeter herself. Meter is mother and the "De" comes from delta of the Greek alphabet, a triangle, symbolic of Demeter as Triple Goddess. The triangle was widely associated throughout the world with the vulva, the doorway of the mysterious feminine. In Mycenae, an early cult center of Demeter, tombs had triangular doorways, short vaginal passages and round domes, representing the womb and birth passage through which, it was obviously hoped, rebirth might come.[15] Demeter, like other ancient Goddesses, was Creator, Preserver and Destroyer.

Demeter is Goddess of all earthly vegetation. In the most familiar of her myths, her lovely daughter Kore plays happily among the fields and flowers with the other maidens until one day, when Demeter is not paying attention, Kore is taken away by the Lord of the Underworld (Hades/Pluto) where she becomes his queen, Persephone. Demeter is devastated and searches the world for her child. She is desolate that all plant life on earth dies and she refuses to function until her daughter is returned. Finally through intercession by Zeus, the Olympian king of the Gods, it is agreed that Persephone will return to Demeter for two-thirds of the year, but must return to Hades for the other third. Demeter agrees, apparently thinking that once she gets her daughter back, she will stay. But before leaving Hades, Persephone eats three seeds of a pomegranate, an act symbolic of indissoluble marriage. When Demeter found out about that, she felt somewhat defeated still, but the agreement stood, and thus do we have our seasons. On Persephone's return to Earth, spring comes, and when she descends once again each year to her nether realm, winter comes to Earth.

The Demeter myth varied considerably from its onset through the later influence of the patriarchy. You will notice that in the basic story I have just told, there is no rape of Persephone. Earliest myths had her choosing her dark lover quite voluntarily. But enough of that for now. In relating the myths of Demeter to the Moon signs, I will sometimes refer to her as Kore or Persephone, but it should be understood that all are a part of

Demeter. Though I see some progression in process through the modes, the daughters do not fit so neatly into Cardinal and Mutable, nor does Demeter the Mother belong solely to Fixed. You will meet all three in each sign.

## Capricorn—the Cardinal Earth Moon

In a retelling of the pre-patriarchal Demeter myth, Hecate, Goddess of the crossroads, appears in the meadow where Kore and the other maidens rest. Hecate whispers into the ear of the sleeping Kore and gives her a vision. Kore sees into the Underworld where the Dark Lord sits lonely and sad. Behind him is an empty throne with a silver crown upon it. Kore is drawn to him and longs to go to him, bringing light and beauty to his realm. As she gazes, he sees her, too. They are connected, she knows it, and her feminine magnetism calls to him. He mounts his chariot drawn by black stallions and comes to get her. As she vanishes with him into the netherland, the silver crown appears upon her head and she magically becomes Persephone, Queen of the Underworld.[16] In this version of the tale, Kore/Persephone is no victim—not at all. She has a dream, a vision, that calls to her and she goes after it. That is Capricorn, ready to use cardinal initiative to go after a dream and make it reality.

Now, don't let the idea of the Underworld lead you to make wrong assumptions about what I mean by the Capricorn initiative. The Underworld and its Lord have a bad rap that comes from linear philosophies of heaven and hell that do not apply here. Demeter is the Wheel of the Year, the eternal cycle, and in that cycle death is not a fearsome thing, but only part of a natural process, and an important one at that. The point here is that Persephone saw where she could fulfill her destiny by creating something good, and hey, if she can become a queen in the process, that is good, too! She, like you, is a benevolent queen, who blesses the souls under her care and brings them comfort and welcome when they arrive. She assists their return in rebirth— just as the seeds that fall from earth's harvest death are protected beneath the surface through the winter, where they germinate to be reborn with spring.

In another tale of Demeter's travels to many places, searching for her lost daughter, she disguised herself (just as Capricorn Moon often suppresses emotions) as an old woman (a lunar Capricorn is likely to seem old even as a child). Demeter came to Eleusis, where she was hired as nursemaid to a little boy named Demophoon. Under her care, he grew up like a God. She fed him ambrosia and each night secretly held him in a fire, with the intent of making him immortal. One night his mother walked in on this and screamed in fear. Demeter reacted with fury, berating the mother for her stupidity and revealed herself as the beautiful Goddess. Demeter commanded that a temple be built to her in this place, and there she installed herself, but in her grief, still refused to function, so Earth remained barren. Thwarted once again in her quest to mold a "child" of her creation, and criticized to boot, Demeter is depressed. The lunar Capricorn needs a goal, and may, in fact, be driven to succeed, but wants to be recognized favorably for it. There's also a very strong sense of personal responsibility and a need to have control. Frustration can lead to depression.

Capricorn tends toward a bit of pessimism anyway. Fortunately, there's also a sense of humor. In an alternative myth of the founding of the temple, Demeter came to the well of Eleusis, where Bardo, a farmer's wife came for water and taking pity on the sad old woman, invited her to her home. There she gave Demeter refreshment and danced for her, making licentious jokes in the process. Demeter laughed, and when she did, the light of her divine form showed through. The home of Bardo was bathed in light and the glorious Goddess appeared in all her splendor. She honored the family of Bardo by commanding a temple to be built and there she stayed. But the land still remained barren until Demeter got her daughter back!

So, Capricorn Moon, set goals and work responsibly toward them, as you will. Don't let pessimistic moods get the best of you. Sometimes you just have to let go of the struggles of life for a while and laugh at yourself and your situation a little. In fact, frequent doses of humor are good medicine, and may be just the thing to renew your energy.

**Taurus—the Fixed Earth Moon**

Consider Demeter, sitting in her Eleusian temple, refusing to allow the land to become fertile again until she got what she wanted, the return of Persephone. Her people brought her offerings, and even Zeus, the great

Olympian king, sent his messenger to plead, but Demeter remained adamant. Famine threatened, but still Demeter held firm. If she could not have her daughter, she had no will to make the land bloom again. Stubborn? No question. Stubborn is a word that is often attributed to Taurus. But here is a nicer way to put it: Moon, in any sign or mode, is said to be changeable, but in Taurus, of all the Moon signs, she is solidly reliable. You, as a lunar Taurean, are extremely loyal and supportive in your relationships. You are "there" for those you love, and will always care, regardless of what may happen over time. Persistent in your work, as well, you'll stick to your goal until you're satisfied, and you do not want to be rushed in the process.

What is not so immediately apparent in your loyalty and support for others is that you need them as much as you hope that they need you. Your emotional security depends on reliable relationships. If you are let down by another, it can be very difficult for you to get over that and move on. One of your big challenges in life could come through having to learn that your true security lies not in another, but in the strength you have within you.

In the Demeter story we can see both challenge and resolution of security issues from the perspectives of both Demeter and Persephone. Demeter is an able mother, but also an all-consuming one, to her detriment. Eventually, she got what she wanted when her daughter came back—almost. What she had to accept was that her child was not just an extension of herself, sharing the same values, but had found her own life and goals, along with her new love. Fortunately, Demeter accepted that with love, and returned to her own work of blessing growth and harvest. Winter's rest became but a cyclical season, blessed in its own way. From Persephone's view, she loves her mother enough to please her—partially. But she has moved on and found her own identity. Whether we consider the Dark Lord as abductor and rapist, or the lover of Persephone's own choice, it is not he who binds her to her new realm. Now a mature queen, she has found her own identity and satisfaction in her role and her work which she willingly fulfills, whether on Earth in her work there with her mother, or within her own realm.

If your own mother was a strong, reliable presence in your life, you have probably developed a good deal of emotional strength yourself. If your early nurturing was not dependable, you may be prone to overcompensation in nurturing yourself more than may be good for you, such as overeating or excessive sensuality or the acquisition of things. You dislike change, but have great powers of strength and perseverance, such that when you do make up your mind to change, you can and will.

Like the Earth Goddess who is within you, you are down-to-earth in many ways, sensual and practical, good at acquiring, building and maintaining what you have. In these contemporary times, those traits may be directed toward business, and you have a good instinct for it, as well as the prudence and stability to make it succeed. Remember, though, your direct connection to the Earth Mother, for she can bring you deep satisfaction and serenity when you take some time to put your hands into the earth, plant seeds, and bring forth and nurture new growth. Even in the midst of a concrete city, find a spot to do this. Make it a meditation through which your soul can sing.

**Virgo—the Mutable Earth Moon**

To cast Virgo the Virgin as a Crone figure, in Triple Goddess comparison with the astrological modal families, will seem strange to some at first, for Virgin in modern times has been associated primarily with youth and chastity. That image is of a girl who has not yet experienced sexual penetration (or, if the word does refer to an older woman, she is spinster— and if Virgo, most likely characterized as picky). From the understanding of Virgin that comes down from pre-patriarchal cultures, we have a quite different picture. Then, Virgin meant independent, belonging to no man. It did not necessarily mean chaste at all. In temples, holy virgins served a role that was sometimes sexual, as comfort for supplicants, or they would participate in the rites of *heiros gamos*, the sacred marriage, without which no ruler could be considered legitimate by his people. King-making required acceptance by the Goddess. This was accomplished when the would-be king, after proper ceremony and within the temple, had sexual intercourse with a priestess who ritually embodied the Goddess.

So much for Virgo interpretations that focus on barren, critical, picky, etc. I never liked them. They derive, I think, mostly from the very arbitrary assigning of Mercury as ruler of Virgo only because it was the next sign from the Sun, ruling Leo, and Mercury was Sun's closest planet. Then one has to rationalize androgynous, barren, intellectualism for the only zodiacal image of Goddess, who obviously fruitful, holds the grain of harvest in her arms. Well, enough of that. Virgo is quite capable of earthy sensuality. As a lunar Virgo, you are discerning and practical, with a real need to be useful. If "useful" includes contributing to the sensual comfort of…well, perhaps that, too. But you'll most likely be discreet about it, and fastidious.

With a slight bow to Mercury, and a reminder that the Moon is also a mental force, you with Moon in Virgo place a high value on knowledge, primarily for what can be gained from it for practical purpose. Your Virgin could be Eve, for in her situation, you, too, would pluck and eat that apple from the Tree of Knowledge. Whatever you think, do, have or are must be useful in a way that you can clearly define. If not, you'll likely discard it. You set high standards for others and, likely most of all, for yourself.

So, how does Moon in Virgo, and specifically the Demeter myth, fit the transformative Crone image I have assigned to the mutable mode? I see it as the acceptance emerging from transformative experience that finds both Demeter and Persephone willingly, and with love, taking up their respective responsibilities of service to others. Demeter fully accepts her role as the seasonal Wheel of the Year, in all of its phases, including the winter absence of her beloved daughter. Persephone fully accepts her responsibilities to mother, husband and to the souls of her nether realm.

Even more significantly, the Demeter myth speaks to the soul of Virgo Moon through the great Eleusian Mysteries that grew out of it. For many centuries Demeter's temple at Eleusis was the center of an elaborate mystery religion that drew pilgrims from far and wide to experience the seasonal rites and initiatory experiences derived from the stories of Demeter and her daughter. This temple served the spiritual needs of the people, with openness to large-scale participation, where other temples belonged only to the deities, with offerings to them received only in an outer court. The Eleusian Mystery rites gave hope and with that hope, healing. Socrates wrote:

> *"Thrice happy they of men who looked upon these rites ere they go to Hades' house; for they alone there have true life."* Isocrates said, *"Demeter…gave us the greatest of all gifts, first, those fruits of the*

*earth which saved us from living the life of beasts, and secondly, that rite which makes happier the hopes of those that participate therein concerning both the end of life and their whole existence."[17]*

Here is the process of Crone, where knowledge becomes wisdom, acceptance turns to serenity, and service brings hope and healing. Your joy and purpose are fulfilled when you can be truly be of service.

**Public Figures with Moon in Earth signs:**

**Taurus: Ronald Reagan**; **Bill Clinton**; **Prince Charles**; rock star **Mick Jagger**; great actress **Katharine Hepburn**, union leader **Jimmy Hoffa**; astrologer **Maritha Pottenger**

**Virgo**: singer/actress **Madonna**; actress also known for her "New Age" activities, **Shirley MacLaine**, the **Dalai Lama**; actors **Sean Connery**, **Jack Nicholson** and **John Travolta**; noted philosopher and educator **Rudolph Steiner**

**Capricorn:** First President of the USA, **George Washington** and Civil War era President **Abraham Lincoln**; country music star **Patsy Cline**; comedienne **Lucille Ball**, founder of American Red Cross, **Clara Barton**; movie star **Susan Sarandon**

# Goddess of the Air

*I call, oh Queen of Wind and Air*
*Breath of life is yours to share*
*Wisdom I now seek from you*
*I need to know*
*How truth be seen with clarity*
*Cosmic cycles, land and sea*
*All continue, all renew*
*Oh, help me see!*

*Live within me, I will serve you*
*Breathe your truth within my soul*
*May it grow now, ever stronger*
*As I live in peace and joy and love.*

## Isis and the Air Moons

For our Goddess of the Air we go to ancient Egypt for Isis, whose powerful presence has prevailed throughout the ages. She is often portrayed with golden wings, but this alone is not my reason for choosing this universal Goddess for the air signs. Air is the element most closely associated with the intellect. The civilization of ancient Egypt still fascinates for its vast accomplishments in such intellectual disciplines as mathematics, engineering and astronomy—feats that would be challenging, if not impossible, to duplicate even now. This has led to wide speculation that a lost but even more advanced civilization, perhaps even an alien one, may one day be discovered to have contributed to the construction and precise alignments of the Great Pyramids.

It is here in Egypt that Isis arose, reigned and on the winds of communication spread her wings throughout the world and still is revered in many countries even today either in her own name, or as the forerunner of much of the lore that later became associated with Mary, Mother of God and the Black Madonna. The mystery religion of Isis persisted in the Christian era with such dominance even in Rome, itself, that the Catholic Church had little choice but to incorporate her. Mother of God, one of the many titles by which Isis was called, became the Christian Mother of God, and art depicting Isis with her infant son Horus was revisioned as the Madonna and Child.

Isis was called the Goddess of Ten Thousand Names. Though her beginning can't be dated for sure, it is known from the pyramids that she was the Great Isis from at least 3000 BC. Her public worship was finally suppressed by the Theodosian Law of AD 426, a century after Constantine had made Christianity the official religion of the Roman Empire.[18] Since then her worship may not have been officially recognized, but it has persisted, and is still practiced by many Neopagans. Particularly notable is the Fellowship of Isis, an international organization based in Ireland that, according to its web site stats for August 2004, there are 23,276 members in many countries.[19] That is a gain of about 8000 members over the data printed in the 2001 publication of *The Mysteries of Isis*, by DeTraci Regula,[20] who is an ordained priestess through the Foundation. The FOI, a multi-faith organization "dedicated to the Goddess in all Her many forms" has named itself for Isis because of her universality.

Though Isis is both light and dark and represents all aspects of the Triple Goddess, I will refer to other Egyptian Goddess names, in part, for the specific imagery they bring to Libra and Aquarius. I have often read, in the multiple sources I consulted, that all other Goddesses of this pantheon could also be considered as aspects of Isis.

### Libra—the Cardinal Air Moon

Libra's symbol in the heavens is the Scales of Balance, and Isis, Queen of Heaven, was considered to be the lawgiver and the source of wisdom, counsel and righteous justice. Libra is the sign astrology most associates with peace, and Isis, among her Ten Thousand names, is Queen of Peace. In this synastry of Goddess images with the concepts of Maiden and the cardinal-initiator mode, Isis is said to have created and taught the skills of civilization to her people. Egyptian writings said of her, "In the beginning there was Isis, Oldest of the Old. She was the Goddess from whom all becomings arose."[21] Called Goddess of the Rosy Dawn, morning rites were chanted to her at every sunrise in ancient times, and by her modern devotees, still are.[22]   The glyph for Libra depicts the sunrise! As Lady of Beauty and of Love, she is considered to be a forerunner of Aphrodite/Venus.

You of the Libra Moon are refined souls of inherently good taste, who appreciate the proprieties of civilized behavior and have a real need to feel that things are fair. Exposure to unfairness or discord or crudity upset you emotionally, likely such that you cannot bear to be around people who behave that way and will avoid them, if you can. You may be known as a peacemaker. Certainly you prefer peace, if at all possible, so will seek compromise in any disagreement. Your skills at diplomacy and charm are probably quite good. Your challenge may be to find the proper balance between giving in and standing firm, for your need to get along with others and have their approval may lead you to over compromise.

With Moon in Libra you have the emotional detachment typical of any air sign. Able to see both (or multiple) view points of any situation in an objective manner, you may find it difficult to commit to just one, preferring to reconcile things so that everyone is satisfied. This could mean being stuck in indecision wanting to "have your cake and eat it, too" or at least to wait for some wind of what others are thinking before you commit yourself.

Isis, as Mistress of Magic, often collaborated with Thoth, the Egyptian God of Wisdom, who was married to Ma'at, Goddess of Truth and Justice. Ma'at's primary image was the Scales, and all judges were her priests. Her trademark was a red feather, worn in her hair. All souls were weighed against Ma'at's feather when they came into the Hall of Judgment, either when entering this world or leaving it, for none may evade natural order.

Ma'at (most specifically, but also Isis) symbolized the natural order of things and the inescapable laws of the Cosmos. Thoth represented the more linear, logical mind more often associated with the masculine. Ma'at is the feminine complement to Thoth, representing the cyclical and organic natural order to which forms of learning, measurement and legislation must be attuned if they are to be effective. And so we have the relationship, the complement and balance for which your Libran soul yearns. Isis' magical power combines the two, for the success of magic, so matter how focused the conscious mind, depends on attunement with natural law—Divine Order.

Perhaps meditating on Isis, Ma'at and Thoth, with their magic of balance and attunement, will be of value in reconciling your needs for external approval with your internal sense of rightness, harmony and balance. Nothing or no one outside yourself defines you unless you allow it to be so, nor can anyone else substitute for the completeness you find within when you are serenely at peace with yourself. Discover your own truth within, and then live it, such that "as within, so without" you will attract from the Universe the harmony you seek.

## Aquarius—the Fixed Air Moon

In ancient Egyptian mythology, Nut was the sky, pictured as a Great Mother arched over the earth, touching its "ends" with her fingertips and toes. Her breasts poured out milk to nurture the people, hence the Milky Way. An interesting image, this, for the Aquarian Waterbearer!

Isis, who is a daughter of Nut, grew in power to become the premier Mother Goddess of Egypt, and over time her cult spread throughout the Middle Eastern and Western world. She, too, fits the Waterbearer in what is said to be a probable origin of her name from Ashesh, which means "pouring out" and "supporting." This implies her divine essence (blood or milk) that kept the Gods and all other creatures alive.[23]

Isis fits well the fixed nature of Aquarius in the persistence of her worship for millennia, longer than any other major deity known. She comes from the distant past of the Great Pyramids and she projects forward into the future, in the universality of her image within the fast-growing Neopagan spiritualities.

Of all the air signs, Aquarius is the stubborn one. Stubborn? Freedom loving, far-seeing, eccentric Aquarius? Yes, once an idea is adopted, Aquarius will push boundaries to the limit to convince, persuade and prevail. Of course, you can change your mind, too, and might do so in a manner that may seem unexpected and unpredictable by others. The point is, you've decided your truth on your own terms, in your own way, and in your own time. It's just too bad for others if they can't catch up with your logical, objective reasoning until after you tell them about it. After all, you're ahead of your time, and you like it that way. Independence of thought is important to you, as is personal freedom.

You aren't particularly comfortable with your emotions. They just aren't reasonable and logical. But you do have them, like it or not. Even if you don't quite understand your feelings, don't stuff them down. It is best that you learn to honestly express how you feel at the time you feel it—even if it comes out in logical phrases.

Nurturing Mother qualities are seen in the Aquarian openness and friendliness that wants to take care of the world, likely through the adoption and promotion of humanitarian causes. You're a revolutionary who wants to change things if you see them as "not right" and are capable of speaking out zealously for what you believe, and to make things better for others. In that you are like Isis, who from her beginnings, looked kindly on the people of Earth and taught them patiently the skills they needed to care for themselves—how to plant, grind corn, spin flax and live together peacefully.

You can, when you wish, be persistent beyond all imagination, as was Isis in determined search for her lost consort Osiris who was murdered by their evil brother Set, encased in casket and thrown into the Nile. Isis searched and eventually found him, only to have Set kill him once again, this time cutting him into pieces and scattering them all around the world. Isis found the pieces, every one of them except the phallus, which had unfortunately been eaten by a fish. She put Osiris back together again, even fashioning a gold phallus to replace the missing one, then brought him back to life and lay with him to conceive Horus. Top that one, Aquarius! And perhaps you might, in emulation of the all-powerful Isis who alone could boast, "I will overcome Fate."[24]

**Gemini—the Mutable Air Moon**

Isis and Osiris were born together and mated while still in Nut's womb, brother and sister but also married (a perfectly OK thing in some ancient cultures, and even preferable in the case of royalty). So we have the imagery of the Gemini Twins, but they weren't just twins, but quintuplets. This is explained by an ancient myth that answers why we have 365 days in our year instead of what you'd think would be the more logical 360 of a full circle with an equal 30 days for each month. The Sun (Ra) ordered Shu (Air) to separate Nut (Sky) from her brother-lover Geb (Earth), and he ordained that Nut should never bear children in any month of the year. Thoth, God of Wisdom, felt sorry for Nut and played a game with the Moon that won him a 72nd part of her light. This became the five intercalary days that belonged to no month. On these days, Nut bore Osiris, Horus the Elder, Set, Isis and Nephthys.

The children of Nut make a neat story to introduce the idea that you, Moon in Gemini, are a multiplicity of moods—changeable as the quicksilver in a thermometer that bears the name of your sign's ruler, Mercury of the winged feet. You are restless, distractible and androgynous—like the siblings of Nut's womb, light and dark, feminine and masculine. You may respond quickly to emotions around you and will, more easily than most, shake them off and go on your way, not buying into the watery and weepy, fiery passionate or muddy earth feelings that might plague other types. You adapt easily to new circumstances, are seldom at a loss for words and like to keep on the move both physically and in your mind, ever curious to learn something new. You take little for granted and question everything.

Usually cheerful and vivacious, you can be a Jack or Jill of many trades and the spark that keeps a party going. Most likely you are good with children because you've never lost the curiosity and wonder of a child, and can communicate with them as quite easily.

The dual quality of Isis-Osiris can also be seen with Isis-Nephthys, and here we see the aspect of Crone as symbolic of the mutable, transformative quality of each element. Nephthys is the dark sister who with Isis represents the life/death-Mother/Crone aspects of the Goddess trinity. Still, Isis was also both, as when she found the dead Osiris, *"O, Osiris, live, stand up thou unfortunate one that liest there! I am Isis. I am Nephthys."* And Osiris stood up and lived, and life continued.[25]

We all have our expressions of darkness. Unrecognized, the dark can be problematic, but when acknowledged, healing. You'd rather fly freely over the surface of emotional problems than to dive into them fully, especially those that murk beneath the surface where you'd prefer to pretend they don't exist. It's easier to tell others—and yourself—what they/you want to hear, rather than to probe a little deeper and chance conjuring unwanted truths. This isn't lying…amoral, perhaps, or maybe just self-protective. If nervous tension is a problem, the path to healing might be to slow down and really open yourself to heart-to-heart communication.

Gemini is a sign most commonly associated with youthfulness, but I have compared mutability to the transformative Crone, who is both she who ushers souls through the gates of death and she who is midwife to those reborn. The mutable signs are disseminating, and certainly the lore of Isis has been widely disseminated throughout the world as a most universal of deities. Of images of Isis, the most familiar in our current era is that of her widespread golden wings. In ancient Egypt, the Winged Isis most commonly appeared in funeral statuary or in her persona of Mistress of Healing. Birds in ancient Goddess symbolism are associated with cyclical change and transformation.Birds are twice-born, first as egg and then as chick. Of the sky they are close to Spirit. In the myth of Isis and Osiris, once Isis had collected all the pieces of Osiris' broken body and reassembled them, she spread her wings over him and fanned him until the breeze breathed life into him once again. So it is that coffins often depicted the wings of Isis wrapped around, so that she may breath new life into the souls that have passed beyond.

You have a talent, lunar Gemini—a real gift—in that through your own transformative experiences, you can help and heal by articulating what you've learned to others, lifting their spirits. With your insatiable curiosity and ability to communicate you can report, teach, inspire and share your sense of infinite wonder in the world.

**Public Figures with Moon in Air signs:**

**Libra:** poet **Elizabeth Barrett Browning**; **Walt Disney**; astronaut Moon walker, **Buzz Aldrin**; Presidents **George W. Bush** and **George H.W. Bush**; astrologer/author **Gloria Star**; distinguished poet **Maya Angelou**; recording star **Bruce Springsteen**

**Aquarius: Diana, Princess of Wales**; boxing champ **Muhammad Ali**; British Prime Minister **Tony Blair**; author of *Little Women*, **Louisa May Alcott**, Beatle **John Lennon**, '60s radical known for LSD, **Timothy Leary**; astrologer-philosopher, **Dane Rudhyar**

**Gemini: Pope John Paul II**, **John Kerry** and **John Edwards**, Democratic candidates for President and Vice-President, respectively, in 2004; highly influential psychologist **Sigmund Freud**, former child actress turned diplomat, **Shirley Temple Black**; astrologers/authors **Zipporah Dobyns, Ph.D.** and **Demetra George**; movie star **Kirk Douglas**

## Endnotes

[1]"Transit" refers to "real time," the position of the Moon at the current time.

[2]The verses of invocation to each elemental Goddess are adapted from the music section in *The Witch's Circle*. They are my own words, written to fit the melody of "Here I am, Lord" by Dan Schutte, S.J., from *Glory and Praise, Vol. 3,* Northern Liturgy Resources, Phoenix, AZ.

[3] *The Witch's Circle*, pg 55-57

[4]Walker, Barbara, The Women's Encyclopedia of Myths and Secrets, San Francisco: Harper & Row, 1983.

[5]Farrar, Janet & Stewart, *The Witches' Goddess,* Custer, WA: Phoenix Publishing, 1987.

[6]ibid

[7]The Ishtar myth of descent is composited from several sources: *The Witches' Goddess, Luna: Myth & Mystery, The Book of Goddesses & Heroines, The Women's Encyclopedia of Myths & Secrets*. See bibliography.

[8]Seven relates to the seven visible planets known to the ancients: Sun, Moon, Mercury, Venus, Mars, Jupiter and Saturn. In the cosmology of Ishtar's time, it was thought that seven spheres of planetary influence were both above and beneath Earth such that a soul seeking entrance to heaven or descending to hell must pass through each of them (the gates). Temple initiations dramatized these journeys. Very early Christians added the concept that souls descending from heaven to enter their physical bodies on Earth, took on faults and passions from each of the celestial spheres, and this is the origin of the Seven Deadly Sins: sloth for Saturn, gluttony for Jupiter, anger for Mars, lust for Venus, greed for Mercury, envy for Moon and pride for Sun.

[9]I've read this in Goddess books in reference to Salome's dance that led to the beheading of John the Baptist, but my Pisces Moon daughter, a Middle Eastern dancer, is a stickler for detail since she's studying history of dance toward her master's degree. She says the Salome reference is not verified by any serious research and therefore should not be stated as such. So, it's apparently a fairly recent idea, but an interesting and colorful one, isn't it. Whoever first thought of attaching seven veils to the dance of Salome must have had the Ishtar myth in mind.

[10]Cain, Kathleen: *Luna: Myth and Mystery*, Boulder, CO: Johnson Printing, 1991.

[11]Public figure examples appear at the end of each interpretive section. See Appendix IV for a complete list, data references and basis for my choices.

[12]Sister Mary is one of two nuns who have formed *Solas Bhride*, a Christian Community Centre for Celtic Spirituality in Kildare, Ireland. A festival is held there each year at Imbolc. For information: *www.ordbrighideach.org* or Sister Mary Minehan, Solas Bhride, 14 Dara Park, Kildare, Ireland.

[13]Farrar, *The Witches' Goddess*

[14]*Witches' Goddess*, quoted from *Celtic Mythology* (Hamlyn, London, 1970).

[15]Walker, *Encyclopedia of Women's Mysteries.*

[16]Reif, Jennifer, *Mysteries of Demeter,* York Beach, ME: Samuel Weiser, Inc., 1999

[17]Walker, *Encyclopedia of Women's Myths & Secrets,* pg 219, as quoted from Lawson 563-64, Lawson, John Cuthbert, *Modern Greek Folklore and Ancient Greek Religion*, New York: University Books Inc., 1964.

[18]Farrar, *The Witches' Goddess.*

[19]Fellowship of Isis web site: *www.fellowshipofisis.com*

[20]Regula, DeTraci, *The Mysteries of Isis*, St. Paul, MN: Llewellyn, 2001.

[21]Stone, Merlin, *When God was a Woman*, San Diego, CA: Harcourt Brace Jovanovich, 1976.

[22]Regula, *Mysteries of Isis.*

[23]*Encyclopedia of Women's Myths & Secrets*, page 454, as quoted from *Gods of the Egyptians* by Sir E.A. Wallis Budge, Vol. 2, New York: Dover Publications, 1969.

[24]Monoghan, Patricia, *The New Book of Goddesses & Heroines*, St. Paul, MN: Llewellyn, 2001.

[25]Frazer, Sir James George, *The Golden Bough*, New York: Collier Books, 1922

## Chapter Three

# The House of Your Birth Moon

The *Moon Tides* report, under the heading **At Time of Birth** gives you a number for **House of Moon**. This is the only place on the report that houses are mentioned. You do need your birth time in order that this feature can be useful, for House of Moon cannot be reliably known without accurate time. For the benefit of readers who have studied houses enough to have an opinion on which system they prefer, the default in *Moon Tides* software is Koch, because that is what I use. If you don't like that, go into Settings and there you will find the means to switch to the house system you prefer.

For novice readers, experiment with house systems if you like, especially if you read my interpretation of House of Moon and can't relate to it. In one of the other systems your Moon may just possibly show up in the house before or after the one yielded by accepting the default. This is because house systems vary according to the mathematician who invented them. Koch Houses were used for public figure examples in this chapter.

The means of interpreting House of Moon in this book must, in sync with the report information, rely entirely on the number of the house. This will work if you know your birth time. If, however, you did not know your birth time, I suggest that you do not use the default for House of Moon. Instead, use the time of sunrise in standard time for your birth date in your location of birth, and select Equal Houses under Settings. That will put Sun on the cusp of the first house, resulting in equal houses from the Sun. It's not perfect, but it maintains the idea of relationship of Moon to Sun, while also giving you the solar houses that many Sun Sign columnists use to write their generalized interpretations.

A House of the birth chart always has an underlying theme that is derived from its "natural" house, i.e., the division and order of the zodiacal 12 that begins with Aries. In other words, House One relates to Aries and its planetary ruler Mars, House Two relates to Taurus and its planetary ruler, Venus, and so on. The meanings are similar, but not exactly the same. It is useful for you to understand the basic differences in how planets, signs and houses are interpreted.

**Planets do**— (Or more accurately, they reflect what we do). Think of them as verbs (Moon feels), or visualize them as the **light** shining through a stained glass window.

**Signs describe**—think of them as adverbs or style. (To oversimplify, Moon in Aries feels impulsively; Moon in Taurus feels steadily; and so on.) Or, think of signs as the **color** of the stained glass that the light coming through picks up and reflects on the floor.

**Houses show where**—the environment, the area of life, in which the planetary function is seen to operate in reflecting what we do. In the stained glass analogy, the house is **where** the light is reflected (on the floor, or if you are standing in that spot, on you, or on whatever else may be in the path of that colored light. For example, House 1 is where "I" am, my identity, while House 2 is what's "mine," which includes my finances.

## The Natural Zodiac

Each house takes on an interpretive theme derived from its natural sign, ruling planet and their element and mode as determined by zodiacal order, e.g.: Aries is the "natural" House 1, Taurus is the "natural" House 2, and so on. As such, you will notice similarities in my interpretations with themes from the sign interpretations, though the interpretive paragraphs and examples to follow are derived much more from basic astrological theory than from Goddess mythology. Considerably more depth could be covered on houses, but since this book and report deal with one factor, the house of Moon in the birth chart, this section will be relatively brief.

Following is a list of houses with short keywords and phrases to identify areas of life associated with each of them, with the ruling planet, sign, element and mode naturally associated with that house. You may find it well worthwhile to re-read the Goddess mythology from the last chapter corresponding to the sign, element and mode of the House your Moon occupies, and reflect on whether the myth might also have some application to the area of your life that the House covers. In some interpretations in this chapter, I've referred back to myths, in others not. Still, they may apply. In the case of my own eighth House of Moon, I find, in retrospect, the Scorpio myths to be more evocative of real insight for me than I can glean from traditional house interpretation alone.

## Areas of Life: The Houses

**House 1**: you, your identity, your appearance and behavior
*Mars, Aries, Fire, Cardinal*

**House 2**: possessions, money, security or lack of it, material comforts
*Venus, Taurus, Earth, Fixed*

**House 3**: communication, movement within local area, early schooling, relatives, neighbors, movement & interaction within local environment
*Mercury, Gemini, Air, Mutable*

**House 4:** home (real estate), family, ancestral roots, nurturing parent(s)
*Moon, Cancer, Water, Cardinal*

**House 5:** creative expression, your children, romance, leisure, games, speculation
*Sun, Leo, Fire, Fixed*

**House 6:** work, co-workers, employees, health, nutrition, service, daily routine
*Mercury, Virgo, Earth, Mutable*

**House 7**—one-to-one relationships, marriage, spouse, partners, competitors, enemies
*Venus, Libra, Air, Cardinal*

**House 8**—shared resources, sex, debt, inheritance, taxes, secrets, power, the occult, death
*Pluto, Scorpio, Water, Fixed*

**House 9**—faith (religion), philosophy, higher education, law, ideals, ethics, distant travel
*Jupiter, Sagittarius, Fire, Mutable*

**House 10**—career, status, reputation, reality, reputation, authorities, disciplinary parent
*Saturn, Capricorn, Earth, Cardinal*

**House 11**—friends, peer groups, organizations, hopes and wishes, humanitarian concerns
*Uranus, Aquarius, Air, Fixed*

**House 12**—withdrawal, retreats (including hospital stays), privacy, secrets kept to self
*Neptune, Pisces, Water, Mutable*

## Moon in the Birth Houses

### Moon in House 1

Your emotions are out front and they show more than you may realize. The old adage of "wearing your heart on your sleeve" applies. Emotionally vested in your sense of personal identity, you have a real need to be seen as central, "number 1," to have the freedom to move around when you want to and do things your way. You feel safest and happiest when you can express yourself freely, but at the same time, you really don't want to hurt those who are close to you. Obviously this combination of concern and self-centered feelings can provoke mood swings when the two don't mesh. Think of your moods as being a combination of fire and water—Moon is a water planet, and House 1 is the natural house of Aries, cardinal fire. Water sizzles, warm and upbeat, or on the other hand, can boil over into hot anger. Or the water douses out the fire and you withdraw into a blue funk. A lot of how you handle yourself emotionally depends on how you, yourself, were parented, especially mothered. If your initiative was squelched, you may be more inclined to those blue funks, but if you were supported and encouraged to express yourself freely, albeit with consideration for others' feelings, you probably stick up for yourself quite well, and are more often in an upbeat mood. Think of Brighid's creative fire, and let her be your guide in expressing yourself. That can be you, at your best. You can use your emotional power, your natural warmth and your independent spirit to attract and to inspire.

**Madonna** has Moon in Virgo in House 1, creating a mix of Mutable-Earth in a Cardinal-Fire House. She expresses a wealth of earthy sensuality, a perfect example of why the nitpicky, modest descriptions of Virgo sell the celestial Virgin far short of her potential. But Madonna seems to have an identity problem, reinventing herself so often that it's difficult to keep up. Certainly she has the creative fire of a media goddess. Perhaps her apparent inability to decide just who she is and stay with it is a combination of the impulsive moodiness of House 1 with the seasonal return of Persephone to the Underworld. She periodically "dies" and emerges again with a new springtime persona. **Others with Moon in House 1: Lucille Ball, Lyndon Johnson, Walt Disney, Elizabeth Barrett Browning, Betty Friedan, Gloria Star, Zipporah Dobyns, Ph.D.**

## Moon in House 2

You may have been one of those kids who had extra trouble with the "mine" stage. Emotionally involved with what you have, you collect things and have a tough time letting any of them go. That also applies to people. But, like the little kid who finds others may not want to play if she won't share, you could have a few similar adult-sized issues, if you hold on too much. That's tough for someone who is also sensual and really likes comfort and cuddling. Much depends on how you were nurtured by your childhood family. If you felt safe and loved there, then you may share easily, both materially and in your ability to let those you love be themselves. It's important to realize that that true security is not in what you have but in what you are inside. Think back to Demeter, as was expressed in the Taurean Moon. She was stubborn and persistent in insisting that Persephone come back, refusing to work or share until she got her own way. But, finally she realized that this was more her own need than Persephone's. When she came to terms with that—her own deep need for emotional security—she could love her daughter without depending on her always being there. She returned to her own work and became productive again. As for the acquisition and protection of material things, if you find yourself surrounded by clutter, or holding onto too much weight for your health, this may be a signal that you're using material gratification as a substitute for soul gratification. Your real strength is not in what you've acquired but in your practical, steady, persistent ability to create the comfort that you desire in the first place. That can never be taken away from you—it is always there, within you, so nurture it and develop your resourcefulness, the true source of your security.

**Martha Stewart** has Moon in Sagittarius in House 2. Blending her fire Moon with Fixed-Earth determination, she propelled her lunar domestic skills into a huge business empire. It appears from the many news, magazine and TV stories about her, amid extensive publicity about her legal problems at the time of this writing, that her fiery zeal to get there fast has also brought serious problems. **Others: George H.W. Bush, John Travolta, Maya Angelou, Coco Chanel**

**Moon in House 3**

No matter what the sign of your Moon, you are likely to express it through the airy and flexible affairs of this house. With an emotional need to learn, to develop dexterity and skill, you move actively in communicating with others. You're likely a "people person," even if your Moon sign is one of the quieter Earth or Water types that might incline you to communicate through writing more easily than through talking. Interested and curious about many things, you may be a "jack-of-all-trades" with versatile talents. This is a mix of a Water planet with an Air house, which means, for one thing, that feeling and thinking are working together whether the two sides of this house's Gemini-twin theme like it or not. Sorting out what you feel from what you think can be problematic at times. Your mood influences how you think, how you express yourself, and also in how you listen, and listening is half or more of the art of good communication. This can come out in a number of ways. On the downside, here's one that could be imagined from the water/air combo: morose mood means you failed to hear something important and then failed the test or offended someone who thought you knew. Or, you snap at someone who doesn't deserve it because you felt, well, irritable. On the upside, your emotional flow can be an advantage when you can project it outward positively rather than dwelling on it inwardly. You can project great empathy in your communications.

**Diana, Princess of Wales**, had Moon in House 3. Even though we know now that she often felt miserable inside, her warmth and ability to empathize in communication earned accolades as "the Peoples' Princess." Diana, who was a Cancer Sun, also exemplifies well the Isis-Mother nurturing and humanitarian image of her Aquarius Moon. She spread her golden wings over the world, and the world became her neighborhood in the archetype of transformative Isis—a great image for a Third House communicator. **Others** with this placement: **Karl Jung, Timothy Leary, Elvis Presley, Yoko Ono, the Dalai Lama, Catherine Zeta-Jones, Jack Nicholson**

**Moon in House 4**

Moon in her natural house is at home and comfortable, regardless of what sign she's in, expressing her homebody nature to heart's content. This is a good placement for a home business entrepreneur, and I can think of several people whom I know personally with Moon in House 4 who have done just that. If they have employees, they treat them like family and are more parent more than "boss." Or if the business is separate from the home, they may treat it like a home—homey office, parental attitude. Regardless of your Moon sign, you derive emotional security from familial relationships and surroundings. You need a warm, cozy, supportive home environment in order to go out into the world and interact with confidence. If the home environment is stressful, you'll pick up the stress like a sponge, so be aware. Do what you can to calm the troubled waters. This will be easier if you received good nurturing in your home of origin. On the other hand, stress in your home now might stem from inner stress from your home of origin. The first step to fix it is to be aware of it: Don't withdraw inside the figurative crab shell and block out what hurts. Nothing outside yourself can cause you undue stress unless you open yourself to let it in. Take a deep breath, and like Ishtar, set out to meet Ereshkigal, your dark inner sister, but don't storm the gates. Just confront her, acknowledge her, learn from her, and then come back calmly and look up to see the rainbow. Breathe in serenity—and then perhaps cook a nice, comfort food meal for you and your family.

**Elizabeth Kubler-Ross**' Moon is in Cancer in House 4. I do not know to what extent she has worked at home, but her nurturing qualities and ability to ease the pain of others through her work and give them hope is very evident. She is prominently known for her research into the life after death stories collected from people all around the world who have briefly died and then were resuscitated, revealing experiences that were very similar. **Others with Moon in House 4 include: Johann Von Goethe, Maria Montessori, John McCain, Michael Jackson, Marlon Brando, Ringo Starr.**

## Moon in House 5

Moon in this fixed fire house of creative self-expression feels the Lion's sense of pride, or lack of it, right in the pit of the stomach. You need to be regal in the sense of receiving admiration for what you do in the areas associated with this house—what you create (including such things as art and performances, but also your children), how you play or compete or entertain and how you love. Remember Brighid and Bres, and how difficult, even humiliating, it may have been for her to share all his self-caused troubles through mishandling his kingship? She probably mothered him, though, just as you may mother your children, your lovers and your own creative work, nurturing them and then basking in glory when they receive admiration and approval...or, feeling shadowed like a big dark cloud when they receive disapproval. You are emotionally vested in the success of your children—after all, they reflect you. This can be a problem for them, if you are too pushy about it. Again, much can depend on how you, yourself were nurtured and received approval, or didn't. Lack of self-esteem could cause some overcompensation here. Your children are not you, so don't try to make them be. You are emotionally involved with the product of your creation. Approval gives you a warm glow of security. You like to have fun, and you can spark it. You've never lost the natural magic and wonder of childhood, and so you are probably quite good at playing and laughing with children on their level, whatever their age.

Two famous artists, **Vincent Van Gogh** and **Pablo Picasso** have Moon in House 5. Picasso, over his 75-year career, dominated 20th century art, receiving worldwide approval long before his death at 91, enjoying his celebrity and becoming very rich. Van Gogh, the major Post Impressionist, received no accolades within his lifetime. He painted prolifically between bouts of depression and madness, but had only sold two paintings prior to shooting himself in 1890. Years after his death, his work had appreciated beyond imagination, when a collector paid nearly $54 million dollars for his painting, *Irises*. One can hope that somewhere his spirit is smiling broadly and is at peace. **Others include: Ronald Reagan, Al Gore, Albert Einstein, Bruce Springsteen, Kirk Douglas, Buzz Aldrin, Sybil Leek, Lois Rodden, Rob Hand**

## Moon in House 6

With Moon here you are emotionally vested in efficient work and in maintaining your heath. Mother was likely your role model for a good job at whatever task is taken on, either because she was efficient, or maybe because she wasn't. Either through imitation or in compensation, you developed a real need to be effective and to achieve a high level of skill. Something also triggered in you a more than average concern about health. This could possibly have begun by your experience of the illness or poor health habits of someone close to you, or from a general empathy for those whom you perceive need your help. You may have been the child who always managed to find a stray animal or less fortunate friend to help. You need to feel needed, and are glad to help when you see a need in others you can serve. There's a potential downside of that, if your own need causes you to either be taken advantage of beyond what is good for you, or to begin thinking of yourself as necessary to someone who would be better off learning to become more independent. Becoming too emotional over health issues, at the extreme can become hypochondria, or it can become your work in the world as a healer. Certainly you'll be fastidious about it in some way, likely to considerable detail.

My youngest daughter has Moon in 6, and in Pisces, a sign often associated with healing. **Elizabeth** became a vegetarian at the age of 11, entirely of her own choice, at first in sympathy for animals. Later she also became convinced vegetarianism was best for her health, and she's become adept at properly balancing her diet with mostly organic foods. She's also a yoga teacher and a professional Middle Eastern dancer, *Mariyah*, with a notable quality of sacred dance. This Mutable-Earth house recalls the Demeter myth at the transformative Virgo-Crone stage where spiritual ritual in the Eleusian Mysteries provided hope and healing for participants. **My list of Public figures who have Moon in House 6 include Woody Allen, Indira Gandhi, Jaqueline Kennedy Onassis, Louisa May Alcott, and Muhammad Ali.** Ali's life story particularly strikes me in his determination and integrity expressed by sticking with his personal choices to become a Muslim and then a conscientious objector, even though, for a time, he lost his heavyweight boxing title as a result. Now he displays quiet courage and stamina in managing his increasingly debilitating Parkinson's disease.

**Moon in House 7**

Moon in this house of relationships emphasizes security needs for an "other." As a child you needed someone to play with, and may have created an imaginary friend if lacking a real one. You feel most secure with a partner—a "right" partner, that is. The level of security or insecurity you have in relationship issues may stem, in part, from how your mother handled hers. If feeling insecure, you can become over-compromising rather than relying on yourself and sticking up for yourself. Fairness in all things matters. When you feel off-balance or treated unfairly you can be pretty emotionally stressed. An egalitarian relationship is probably best for you, but you may vacillate between partners that are too stifling or too free-wheeling and undependable before you learn the proper balance point that will allow you to feel safe in a relationship without sacrificing your own individuality. With a gift for grace and charm, you are probably quite sociable, unless with a very quiet Moon sign. You prefer peace, harmony, refinement, good taste and aesthetically pleasing surroundings, and can feel emotionally rattled if things are not, well…nice. Balance is the key—keep within your mind and soul the scales of balance on which Ma'at weighed souls against the red feather from her hair. You must find the balance that is right for you of when to give in, when to compromise and when you must stand firm for your own preferences.

Two public figures exemplify facets of the Moon in House 7 theme very well. **Queen Elizabeth II,** whose Moon sign is regal Leo, has always been a model of refinement, grace and dignity, as well as a symbol of unity and continuity for the UK. **Albert Schweitzer,** German medical missionary and Christian theologian, richly exemplified his own creed of reverence for life. He was awarded the Nobel Peace Prize in 1952. **Others with Moon in House 7: VP Dick Cheney, Jane Fonda, Oliver North, Cher, Patsy Cline, Katharine Hepburn, Marilyn Monroe, Senator John Kerry**.

### Moon in House 8

Here we have a playing field, or sometimes a battleground, for sharing. It's about the give and take that goes on with others. Sometimes grown-up versions of dealing with this are not so radically different from the small child's having to struggle with what is rightfully "mine," what is "yours" and what we can comfortably agree is "ours." The resolution can be emotionally intense. In close one-to-one relationships we may share space, possessions, ideas, time, secrets, control and power. In marriage, there's also sexuality, and that hasn't been unknown in business relationships, either. Then, have you heard the phrase to the effect that the two things you can't avoid are death and taxes? Well, both of them are matters of this house, too. Also, so is the occult (an extrapolation of the term "secrets"). When one's sense of emotional or material security is closely tied to someone else, and then feels threatened, obviously there's emotional upset and the potential for power struggles and manipulation. It can be a major Ishtar and Ereshkigal face-off, but here I do not refer to you and the other confronting each other, but instead to you confronting the darker side of you. Interacting and sharing with others helps you learn about yourself. A challenge is to find a balanced place of egalitarian commitment and mutual respect, somewhere in between dependency or dominance. A lesson of this placement is self-mastery. You learn to master yourself, but you do share, often giving a good deal of yourself. Moon in House 8 people are often seen in roles through which they facilitate the interests and advancement of others.

**Eleanor Roosevelt,** one of the most admired First Ladies of all time, had Moon in House 8. Also, **Sigmund Freud** (you did note that I said sexuality is an affair of this house?), **Lucianno Pavarotti,** world renowned operatic tenor, **Pope John Paul II**; abstract expressionist painter **Willem De Kooning;** football star tried and acquitted of murder, **O. J. Simpson;** and also **President Bill Clinton, Jim Bakker and Isadora Duncan**

## Moon in House 9

With this house of your Moon, you're emotionally vested in your ideals and beliefs, and if questioned, will defend them with spirit, and perhaps even evangelistic fervor. Whatever you care about you're inclined to idealize, put on a pedestal or hold as Truth—with a capital "T." The quest to learn and seek Truth is lifelong. It is likely that your mother had a good deal of influence on your belief system. Either you've followed that lead and developed it further on your own, or if you feel she let you down, you were highly motivated to seek a different Truth. As you evolve in that direction you'll also develop a moral and ethical code of utmost importance to you. You may travel far in seeking and developing your philosophy and worldview, if not in miles, then via the mind through higher education, books, media, internet and in philosophical conversations and debates. Attracted to foreign countries and diverse people, you'll want to experience the stimulation of the new and different. With your lively sense of adventure, personal freedom is highly important. You need the space to do what you like to do, to think your own thoughts. You're gregarious and like to be with people, especially when there's something new to learn. Your sense of justice may also be an important issue. It can drive you to "fight for the right without question or pause" in your quest to reach "the unreachable star."

That's from *Man of La Mancha,* the story of Don Quixote, a good myth for this placement. Seek your Truth and your destiny!

> *...My destiny calls, and I go!*
> *And the wild winds of fortune*
> *Shall carry me onward....*
> *To wither so ever they blow...*

—from *The Impossible Dream,* lyrics by Joe Darion[33]

**George Washington,** our first US President and "Father of our country," a model of unquestionable high ideals, had his Moon in House 9. **Others include** ardent feminist **Gloria Steinam** and also **Sean Connery, Marc Edmund Jones, Sidney Omarr, Margaret Thatcher, Charlton Heston, Giaccomo Puccini, Bob Hope, Oprah Winfrey**

## Moon in House 10

Structure and organization represent emotional security. It is important to you to be seen by others as a responsible person of good reputation. There's a real need to achieve something of importance. You'd prefer to be seen as a role model, a leader, a maker of rules rather than a follower of them—though you do tend to follow rules, especially those you see as necessary for you to carry out obligations, to feel "right" with your world, to get practical results and to advance in your career. This does not mean you don't innovate, for you may indeed do that, creating an advance of benefit to many. But, you are not likely to take undue risks in doing it. You'll move cautiously, making sure your base is secure before launching the new. Attitudes that were formative in your sense of responsibility and discipline were generated in childhood most likely by parents who expected it of you, through their basic conservative values. On the other hand, sometimes the motivation to assume these traits can emerge from the opposite experience, such as if you were the big brother or sister who had to learn early responsibility out of necessity to help take care of the younger siblings while your parents were, for whatever reason absent. Moon in the 10th house is often found in the charts of people who have a strong connection with the public. It is a good placement for public service. Your career may have a nurturing, somewhat parental, aspect to it—you'd like to take care of the world.

The public figure reports I compiled have a few good examples of Moon in House 10 "care of the world" motivations among them: **Clara Barton,** who founded the American Red Cross, **Franklin D. Roosevelt,** President noted for his "New Deal" and leadership during WWII, **Nancy Reagan,** who as First Lady took a leadership role in her "Just say No" program against drug abuse, **Tony Blair,** charismatic Prime Minister of Great Britain and **Bill Gates** of Microsoft fame who spends much of what he's gained on humanitarian causes.

## Moon in House 11

Here emotional security is most likely tied to whether you can see yourself as unique and independent, and how well you are able to express your individuality. Probably you've developed a style or field of interest that sets you apart from the mainstream, and you like it that way. You may have acquired that trend early from an independent Mom who had out-of-the-mainstream careers, interests or causes she espoused. Mom likely had a flair for the unusual, and was perhaps more detached that you may have preferred her to be at times, perhaps preoccupied with her own career. Early family experience encouraged you to be a free thinker, tolerant of differences and egalitarian in your expectation of your own relationships, both family and friends. You may have a humanitarian outlook that drives you to speak out if you feel unfairness, and you may join or structure a group that lobbies for change. You probably have many friends with whom you enjoy a variety of activities, and yet, at the same time, you keep a certain level of distance and space. Groups are your style, rather than one or two best friends. You can enjoy friends greatly when they're around but if you don't see them for months, or years, that's OK, too. You can stay in touch via email and when you get together again, take up where you left off. You need intellectual stimulation, changes of scene and a sense of personal freedom. You're not scattered—far from it.

The natural sign of this house is fixed in quality. Remember Isis' extreme persistence in finding all the pieces of Osiris, reassembling him and then breathing life back into him? That's you, when you really make up your mind to something. You'll push the limits with logical debate that anyone should be able to understand and agree with. Right? Of course. For a free thinker you can be pretty stubborn about getting your point across. While you are quite ready to break boundaries if you don't like them, you are pretty adept at keeping your own intact.

Moon in House 11 people are a mixed group, but then I did describe them as unique: **President John F. Kennedy**, perennially famed movie actress **Elizabeth Taylor, Krishnamurti,** the East Indian religious leader and philosopher who was considered Avatar by the Theosophical Society, **Tammy Faye Bakker** of TV evangelist fame marked by scandal, **Helen Gurley Brown,** the hardworking and glamorous author of *Sex and the*

*Single Girl* and editor of *Cosmopolitan* and **Senator John Edwards,** '04 candidate for Vice-President.

**Moon in House 12**

If your Moon is here, you have a strong need for privacy and at least occasional, if not frequent, solitude. Something about your early nurturing triggered a need to escape from the mundane world. There are multiple forms of escape, some of them very negative and to be avoided. Don't allow yourself to fall into feeling like a victim or becoming so dependent on someone else that you sacrifice yourself in the process. Security comes from expressing your own soul and discovering its beauty. If you came from an artistic or spiritually attuned early environment, your continued expression of that is a wonderful form of escape. It could be that your need to withdraw had its roots in dealing with negativity or illness and now you react against that by searching for beauty, healing solace and spiritual serenity. There's something very empathic and intuitive about this house, its natural sign Pisces. The Moon is about feelings, no matter what her sign, so you have a triple dose of sensitivity here. You easily pick up moods around you, and may misinterpret them as your own, if you're not aware. If you feel your mood dropping for no good reason, that may be why. You can learn to shield yourself from such exposure through meditation. You will do well to develop yourself in some art media: visual, musical, and movement. Through art you can channel and express your vivid imagination, deep emotions and need for beauty, and find a means to transcend the mundane. You may also find your expression and transcendence through mysticism or through charitable or healing work. By one of these means you will find much of your security through seeking and becoming centered in something higher than yourself, a sense of wholeness and spiritual unity.

Actress **Shirley MacLaine,** who has Moon in House 12, found peace and enlightenment through her work within "new age" spirituality. **Others** with this placement include **Liberace,** who found and created beauty with his music, **Dorothy Hamill,** Olympic champion figure skater who created beauty in motion; astrologer and author **Marion March,** who inspired, healed and enlightened many with her teaching and leadership; and **President Abraham Lincoln,** who saw this nation through its Civil War, his words ringing down through the ages in his *Emancipation Proclamation*.

**Endnotes:**

[33] Darion, Joe and Mitch Leigh, *"The Impossible Dream"* from *Man of la Mancha*, Andrew Scott, Inc. and Helena Music Corp. 1965.

*Spirit of the Snow*
pen & ink drawing by Maria Kay Simms

# Chapter Four

# *New Moon and the Waxing Phases*

*Romeo: Lady by yonder blessed Moon I swear*
*That tips with silver all these fruit-tree tops—*
*Juliet: O! Swear not by the moon, the inconstant moon,*
*That monthly changes in her circled orb,*
*Lest that thy love prove likewise variable.*

—Shakespeare, *Romeo and Juliet*

## Your Birth Phase and Your Progressed Moon

The seasons of your life—constantly changing seasons—are marked by the phases of your Moon. The phase you were born with has a life-long theme for you that is as much a part of your soul as your Moon sign or Sun sign. I hope to provoke you to think about your birth phase and how your life expresses it.

It is also worth thinking about the very first New Moon cycle you ever experienced. If you're a New Moon baby, then you entered this world at the very beginning of a new cycle. If you were born in any of the other phases, then what about the New Moon that occurred while you were waiting in the womb to be born? Might your prenatal New Moon tell you something about the cycle you've entered the world to continue?

You can live your Moon through phases and truly see the seasons of your life! Astrologers call this method "secondary progression." You'll see how every 29 to 30 years of your life you experience all eight phases of the Moon in progression. Remember how within one synodic month of about 29-1/2 days, the Moon changes her phase about every 3-1/2 days? In the symbolic system of secondary progression, a full cycle is 29-1/2 years, so about every 3-1/2 years your Moon will progress into the next phase. When she returns to the same degree and phase as she holds in your birth chart, she begins a whole new 29-1/2 year cycle. Most people, according to current life expectancy, will live through close to three complete cycles. A person living past 90 will experience part of a fourth cycle.

The basic symbolism of secondary progression is simple: 1 day = one year. For example, the planetary positions used to calculate a secondary progressed chart for age 35 are the planetary positions of the 35th day after birth; progressed planets for age 20 are taken from the 20th day after birth. *Moon Tides* software makes it easy and quick to calculate the progressed phases for yourself and anyone else whose birth data you have. On the first page of your report you'll see a listing of three complete progressed lunar phase cycles—all or most of a lifetime. I suppose we could have gone for a fourth cycle in these days when more people are living to be 100 or more, but truly I believe (after having experienced two complete cycles and part of a third) that any of us who live through three of them will be sufficiently experienced in life and living that we'll have no need to consult a chart to analyze how we feel. We'll feel the changing phases in a deep internal way beyond any desire to know exactly which day they change.

This chapter will take you through the first four waxing phases one at a time. The next chapter will cover Full Moon through the waning phases. Though I will begin each phase with birth phase, and then go on to the temporal progressed phase, my descriptions tend to be fluid, rather than neatly separated. Birth phase paragraphs will add to your understanding of the progressed phase, and vice versa. Both will relate to the transiting phases in Chapter Eight. The transiting phase interpretations may contain practical advice for advantageous short-term actions that can also be applied to the longer-term life cycles of your progressed phases.

**Whether you are born in a phase, passing through it
by progression, or just experiencing it in "real time"
within any given month, the core theme is the same.**

You'll understand this technique and your own process best if you read everything about every phase, think about when you may have gone through that phase before, and then journal whatever you can remember about your own life, as it does (or does not) seem to apply to what I've written. Don't be surprised if what at first seemed like it didn't apply makes sense after you've had time to think about the sequence of phases and how each one fits into the flow of the whole cycle over time and repetition.

**The heart of this book is the lunar phases.**

Everything else in it is supplementary to your understanding of the power of their pattern in life—the Earth's, yours and everyone's—and how that cyclical pattern reflects the evolutionary flow of the soul's journey.

**The Importance of Journaling…
      We Learn from Our Past to Create a Better Future**

There is nothing that I can say that will teach you more about how the phases work in your life than you can learn by meditating on the time each phase occurs, and then writing notes about what you remember of what happened then, and what you were going through emotionally and mentally. Even I, as long as I've studied and experienced this 8-fold cycle, received eye-opening insights about my own issues and development as I worked on this book and while doing so, also thought about and wrote about my own life during each progressed phase. Before, I knew that the phases had shown definite synchronicity with many of the changes in my life, but I'd never before written out what was going on during each and every one of them. I am too sporadic about journaling—some years I do it, and some I don't. Especially when I'm writing about astrology, I've thanked myself for every year I'd bothered to journal and mentally kicked myself for every year I hadn't. There is no better way to learn than to keep track of your experience.

I highly recommend that you take a good look at the dates on your *Moon Tides* computer report for the three to four year period of each of your progressed phases, and think about what events were happening in your life at each time, and even more importantly, what you were thinking about and feeling then. Go over old scrapbooks, albums, calendars and even checkbook registers if you don't remember. Ask others who might know. Check recent history for world events that might trigger memory. Events in your life may be descriptive, or maybe not, but they do supply context. Progressions, I believe, reflect mostly an inner process that may possibly manifest in outward changes, but sometimes may remain only inside, unnoticeable to others but very significant to you.

As you reflect on your phases, also consider the sign of your birth Moon and also the signs of progressed Moon during each progressed phase. Though I didn't think much about the progressed Moon signs until after I'd written the sign interpretations from my meditative inspiration to use elements and Goddess mythology, I was surprised to then look at my own Progressed Moon passages in that context and discover how much the myths reflected what I was going through at the time. It made sense to me, it fit, and I learned from it.

Journal! It's important. There's never a need to show it to anyone else, but writing down your thoughts and then rereading them later will help you see the patterns of your soul. You'll see more clearly what you've learned about yourself, your feelings, your emotions, how you handle things—and you'll likely also see what you have not learned yet. The things that cause us pain are often found to involve similar patterns of behavior, similar mistakes. In the process of thinking these things through, you may also discover a path toward healing. I believe that we are here to learn, on a deep soul level, the path to serenity and spiritual attunement.

# New Moon

*Everyone is a moon, and has a dark side
which he never shows to anybody.*

—Mark Twain, from *Following the Equator*

*This night of no moon
There is no way to meet him,
I rise in longing—
My breast pounds, a leaping flame
My heart is consumed in fire.*

—Kokinshu, 9ᵗʰ c.

*I'm dreaming in the dark, walking in the deepest shadows, there's no light anywhere to be seen…but what is that? A twinkling star? A firefly? Reach out and grasp it! Missed? Darn! Oh, well, I'm sure there's another here somewhere, and if not, I'll spark one myself! I've been walking in the dark long enough now. At first it was interesting. I was ready for change from how I used to be, ready to try something new, and so I did—several new things, in fact—but much of it just didn't quite reach the satisfaction I'd hoped to find. In fact, it was downright discouraging at times. But now, something new is happening, I feel it, I sense it, the energy is building—ah! That bright star, that one! That's what I want! Now where's that wagon I can hitch it to?*

An inner dialogue similar to the one above might be in your thoughts after emerging from the past three and one-half years of your passage through progressed Balsamic Phase. You've experimented with things that were a break from your past, but the energy you now feel stirring within your soul is somehow different, something new, something charged…you are beginning to feel the energy of New Moon stirring within your soul.

In real time, the real world of time and space, the New Moon sky is dark, save for the distant stars, and the night is inky black, though few people think of it as New Moon. Most people, unless they are aware of lunar cycles through studying them, name only what they can see. Throughout the ages countless people around the world have greeted the New Moon, but what they greet is the slender Crescent appearing in the sky. The true New Moon is when she's conjunct the Sun, so close to his fiery glow that she can't be seen at all. Her orbit around Earth has taken her to the same sector of the ecliptic (sign) in which we earthlings see the Sun. She rises and sets with him, all the while hidden by his blinding light, and during the night, like the Sun, is gone from our view. But, though the Moon may not be visible to us, deep inside we feel her energy, alive within, like the seed beneath the ground that is practically bursting with life but hasn't yet shown itself to the world. All the world feels something of this sense of newness at the beginning of each lunar month, but we'll leave that for now, to be covered in Chapter Eight on timing. Here, we focus on the lunar phases that are unique to you.

## Born in New Moon Phase

If you were born at or within the three and one-half days following the conjunction of Moon and Sun, you are marked by the New Moon's magic for your entire life. Undaunted by the dark, you project yourself onto the world, generating your own light and energy, with unflagging faith that you can catch that bright star and fly with it. You don't analyze things much, or at all, before you act on them. Your style is subjective. What impact your choices will have on the rest of the world and how others might regard those choices seldom, if ever, has much bearing on what you do. You act on pure instinct, spontaneously and often impulsively. Others might interpret what you've done with various epithets of disapproval such as "lacking in foresight" or "rash" or "irrational" or "audacious" or "self-serving" at times, but whatever they may think, it's their problem, not yours. More often than not your instincts, for you, were just what you needed at the time.

Dane Rudhyar described New Moon subjectivity and emotion as producing a "state of confusion" leading one to "project oneself upon others and the world at large, to live life and love as if they were dreams or screens on which to cast one's image—and often one's shadow."[1] He suggested that people and situations are seen not so much for what they actually are, but instead as symbols.

A number of private individuals, who've been part of my life, have demonstrated to me the validity of Rudhyar's projection description. I've seen it at work in ways that were very positive, and in other ways where their shadow was definitely cast—shadow, in the sense of the Jungian concept of the darker side of one's psyche. In addition to that, I have also often found myself noticing traits (no matter how old the subject) that might be associated with a little boy or girl who is still very much alive inside the adult. Like a cute kid, the "child" can charm. Common to those I have in mind is the vivid projection New Moon people have to draw you into whatever they are creating. Marc Robertson defined New Moon individuals as having "star" quality, the "actors and actresses of our world."[2]

Like the actor on a stage, the New Moon born want to be seen, to be noticed, to be admired. Ego, to some extent, must be part of that projection, and as such can be a big part of the charisma that attracts, or in some cases it can get to be just a little too much, causing people who at first were taken in, to shy away. At worst, the shadow projection is like the child that demands his or her own way no matter what. At this point it becomes clear, as Rudhyar suggested, that they see others as "symbols" within their own personal drama, rather than as individuals with feelings and motivations of their own, along with a perfect right to express them.

I encountered an extreme example of being the "symbol" of a New Moon shadow projection many years ago, in connection with a small bookshop I had in an old colonial house I'd rented. From being drawn into the vision of a subtenant who opened a café within my business to the point of assisting him to get started, I became his symbolic obstacle. His grand expansion desires where thwarted by the fact that I (with my children) lived upstairs and owned the business within which his business existed. When he saw I had no intention of leaving, he first tried charm, then persuasion, then sly attempts at slandering me to the town, followed by outright scare tactics in his attempts to get me to give up, move away and allow him to take over the whole operation. (I prevailed, but not easily.)

I have personally known and admired New Moon individuals who are successful, charismatic leaders, but I have also known a few born in this phase for whom success in life has been elusive time and again. In thinking of why the latter may be so, it seems to me that it is because early impulses were directed in ways that were self-destructive or just didn't pan out as hoped. The individuals began to blame others or situations outside themselves as the cause of their problems and were somehow unable to grow out of that mode. Again, the "other" became the symbol of the New Moon's personal drama. The child within was stymied in an impulse that caused hurt, and in nursing the hurt, simply failed to "grow up," with future impulses tending to be expressed with bravado rather than true confidence.

Still, others who have written about lunar phase personalities (Rudhyar, Robertson, George) all agree with my own observation that if you are New Moon born you are at your best when you live spontaneously and act according to instinct, rather than by a set plan. You don't like to work within someone else's schedule and structure, so having work that provides at least some degree of independence is important to your ability to function well. You have entered this world in symbolic darkness, at the birth of a new cycle of experience. Now you must create your new cycle, a new drama. Your self-esteem and personal growth demands that you establish an identity for yourself that you can project onto your environment and see its influence. Plunge in! Your instincts about what you want to do are most likely right. Like the Fool in the Tarot, you step off the edge of the cliff in blissful trust, and more often than not, your trust will be rewarded. So long as you can deal with an occasional fall with awareness that it was your impulse, not the cliff, that caused it, then go for it! Let your instincts be your guide. You live in the present moment well because you, like that moment, are unique. The past is gone and the future, well, you'll know when you get there!

## Public Figures Born During New Moon Phase

Well-known New Moon personalities include **Pope John Paul II; President Lyndon Johnson; Vice-President Dick Cheney;** former **First Lady Nancy Reagan; Muhammad Ali,** of boxing fame who went on to champion causes; singer and actress **Madonna;** actor **Sean Connery;** famed psychiatrist **Sigmund Freud;** drummer with famed foursome, the

Beatles, **Ringo Starr**; **Clara Barton** who founded the American Red Cross; **Elvis Presley,** legendary rock star; **Bruce Springsteen**, popular singer and songwriter; **Sybil Leek**, astrologer and Witch, author of over 60 books and syndicated columnist; **Pablo Picasso,** prolific, famous and highly influential artist; muliple Oscar-winning actress **Katharine Hepburn**; and famed comedian **Bob Hope**.

## New Moon Phase by Progression

If you're studying the astrology of the lunar phases for the first time, you may be, like I was, only clear about what was "new" in retrospect. Even at my second progressed New Moon, after I'd begun practicing astrology but had not yet explored this particular technique, I identified what had been new only after first having it pointed out to me by Zip Dobyns, and then later through reflection, and even much later than that, in the process of writing this book! When you're passing through the New Moon phase you don't analyze, you act. You do what feels right. You invest little, if any, time or effort asking others whether or not they think it's a good idea. You just do it. You don't particularly want to be questioned as to why, either. What's new may be something for which the seeds were planted during the Balsamic Phase just past. You experimented then, but what you do now has a different feel, more decisive, even if not immediately seen as such. The seeds of the new are germinating, but have not yet sprouted. Still,they are within you and are very much alive. Change is felt, and the past cycle is falling away, either by external changes or by your own initiative, and very likely as an outgrowth of a dissatisfaction with the status quo that has been growing within you over the two waning phases you've been in through the previous seven or eight years. You make changes, driven by instinct, and these require that you reorient to whatever the changes have wrought both in you and in your environment and relationships. The reorientation may be gradual, such that what has truly occurred may not be entirely clear until some future year when you reflect back on what happened in the past. In looking back, you'll define a significant new direction in your thinking that began during the years of your progressed New Moon.

Now, what may happen in the case of an astrologer who knows he or she is about to enter New Moon phase by direction? That I cannot answer from personal experience. If I'm still around and writing in my 70s, I may let you know! I know that I felt validated in the new direction I'd already instinctively chosen when in 1981, Zip Dobyns informed me that I was in my first year of Progressed New Moon. This validation, within New Moon phase, of a choice already made also fits a woman who has recently become aware she is in this phase through my Circle classes. She is a published fiction writer who'd been practicing Wicca in a very private manner for quite some time, until a month into her New Moon phase when she saw me at an astrology conference and asked if she could visit for a Sabbat ritual with my Circle of the Cosmic Muse. Around that time she'd also linked with several other writers who were Witches or interested in Wicca, and agreed to contribute a story to an anthology called *Words of the Witches*.[3] She wrote under the pseudonym Zelina Winters, but it was still a definite "coming out." By the time of publication she was actively participating in my Circle. Since then she has progressed to Third Degree initiate and is busy writing a solo novel about a Witch.

With *Moon Tides* reports run on public figures and subsequent research for their biographical information, one can find events—facts—but usually can only surmise the inner process that might have been going on at the time. In writing my interpretations and examples, I've drawn most heavily on personal experience observed or related to me, but in order to have examples that I could cite by name, I also searched *AstroDatabank* for public charts containing sufficient biographical data to compare with their *Moon Tides* reports. It is fairly easy to find biographical facts that support Progressed New Moon as a time when something decidedly new transpires. Here are a few of the "new beginnings" I found.

## During Progressed New Moon

**George W. Bush**, who won his second term Governor of Texas early in this phase, had before the end of the phase, become President of the USA.

**Dick Cheney** was nearing the end of his New Moon phase at the time of his election as Bush's Vice President. He'd entered Crescent phase just prior to Inauguration.

**John Glenn**, first man to orbit the earth, went into space at age 77, in part to test how space flight would affect the cardiovascular system of elders.

**Jacqueline Kennedy**, seeking respite, in her widowhood, from the constant glare of publicity, and a new life, married Aristotle Onassis.

**Mike Tyson**, at age 18, became heavyweight champion.

**Hillary Clinton** experienced the scandal over her husband's affair. We can imagine this precipitated her inner process that would lead to her decision to forge her own independent career.

**Charles Emerson** founded National Council for Geocosmic Research, Inc (NCGR).

**Margaret Thatcher** won her first seat in Parliament. Thirtyyears later, again in New Moon, she resigned as Prime Minister.

**Nancy Reagan,** who was New Moon born, signed her contract for 7 years with MGM and then met Ronald Reagan during her Progressed New Moon phase.

It was during his second Progressed New Moon that **John Edwards'** career as a trial lawyer got a tremendous boost with his winning of a landmark medical malpractice case.

During **John Kerry's** second Progressed New Moon phase he met Theresa Heinz and was appointed chairman of Senate Select Committee on POW/MIA Affairs.

**Martha Stewart,** with the career she'd begun during her progressed Full Moon soaring, divorced at Progressed New Moon. Then, by subsequently claiming residency in Connecticut while living in New York, she created a problem that surfaced in an expensive judgment for back taxes nearly a decade later. In retrospect, that New Moon deception (whether deliberate, careless or unknowing) can be taken as an omen of the greater problems she would experience during her next Progressed Full Moon.

# Crescent Moon

*Think'st thou I'd make a life of jealousy,*
*To follow still the changes of the moon*
*With fresh suspicions? No; to be once in doubt*
*Is once to be resolved.*

—Shakespeare, *Othello*

In real time, when we see the first slender crescent-shaped Moon appear in the night sky, the dark of the Moon is over. The light has become visible, fresh and bright as the Maiden Goddess, with a goal in mind and quickly growing energy. We look at her and share her anticipation, just as we anticipate the spring when we see that first crocus peaking through the snow at the crescent phase of the new year. Or, we may eagerly await the verdict of Punxsutawney Phil, the fabled and famous Pennsylvania groundhog, who lets us know whether spring is on the way. How? Well, if the Sun is out and Phil sees his shadow, he panics and scurries back into his safe hovel. Phil's uncertainty dooms him and us to six more weeks of winter. On the other hand, if the day is cloudy and dark and Phil sees no shadow, he remains outside and winter wanes. Now, this little story in itself—a modern myth that is the secular remnant of the Celtic fire festival of Brighid that became Christianized as Candlemas—has a portent for our understanding of this lunar phase, as you will see. Whether by monthly transit or by the first hints of spring within each Wheel of the Year, Crescent phase is a time of anticipation, but also of uncertainty, often accompanied by challenge.

## Born in Crescent Moon Phase

You who are born during Crescent phase are, in some significant way, trying to pull away from the past and forge something new. You have a vision of what you'd like to become but in order to get there you must overcome something that threatens to hold you back. You are like the little sprout trying to push your way through a resistant, untilled garden from which you're just emerging from winter's freeze.

The resistance you face may be from your environment. You could be wanting to change your religion, your economic status, forge a new educational path uncommon for your family background, or perhaps resist pressure to become part of a family heritage or business so that you can go your own way. You might be trying to grow away from a very ethnic background into a more mainstream culture, or you could be rejecting the mainstream your parents have chosen in favor of a return to ethnic roots.

Alternatively, the darkness and inertia against which you must push in order to sprout into increased light may be not outside you, but within. Perhaps something either carried into this physical life from a past life, or implanted in your psyche in very early childhood, has deeply rooted within your soul and formed an inner blockage or fear against fully succeeding in what you choose to do, such that it is your own lethargy or uncertainty that causes the tension of resistance. In that, you are like Phil, the groundhog, allowing your own shadow to spook you into taking a step backward against your resolve to forge ahead.

Whatever the circumstance that seems to hold you back, the challenge at the core of your life's purpose is to overcome that resistance and move forward! Deep down you probably realize that you need to accomplish this—that if you can't move forward, you'll be dragged back into an even worse situation than the present one. If you've previously made tentative forages forward in your life only to be drawn backwards, fear may have become a factor—beyond just the fear that you might not succeed. You may be afraid that your survival—emotionally, intellectually or even physically—could be at stake. Or, you could have a nagging inner doubt that you deserve to succeed, including guilt that you've no right to reject your past in order to build a better future. There is resistance to the past, and at the same time perhaps a loyalty to it, to a group identification, a culture, and a family who although you want to be different from them, nevertheless, did give you life and nurturance. The past may not be all you'd like, but there's a certain security in it. It could be from a Crescent type that the old saying emerged: "Better the devil that you know than the one you don't."

It may seem a chronic condition of your life, over the years, that for every thrust forward you succeed in making, there's another yank from behind that pulls you back, or an inner nagging that causes you to second guess yourself and see obstacles to your progress that need not exist, if only you can clearly see them as self-created and banish them. But you must resist the resistance and grow, for this is the entire thrust of your birth phase, to grow—to wax in light—to never give up, to persist in the changes that you know deep in your soul that you must make in order to have the life you seek. As you achieve progress—and you will, if you persist in pulling yourself up and dusting yourself off after any backslide—you'll become increasingly able to take bigger steps forward much more steadily, and your confidence and sense of power will grow. You must keep in mind Rudhyar's analysis that this phase of a cross-quarter (semi-square or octile aspect) between equinox and solstice is one of the four phases of greatest momentum and maximum release of power. It is through resistance that momentum gained is most strongly felt, just as without the grain of irritating sand, an oyster cannot grow a pearl. The more you develop yourself educationally, in skill and in confidence, the more easily you will progress and find the faith in yourself and your purpose that you entered this world to develop.

One man I know who accepted of the challenge of the Crescent born and succeeded came from an abusive family with no educational encouragement. He enlisted in the military, rose in the ranks and was eventually sent to college in a special program leading to commission as an officer. He graduated *cum laude* and has risen to steadily higher leadership positions with an exemplary record. A woman whose difficult early relationship with her father was partially a motivation to marry too young, chose a husband who was also abusive, finally divorced and began to get a handle on her own resourcefulness. She recovered, married again, this time much more wisely, and tried out her interest in writing. For years, she went through the experiences of anticipation and rejection, as many authors do, but she persisted through times of nearly giving up, was eventually published and has since published several more books. Another person, from a poor family plagued with alcoholism, struggled to go to college, graduated and forged a substantial career only to become an alcoholic after circumstances pulled him into business with his family of origin. A strong person, he persisted over the years, with major strides during sober periods and significant setbacks through intermittent bouts of drinking, buffeted between his will to move forward with the very considerable intellect, talent and skill he had at his disposal, and the defensive guilt and loyalty that bound him to his origins and the deep fear that he perhaps somehow didn't deserve his success. Eventually, he stopped drinking permanently, and has acquired substance through building a good business, though he still second-guesses himself sometimes. Finally, I have long known another Crescent born individual who overcame strong resistance from his parents who were conservative and business-oriented in order to forge a career in the arts. He has had a substantial career, but has created his own obstacles several times, in part through his own tendency to waver between his freewheeling"show biz" style and his inner "father" urging practicality.

## Public Figures Born During Crescent Phase

Well known people born in Crescent phase include **President Ronald Reagan;** child actress turned diplomat **Shirley Temple Black**; actor **Woody Allen; Indira Gandhi** who was Prime Minister of India; **Maria Montessori**, who originated a highly successful method of pre-school education; **Louisa May Alcott,** author best known for *Little Women*; actor **Clint Eastwood; Ralph Waldo Emerson,** renown author, essayist and poet; the **Dalai Lama**, who exiled from Tibet, is a popular spiritual leader and winner of the Nobel Peace Prize, and most likely (though his birth time is uncertain), the greatly revered civil rights leader, **Martin Luther King, Jr.**

## Crescent Phase by Progression

When you pass through Crescent phase by progression, you traverse a period when it may seem as if every time you take two steps forward you run into an obstacle that causes you to take a step backward again. The light has dawned on a new sense of direction. You most likely know what it is you want and/or where you want to go, but you're not having nearly as much success as you'd hoped in making it happen. The resistance you face may come from outside you. It could be the naysayers around you—the family members, friends or colleagues who are just not ready for the new you and ask, "Why on earth do you want to do that?" It may be from circumstances that seem to weigh so very heavily against your choice to move on, such as factors of economy or proper education or language barrier or any number of other things that must be improved or overcome in order for you to progress. Or, it may be only a problem within you, a sense of inertia that comes from your own fears of not being able to succeed, your inability to concentrate, your insecurities about relationships involved, or just bad habits. Whatever it is that stands in your way, your challenge of this period is to overcome and move forward toward the light you have envisioned as your beacon, your desire. Persist in developing your abilities and if you find you must break away from circumstances or people in your life that are impeding your own growth, then you must face up to that and do it. Be alert to the opportunities that will open up for you as you develop your will to progress.

A few of the forms I've seen the Crescent struggle take include a woman who married in Balsamic Phase and spent much of  Crescent in a depression, facing retrospectively the realization she'd made a hasty mistake. She finally took hold at First Quarter and divorced. Another young woman, very talented in the performing arts, was pursuing in college her childhood intent of following parental example by becoming a professional performer. Halfway through college, during her New Moon period, she fell in love. Crescent struggle brought a soul-searching decision to change her major to education, as she realized that she didn't want her parents' constantly traveling lifestyle after all. The applause was not worth it for her. She wanted a home and family, so she married, still in Crescent phase, and her first child was born during First Quarter. Now, years later with a busy life fulfilled with her husband and children, she has no regrets about her choice. Then, there's a much older woman, who during her second Crescent phase worked outside the home for the first time to ease the difficult transition in her life after her children left the nest. During her third Crescent phase, following her recovery from a broken hip that brought to a head her children's growing concerns about her living alone, she had to face giving up her home of 60 years to live with her daughter.

## During Progressed Crescent Phase

An example of how the past can win over an attempt to pull away can be seen in **John F. Kennedy's** sense of obligation, after the death of his older brother, to assume the political role that would satisfy his father's ambition to have a president in the family.

**Tammy Bakker's** life fell apart with the scandal and collapse of Praise the Lord empire and subsequent imprisonment of her husband.

**Hillary Clinton** passed into this phase during the impeachment trial of her husband, stood by him, but obviously gave serious thought to her own future. Toward the end of the phase she ran for senator from NY and won, thus meeting the challenge to move forward despite odds.

**George W. Bush** describes his first Crescent as his "wandering years," a decidedly unserious period of his life. His second Crescent began just one month before he faced the trauma and challenge of September 11. That phase, ending August 2005, included the attack on Iraq and its aftermath, as well as the 2004 presidential election.

**Vice-President Dick Cheney** was re-elected in 2005, near the end of his Progressed Crescent Phase. He passed into First Quarter Phase just prior to the date of Inauguration.

**Sybil Leek** had a mystical vision that her purpose in life was as an evangelist for the Old Religion. She was running an antique shop at the time. The media spotlight caused her landlord to demand she renounce Witchcraft or lose her lease. Sybil refused.

Another good Crescent phase example of attempting to pull away from the past can be seen with **Michael Jackson's** experience of it when he began the series of cosmetic surgeries to change his nose and chin and lighten his skin color.

# First Quarter Moon

*I'll come to thee by moonlight,*
*though hell should bar the way.*

—Alfred Noyes, *The Highwayman*

Visualize the Moon half light and half dark, poised to quickly overcome the dark with increased light over the next few days to come. Imagine the highwayman charging through the night to claim his lover, prepared to meet any challenge that bars his way. Think of the beginning of spring, when the days and nights are of equal length, but growth emerging through the brown earth during steadily warming days assures the inevitability of "spring forward." Picture the young Bright Lord, still his Mother's child but full of spunk, bursting with an individual identity that is now seen with growing clarity. He's never still, is into everything and even likely to take a few hair-raising risks, as little boys are known to do. The bond of winter's dark and hidden silence is decidedly and finally broken. From a point of momentary equilibrium, the thrust is forward, in no uncertain terms. There's no time to waste. The time to act is NOW!

## Born in First Quarter Moon Phase

Action is your soul urge and an important part of your life purpose, no matter what your elemental Moon sign, or whether you have other chart factors of more subdued interpretation. First Quarter people are born managerial types, forceful in their will to make new things happen.

Rudhyar called the phase the "crisis of action." You who are born in it may find your lives to be full of crisis. At least, other people might call it that—you probably like it that way. If there's no movement and tension already, you'll create it. You like lots of activity around you and if it's noisy, that's fine, too, so long as things are moving ahead. You may enjoy a good debate, and if you do, the other guy had better be articulate and persistent, because you're out to win.

Your thrust is toward the new, the increased light that you know is ahead, even if the shapes and shadows it will illuminate are nowhere near to being clearly in mind. Your style of action is still instinctive, rather than carefully thought through, but it is a different brand of instinct than New Moon people express. You know what you want to do and where you want to go, at least the general idea of it. So it's time to act, to make it happen, and that means to get things in motion. The details can be filled in later.

Step one, in surging forward, is often seen as the absolute necessity to break with something that you see as an obstacle to the momentum you seek. You challenge what is, and if it does not serve, you are more than ready to take action to sweep it away. Unlike the hesitancy with which Crescent types might waver in feeling pulled by the past as they strive to move forward, you have little or no patience with things, circumstances or relationships that you feel are in the way of where you want to move. You'll get them out of the way, decisively so. If this provokes a temporary crisis, well, that's part of the game. You'll deal with it, so you can move on. If you happen to be a sign type who doesn't inherently cope with this style of decisiveness early in life, you'll surely learn how to cope soon enough, because in your life, somehow, you'll get plenty of opportunities for experience.

If other factors in your chart run toward quieter themes, you could find that your first act of decisively sweeping away the past might be banishing your own insecurities or hesitancy and discovering the courage that is within you. First Quarter types seem to attract crisis, like honey attracts bears. Be the warrior bee that sets the bears to running. It is part of your job in life, your choice in coming into the world at this phase, to learn to stick up for yourself, to make the changes as you see the need, to pave the way and move forward. Through handling one crisis, you learn how to handle the next one and your confidence grows.

Then, there are First Quarter types, supported by other action-oriented and strong-willed factors in their charts, who find it only too easy to attract or generate one "crisis of action" after another. If you're one of these, you may like it that way. You may even thrive on it. You find it exciting to make changes, to tear down the old in order to bring new things into being. This may be fine—it is an important part of your soul growth in this life, or you wouldn't have chosen to be born in this phase—but it is well to be alert to how others are reacting to you. If there's annoyance, even silently expressed, when you'd think there should be cheers, then just maybe your ego is showing a bit too much, or maybe the others do have valid points about an alternative choice to the action you advocate. You can be pretty single-minded, even ruthless, when you get an idea in your head—imagine a dog with a bone thinking that someone else may be wanting to take it away. Focused on your immediate thrust, it's not your strong suit to see the big picture. You are not the best person to carefully think things through and weigh all the various aspects that could influence an outcome. One or more of the others involved might have cautionary thoughts that you should consider, or even an idea or two that could move your desires forward without causing a crisis. Crisis isn't necessary, after all…is it? Is it so important that things be done your way only, so long as they do get successfully done? Doubtful about the truth of that? Not surprising—it's not your style to nitpick details before you decide.

Think of our plant that having pushed through the earth now grows strongly upward, stems leafing out in preparation for the buds and flowers that will become fruit in the future. At the same time as we see that happening, there is very important growth not seen on the surface, but equally significant and necessary. The roots are becoming stronger beneath the earth, supporting the plant and reaching out for the waters that will nurture its growth. The plant is maturing both upward toward the light and also inward as it seeks what it needs to grow healthy and be strong. The maturity that you gain though making decisions, committing to a course of action and following through, and through coping with crisis effectively, are absolutely essential to your soul growth in this life. As you learn to couple dynamic action with effective coping, it is likely you'll be called upon to demonstrate that ability through leadership roles. Many First Quarter people become leaders and managers who take charge of projects, businesses, organizations and even nations. They are known for their ability to break up outworn structures and then create new and better ones. Action is your identity. Go for it!

## Public Figures Born During First Quarter Moon

Among celebrity figures born in First Quarter phase are three US presidents, our current one **George W. Bush**, his father **George H.W. Bush** and **John F. Kennedy,** and the monarch of Great Britain **Queen Elizabeth II**. Others of this phase include union leader **James Hoffa; Oliver North**, who during the Reagan administration, was indicted and convicted but later cleared in the Iran-Contra scandal, and much more recently has been seen as an embedded reporter in Operation Iraqi Freedom; **Martha Stewart,** the "domestic diva," a hard-drivingbusinesswoman; famed country singing star, **Patsy Cline,** who died tragically in a plane accident; abstract expressionist painter **Willem De Kooning; Michelangelo,** the Renaissance artist who is considered to be one of the most powerful and renown of painters and sculptors in history; Beatle **John Lennon**; feminist leader **Gloria Steinem;** 60s rebel **Timothy Leary;** movie actresses **Susan Sarandon** and **ShirleyMacLaine,** who is noted for her "new age" connections.

## First Quarter Phase by Progression

When you are passing through First Quarter phase you've become very much aware of that direction that germinated at New Moon and began to show some signs of manifesting during your Crescent years, though not without some mixed feelings and doubts along the way. Now the energy shifts. No more hesitation is allowed. Your engine revs into gear and there's no stopping you from making things happen. It is decision time. No more must the past be allowed to hold you back, as it may have before. Now you will make a clean break, if that is what you think you most need, and move forward without looking back, and likely without even a shred of regret.

That may be the first "crisis of action" you'll face, a confrontation with something or someone that must be left behind. Once that tension is handled and becomes part of your past, new sources of tensions will loom ahead as you meet the challenges of moving forward. Instinct still drives action during this phase, but it is usually a more directed intuition about steps you should take toward progress in your new direction. Moving on pure impulse may be the just right thing to do at times. Success usually involves taking some degree of risk. But, impulsive behavior can also trigger crises that do not serve your larger purpose at all, and in fact, impede it.

This is time to be firm and forceful in taking charge of your life, but a mature person does so with respect for others. Ruthless behavior hurts not only other people, but also you, in the longer run.

Be alert for opportunities you might be able to grasp, at the same time as you take initiatives to create them. This phase of your cycle calls for courage and a fearless will to move forward in your new direction. When you do this, you're bound to encounter some resistance. If you have any residue of nagging doubts about your choices, then obstacles or naysayers could provoke anger to well up inside you—but remember that nothing can make you angry unless you permit it and anger is only another obstacle in your path. You know what you want to create, and now is the time to commit to it, with both will and purpose. A favorite quote of mine, so much so that I have a framed copy of it near the altar in the corner of my bedroom is this one from Goethe:

> *Once you make a commitment, then Providence moves, too.*
> *Whatever you think you can do,or believe you can do, begin it!*
> *Action has magic, power and grace.*[4]

## During Progressed First Quarter

Most of my examples of actions taken during First Quarter phase, illustrate decisions and actions through which those who took them moved forward in a positive way. I've also included two seriously major crises provoked through impulsive actions, and one case where the crisis causing serious problems that led to major life changes was initially forced on the person against her will.

**George H. W. Bush** became Vice President under Reagan.

**George W. Bush** married Laura, a choice widely credited for supporting the life changes that would ultimately lead him to a distinguished political career.

**Bill Clinton** became President.

**John Glenn,** who'd left behind a highly successful first career as a pilot and then astronaut, became a senator. He would serve for four terms.

**Jacqueline Kennedy Onassis,** widowed for the second time, returned to the life in New York that she'd briefly tried after JFK was assassinated, but then left to marry Onassis. At progressed First Quarter she took a job in New York as an editor, beginning a successful independent career, one that also expressed her natal Disseminating Phase.

**Tammy Bakker** married and began her meteoric rise as a TV evangelist with husband Jim, making millions of dollars through their Praise the Lord foundation.

**Jim Bakker** saw PTL crumble in fraud and scandal after he was caught in infidelity.

**Mike Tyson** raped a Miss Black American contestant and wound up in prison as a result.

**Patty Hearst** was kidnapped and then brainwashed by her captors to the point that she collaborated with them in a bank robbery, was caught and then sentenced to prison, all during progressed First Quarter.

**Dorothy Hamill** dramatically burst into international fame as she won US World figure skating titles three years in a row and then the Olympic gold medal.

# Gibbous Moon Phase

*Moon River, wider than a mile,*
*I'm crossing you in style some day.*
*Old dream-maker, you heart breaker,*
*Wherever you're goin', I'm goin' your way ...*[5]

-Johnny Mercer

Now the Moon's light has grown to an orb that appears almost full, but not quite. There's still a dent on that left side that keeps it from being fully round. The magical fairy lights and shadows of Full Moon are enticingly near, almost...but not quite. The plant whose growth we've been following has grown taller with lots of leaves and now has pretty buds, too. The buds are plump with the promise of colorful flowers—but not yet. The flower hasn't opened up to show its full beauty, not quite yet. The Maiden Goddess has reached her menarche, blooming with sensual promise; the young Bright Lord is alert, his hormones raging, and the chase is on! Imagine the colorful and carefree dance of the Maypole, the dancers weaving the magic of their future, sometimes stumbling and mixing up the order, but still the weaving grows in a beauty through which the flaws become barely seen. The Maiden is caught, not unwillingly, taken by her young Lord in sacred marriage. But, they are not yet ready for the full consummation of life they will create through their union...not quite yet. During this fourth phase of any eight-fold cycle—lunar month, progressed Moon or phase of the solar year—energy is sparked with anticipation. Can what awaits the crossing of Moon River possibly match the dream? There's only one way to know! Cross it! Follow your dream and make it come true!

## Born in Gibbous Moon Phase

You entered this world at the second cross-quarter phase of the 8-spoked lunar wheel, another of the points that Rudhyar characterized as one of great momentum and release of energy. Phases may come and go by progression, but for you it is a lifelong quest to create momentum and charge energy toward a fulfillment that is so close you can taste it, but is somehow never quite completely fulfilled to your total satisfaction. Can that be frustrating at times? Of course. But is it bad? No, not at all. What it means is that you will always find something more you want to learn, something more to care about, another goal to which you can aspire, another cause worth your supportive energy.

This is a transitional phase where the instinctive energy of the first three phases becomes less spontaneous and more consciously directed. You ask questions of anything and everything, curious to understand, analyzing what you discover and deciding if and how it can fit into your growing awareness, if and how it can serve your goals. My eldest daughter, the quickest and the by far the most likely of the three to verbalize what was on her mind, constantly asked "how" "what" and "why" as a child, and she grew to an articulate adult who expresses well what she thinks and why, so I've always known with little guesswork that she fits this, her natal phase, quite well. The other two, less inclined to talk about it, have shown me in many other ways how they question, sift through what they observe and hear, decide what they can use and what they can't and grow as a result. Yes, all three of my daughters are Gibbous born, and so, in fact, are both of my parents and also a 90-year old friend whose life story is profiled in Chapter Seven, so I've had close-hand opportunities in profusion to observe this phase type. This makes me wonder, now that I think about it, why I was the family anomaly, born at the following Full Moon phase? Maybe it's because from them I'm supposed to learn something about what tidal forces pulled on my soul before I was born. Perhaps I, for them, exemplify some aspect of what they seek to learn…or hope they can avoid having to learn. I wonder.

You who are Gibbous born have the lifelong task of figuring out how to reach your goals within the context of structures that were set in motion in a previous phase, but if you set those structures by your own soul choice, it isn't likely you remember that you did or why. Still, there is an ideal toward which you strive, and you have a strong drive to reach it. Nothing short of the ideal will completely satisfy, yet like all ideals it is…well, ideal. Dictionaries define "ideal" as a standard of perfection, and perfection is a very difficult, if not impossible, thing to achieve, not to mention the even greater challenge of trying to maintain it if ever you're able to grasp it, even for a moment.

Though you will probably never entirely feel that you are quite as good at it as you could be with just a little more time and effort, it is highly important to your self esteem and to the fulfillment of your life purpose that you develop some skill to a high level and put your own unique stamp on it. Early on you could feel somewhat overwhelmed by all there is to learn. You wonder if you can learn to do really well what you want to do—but you can do it, if you are sufficiently persistent. In fulfilling your challenge of this phase, the goal itself is less important than the growth you achieve in accepting the challenge to stick to your commitment with determination to persist, to improve, to learn, to adjust when necessary, to pick up and dust yourself off and try again when you hit a bump along the way, and ultimately, to master whatever it is you have chosen to do.

This does NOT mean to become perfect. Perfect to whom? The quest for perfection can lead you to obsessiveness with detail or nameless fears that contribute nothing but frustration, and perhaps even a poor excuse for not reaching an "impossible dream." The test is not in your result but in your ability to commit to a purposeful life, and through that commitment and the skills you achieve through it, to contribute something of value in your world. As the light increases, you need to emerge out of yourself and any self-centered worries about your own inner conflicts or insecurities to realize that in the whole scheme of things, they are just that—self-centered and of good use to nobody, least of all you. It's a big world out there, much larger than any one of us. How will you make your mark on it in a way that works for you and also contributes something of value to others? This you must discover!

At this phase of the cycle, the soul needs to evaluate, to analyze and to strive to become less subjective and more objective. You have a great need to understand who you are, where you are going and what meaningful purpose you can fulfill in your life. Once you've found that sense of purpose, you have the ability to focus with will, discipline and devotion to learning all you can about how to perform well in your chosen field, or how best to support your chosen cause. You'll see your cause, your goal as the means through which you can express yourself with ever improving skill and increased understanding. Perhaps you'll come to understand, too, that the perfect moment, movement, brush stroke or phrase is only perfect (if perfection ever truly exists) until the next experience brings a nuance through which another facet emerges and must be integrated into your continual growth in ability, soul and spirit. With openness to such creative growth, life will never be boring, but increasingly rich and of exemplary benefit to all others whose lives you touch, making your life richly worthwhile in the process.

## Public Figures Born During Gibbous Moon

The Gibbous born include comedienne of "I Love Lucy" fame, **Lucille Ball; John Glenn,** first astronaut to orbit the Earth and later a 4-term senator; famed operatic tenor, **Lucianno Pavarotti; Prince Charles,** crown prince of the UK; **President Franklin D. Roosevelt**; recent Oscar winning actress **Catherine Zeta-Jones**; Wiccan author **Margot Adler**; performing artist, writer and poet **Maya Angelou**; **Bill Gates,** head of Microsoft; **Charles Emerson**, prominent Uranian astrologer and a primary mentor of mine; movie actor **Jack Nicholson**; **Senator John McCain**; **Hillary Clinton**, First Lady turned Senator; and **Aleister Crowley**, controversial mystic, magician, occultist and author, who headed O.T.O. (*Ordo Templi Oreintis*).

## Gibbous Phase by Progression

When you pass through Gibbous phase you most likely have a clear goal in mind. A new direction began several years ago. After some faltering at first, the direction crystallized into a more definite focus and now you know what you'd like to achieve, but the end result is still beyond your grasp. At this point you may be feeling somewhat overwhelmed by just how much effort appears to be necessary to get from where you are to where you want to be. You've made that critical breakthrough, and for a short time, back then, it seemed like things would be easier going forward. But, as it develops, it appears you hadn't thought things through adequately. It's just not as easy as it once seemed. Now you can see that what you had was only a good start. Perfecting the technique, refining the structure or improving the method...these things take time, perhaps skills you don't have yet, and there is so very much more you need to learn!

This phase may include realizations that something you missed noticing or thought you might be able to slough through or get away with in the past has now popped up as a frustrating obstacle that you have to somehow overcome in order to get back on track. You can learn a lot from that, but I won't kid you that it will be a quick and easy lesson. Such challenges could involve a painful process (voice of experience, here). But, the only way to pass the test is to forgive yourself for being human, pick yourself up, repair the damage if necessary, analyze how you handled it or might have otherwise behaved, accept the lesson the Universe was trying to teach you, learn from it, and then firmly commit to moving forward again. This phase can be a highly productive period, perhaps one of the more productive of your life. Certainly you will learn a great deal within it, so long as you are open to learn and able to make adjustments as they are called for, in objective evaluation of your progress and with respect for the structures of reality in which you must work. This may be an actual period of apprenticeship that prepares you to take on the master's role during the Full Moon and Disseminating periods to come.

Here is a little real-life story, more extreme than average for this phase, but it illustrates the flow of phases, plus showing how Gibbous can be both challenging and also very growth-oriented. Nan (not her real name), as a teen and then a young woman in her Last Quarter through Balsamic phases, had an unbearable relationship with her emotionally volatile mother and got no support from her father. She escaped her problems somewhat by going to a distant college, and then working during summers and even spending time out of the country on a missionary trip—anything to avoid going home. Coming from a place of feeling unsafe and invisible at home, she had a hard time forming healthy relationships anywhere else. Her new cycle began, and eventually she had to deal with her mother again, but she began to have serious panic attacks even after a phone call home. It wasn't until Gibbous phase that things began to turn around. It began with a challenge, when she'd decided to room with an old friend only to then realize that her friend was an exaggerated version of her mother. The friend was manic-depressive (and Nan came to wonder if her mother might be, too). Nan's panic attacks became more frequent and intense. Realizing that if she didn't do something with herself, and fast, she would never be able to have normal, healthy relationships, she sought help, and chose an intensive form of therapy called PSI (psycho-spiritual integration), while also seeing a counselor who helped her with both talk and a stabilizing medication. A little over a year later, Nan had managed to integrate her mother relationship and acquire a new self-image and coping skills. Now at Full Moon, Nan has found healthy independence with enough financial success to have bought a home and think about a long-term relationship. She no longer fears being with her family and has created a new and much healthier relationship with her parents, with appropriate boundaries that enable her to stand her ground calmly and live life as she chooses, even if Mom and Dad don't always agree with her decisions. Nan has come to feel safe and comfortable with herself.

## During Progressed Gibbous Phase

**Patty Hearst**, in prison during her First Quarter, had her sentence commuted and soon after married, beginning a new life that has since turned out quite full and productive.

**Martha Stewart's** Progressed Gibbous began April 2002. Early that year the story broke accusing her of insider trading for selling ImClone stock the day before the company's stock fell. Despite her close relationship with the company's chief executive and the fact that she had a known background of stock market expertise, she was at first deemed not guilty of any wrongdoing. Then, in June of '03, she was indicted in federal court for securities fraud and obstruction of justice, accused of lying to investigators and changing records. She stepped down as CEO of the corporation that bears her name, but fought back through a personal website that garnered many letters of support. The saga of this highly humiliating challenge of Gibbous phase continues in the progressed Full Moon section in the next chapter.

In his Gibbous phase of 1952, **John F. Kennedy** became a Congressman.

**Mike Tyson** released from prison in Gibbous phase, made a successful comeback as a fighter, but then bit off a piece of an opponent's ear.

**Jim Bakker** went on trial over the PTL scandal, was sentenced to 45 years in prison, and had a nervous breakdown. Tammy divorced him.

**Sidney Omarr** is interesting for the notable biographical information of the beginnings, peak and endings of his long career that occurred during his three progressed Gibbous phases. In his first Gibbous, at age 15, he performed as a magician, until at age 17 he went into the army and assigned in Okinawa, began doing astrology charts. By his second Gibbous phase, beginning in 1970, he'd become a household name in connection with astrology, with several published books, a syndicated column and TV fame. In 1971 he was diagnosed with multiple sclerosis, but it barely slowed him down. At his final Gibbous phase, then 76 years old, he became paralyzed, but persisted in his work. He died in January 2003, still in the final months of Gibbous phase.

Shortly before entering his Progressed Gibbous phase, **John Kerry** was sent home from Vietnam following his third wound in combat. He was promoted to 1st Lieutenant in January 1970, two months into this phase, but requested early discharge and ran for Congress, He didn't win. By 1971, he'd become a prominent leader in Vietnam Veterans Against the War, as well as a national figure for his congressional testimony and various anti-war protests and TV appearances on behalf of the anti-war movement. He ran for Massachusetts State Representative in 1972, while still in his Gibbous phase, but lost again. Shortly after that loss, he entered Boston Law School.

## Endnotes:

[1] Rudhyar, *The Lunation Cycle*.

[2] Robertson, *Not a Sign in the Sky but a Living Person*

[3] Ed. Yvonne Jocks, *Words of the Witches*, Berkeley Publishing Group, 2002.

[4] This quote, slightly paraphrased from the original words of Goethe, but with the same meaning, is frequently seen on greeting cards, plaques and the like.

[5] From *Moon River*, song by Johnny Mercer and Henry Mancini, © 1961 Famous Music Co.

*Illumination*, oil on canvas by Maria Kay Simms

O Moon of Mystery and Magic,
Goddess of Many Faces
Queen of the Marking of Time,
Lady of the Night...
Show me the Illumination
I seek within my soul!

*I Dance in Earth*, oil on canvas by Maria Kay Simms

## Goddess of the Earth

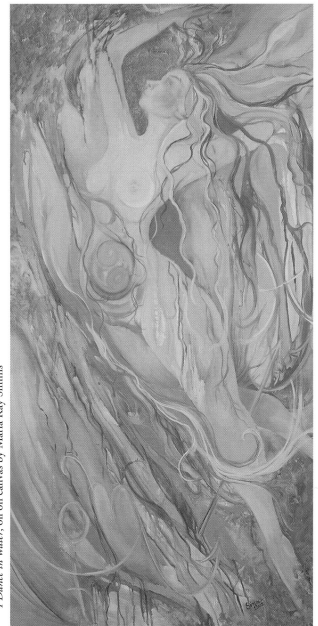

*I Dance in Water*, oil on canvas by Maria Kay Simms

Goddess of the Sea

*I Dance in Air*, oil on canvas by Maria Kay Simms

Goddess of the Air

*I Dance in Air*, oil on canvas by Maria Kay Simms

Goddess of the Fire

Within each element are
three qualities of being. As
the Modes are Three,
so is the Triple Goddess.

By all her names we call Her
Maiden, Mother and Crone.

### The Maiden
### Cardinal ...Creator
The Maiden emerges from
the darkness of Chaos having
gathered the stuff of life.
She brings forth new light.
**Her Mode is:**
## Initiative

### The Mother
### Fixed ...Sustainer
The Mother stays to
weave life—to nurture,
to teach, to preserve.
**Her mode is:**
## Stability

top:
*Ascendancy of Light*

right:
*Magical Child*

Both are oil paintings
by Molly Sullivan

*Spirit Guide,* oil on canvas by Molly Sullivan

### The Crone
### Mutable...Destroyer

*The Crone, at the gateway bestween visible and invisible worlds,  cuts the threads of old life to make way for the new.*

### Her Mode is: *Change*

## *New Moon*

*At New Moon, the night sky is dark—no Moon can be seen, for she is with the Sun, hidden within the blinding light of day. In the darkness, new potential whispers from the Spirit within. The future is uncertain, not yet defined. Anything may happen. Is the moment now? Listening for the voice of the Maiden who dances out of Chaos, we instinctively move forward, looking for the light that is as yet unseen. The light is within, waiting to be born.*

*In this oil painting for the original cover of* **Circle of the Cosmic Muse,** *the zodiac, shown in glyphs against the starry sky with the image of a far-seeing Maiden, reminds us that in our symbols of astrology, infinite potential can be seen, if only we seek the ancient wisdom.*

*Circle of the Cosmic Muse,* oil on canvas by Molly Sullivan

## *Crescent*

*When in the fading light of day, the first sign of Crescent Moon is seen above,*
*we emerge from the dark and the depths of instinctive beginnings and see the*
*emerging light of our new goals.  Like the sprouted seed and the newborn*
*babe, future growth is uncertain.  Comforts of the womb of the past may*
*beckon...but the challenge is to move forward!*

*Crescent Moon,* oil on canvas by Molly Sullivan

## *First Quarter*

*Decision time! With the onset of First Quarter, an energy for action is felt. There's no holding back now! The dance is full of spirit. Past hindrances are swept away, and the action is fully forward!*

**Astrologers:** the painting is an interpretive portrait of both the dancer and her chart.
Look for the symbols, and see what you can read. Hint: Sun in Libra, Moon in Pisces, Virgo Rising
*Astromandala for Mariyah*, oil on canvas by Maria Kay Simms

## *Gibbous*

*At Gibbous Moon, we are almost there!  Our Moon is not yet quite
Full, but in our vision is is...we can see the fulfillment we seek, just a
little further ahead.  We will reach it...soon, very soon.*

*Finding Our Way through the Dark, oil on canvas by Molly Sullivan*

*Fulfillment,*  oil on canvas by Maria Kay Simms

### *Full Moon*

*The Maiden is now Mother. Fulfillment is here—manifest, both within and without—but with it must come illumination.  The light will wane.  The opposing force of darkness cannot be denied and must be integrated.  Balance must be sought, even as we celebrate the light.*

*Green Tara,* oil on canvas by Molly Sullivan

## *Disseminating Moon*

*Our Moon is a little less round now, gradually losing light, but still brightly shining, illuminating the mysteries of the night. Like Green Tara, she embodies wisdom. Compassionate, wise and quick to act with purpose, she shares her enlightenment, just as we share the wisdom and experience achieved from our Full Moon illumination.*

*Last Quarter Moon*, oil on canvas by Maria Kay Simms

## *Last Quarter Moon*

*The "crisis of consciousness" has come. Light and dark are equal, but ahead lies growing darkness. In silent contemplation, we begin the inner process of letting go of the old to make room for what will come. What is she thinking? Where is her focus? Your answer may lie within...*

*Seek Ye the Ancient Wisdom?* oil on canvas by Maria Kay Simms

## *Balsamic Moon*

*Crone's Crescent—life spirals out...and in, and out again.  Be not afraid of my cosmic brew. Rest, dream, experiment, for in that you may glimpse what lies beyond and be guided...toward what? That is for you to discover!*

*One more color page—There's room
for one of my favorite paintings
of Molly's and also a new one of
mine that I completed since the first
edition of this book.*

*At right, is Molly's **Prayer to Tara**.
It reminds me of both the quest for
acceptance and the release of the
Balsamic phase, plus the fluidity
of Mutable-Water...Pisces! The
model, whose Moon is in Pisces, is
also the dancer of **Astromandala,**
which illustrates that moods...and
times do constantly change!*

*Below, my **Awakening**, though
solar, has the feeling of Crescent
Moon, for it is Crescent phase
of our solar year to which the
awakening Earth responds.*

# Chapter Five

# *Full Moon and the Waning Phases*

## Full Moon

*Oh, Moon thou art my guide.*
*Through night more loving than the rising Sun*
*Full Moon that shines a lover to the beloved one*
*Transforming each of them into the other ...*[1]

The magical time is at hand. The round, full orb of poetry and music rises high in the sky so full of light that even in the middle of the night, one can see quite clearly without candle or flashlight. Through the lacy branches of the trees the moonlight shines, casting patterns of light and shadow on the earth like a fairyland, at once both illuminating the darkness of the night but at the same time, deepening its mystery. The shadows…what do they mean? What purpose is illuminated in this intriguing pattern of light and dark that our Lady Moon now translates to us from her consort and lover, the Sun? So much more softly she shines than his harsh glare by day that forces our eyes away. He is hidden from our sight but still perceived, as his light shines forth, reflected from the face of his beloved. In the comforting blanket of night, Moon rises with light full and beautiful that we can gaze upon fully, a light that is his, a light that is hers, blending their energies into one—two that are separate but cannot be separated, for they are one, oh light of lovers transformed…

In the corresponding culminating phase of the seasonal Wheel of the Year, the Sun rises at the height of his glory in the longest day of the year, bittersweet in his realization that this is also the onset of the waning of his power, the gradual progression into increasing darkness. Moonlight must also wane, by month and by life cycle progression. Fulfillment is at hand at the full phase of any cycle of experience, but fulfillment is fleeting. Think of the anticipation of dreaming, climbing and finally reaching the top of the hill. Now what? With no wings to fly, there's only one direction left to go from here. Yes, down. Maturity accepts the rightness, the necessity of that, and illuminates the purpose for it all. The Maiden becomes Mother and her consort realizes and accepts his role as Father. Somehow these two who are one, just as we who reach this phase, must protect and preserve the life fulfilled, while at the same time accepting that the Wheel keeps turning, round and round, light to shadow to dark to shadow to light to shadow…one cannot exist without the other. Where is the balance? Is it within the shadow?

## Born in Full Moon Phase

You who have chosen to enter the world at this point in the lunar cycle have a sense of deep inner purpose that somehow fulfills a cycle that began before you were born. The full round light of the Moon objectifies the sunlight she expresses. Opposite in the sky from him, she reflects his light as his true complement and balance, for opposites are but two sides of the same coin of the material realm, the double edged sword of decision, the wind that blows both hot and cold, and the calm, still pool vs. the tidal waves of the ocean.

More than any other phase type, you must objectively weigh opposing forces, for they are a key to that which you need to find balance in fulfilling your purpose. Look to the signs of Moon and Sun, and the houses into which they fall as potential symbols of the particular polarities that you may be most called upon to balance. It may be that your Moon will not be in the sign directly opposite your Sun, but instead in the sign (or even second sign) past opposition but still within Full Moon phase. Consider, then, that your "balancing act" may involve aspects of both Sun's and Moon's opposing sign. Oppositions are supposed to be complementary, each contributing something the other does not have. Appreciating that complementary energy is part of learning to balance the polarity forces within. Chapter 3 on the signs and houses can add to your insight on what might be your challenge of balance. Following are a few very simple keyword suggestions:

**Aries vs. Libra (or in Houses 1 and 7)**
Balance your own needs and desires with the needs and desires of your significant other. Balance assertiveness with compromise.

**Taurus vs. Scorpio (or in Houses 2 and 8)**
Balance your tenacity in holding on with your ability to know when to let go. Balance concern for what is yours with what is appropriately and fairly shared with another.

**Gemini vs. Sagittarius (or in Houses 3 and 9)**
Find the balance point between the need for logic and reason and the need for inspiration and faith. Balance the benefit of seeing all sides of a question against the benefit of devoted conviction to an ideal.

**Cancer vs. Capricorn (or in Houses 4 and 10)**
Balance home and family with career goals; balance the concern for and the necessity to protect one's own close family with concern for and the necessity to protect the larger community.

**Leo vs. Aquarius (or in Houses 5 and 11)**
Balance individual creative expression with contribution to group creative expression; balance the love you give with the love you receive.

### Virgo vs. Pisces (or in Houses 6 and 12)

Balance that which is practical with that which follows your dreams. Balance discernment with synthesis (sense of wholeness).

Although all Moon phases are aspects of relationship in that Moon's face reflects the light of Sun, it is at Full Moon that relationship issues are most intense. With Full Moon as your birth phase, your relationships with others, especially significant one-to-one relationships, are a primary method through which you learn. Just like the Moon, you pick up light, collect light from others, process it and then reflect it back at them, with of course, your own objective interpretation. (I say this to myself somewhat sardonically, with a bit of sympathy for the "other" so interpreted. Hey, the guy didn't necessarily ask to be interpreted, but a girl has to learn some way.)

Because it is through relating to others that one learns, it is not unusual for a Full Moon type to have multiple significant relationships, some very positive, some hellishly painful and others of various gray shades in between. But, hopefully all of them will sooner or later be seen as having assisted you to learn valuable lessons through which you grew stronger. Mind you, though, just because some Full Moon types have multiple marriages, that does not mean this is the fate of all Full Moon people. I have personal associates among the Full Moon born who have chosen one stable relationship or spouse with whom they've stayed for life. But if so, other significant associations, often through their career life, have provided a multiplicity of experience in reflection through relating. In any case, you who are born at Full Moon should understand that the "other" through whom you process whatever it is you need to learn, is not the cause of your experience, but instead is a foil or symbol of something you need to confront within yourself.

At this phase of the cycle an illumination of full light is essential—an objective realization of just what is going on, what it means in terms of your own growth, and further, what it means in terms of your understanding of your purpose in life and how you are going to fulfill it. Earlier waxing phase types express a good deal of subjectivity, but at this point it is objectivity that is the name of the game. It is not enough anymore to feel your way. Now your challenge is to see it—and that may be why you're inclined to "see" by bouncing yourself off other tangible souls. Or, if meaningful relationships with other humans aren't easily captured, you might set your sights on a cause, an ideology, a grand idea or a famous person (idol, guru).

But, this phase is about culmination, fulfillment, completion, isn't it? Yes, that is true, but it doesn't mean you're finished, not by a long shot. What it means is that you've come into the world at a point where you must have had plenty of experience acting on instinct and feeling, but now it is time in your soul process to learn to think…before you act, while you are acting, and in evaluating after the fact just why you did what you did, and what it is all for. What is your motive? What is your purpose? If there is no purpose, just what is the point?

Do you remember that earlier in this book I spoke of the Sun as energy and the Moon as form? The energy of the Sun represents one's purpose in life, but energy and purpose are worthless unless manifested into form and structure. The Moon is form, inert and lifeless without energy and purpose, but totally magical when fully reflecting that solar light. Neither is complete without the other.  But therein lies the key to the illumination that must be realized. Both Sun and Moon are within you—not outside yourself in another, not even in the idealized "soul mate" you may have sought. The only true completion is that which you find within yourself, when you come to that full realization of your purpose, and then charged with energy and conscious choice, structure your life so that your purpose can manifest into concrete form.  Then, like the plant we've followed through the phases, the bud opens up into a beautiful flower.

## Public Figures Born During Full Moon Phase

Among public figures who were born at Full Moon are **Patty Hearst,** the kidnapped heiress who is now an author; **Elizabeth Barrett Browning**, who is famed for her love **poetry; Saddam Hussein** (most likely, if published birthday is right), brutal dictator of Iraq, deposed in 2003; operatic composer **Giacamo Puccini**; famed fashion designer **Coco Chanel**; innovative dancer, **Isadora Duncan**; actors **John Travolta** and **Kirk Douglas**; actress **Shannen Doherty**; **Carl Llewellyn Weschcke**, head of Llewellyn Publications, **Liberace.** the flamboyant and famous pianist; philosopher and educator **Rudolph Steiner**; **Krishnamurti,** East Indian spiritual leader who was promoted as an Avatar; **Michael Jackson**, famed for both his music and his eccentricities; **Mary Baker Eddy**, founder of Christian Science; and **Johann Von Goethe**, famed German author whose masterpiece was *Faust*.

## Full Moon Phase by Progression

When you come to Full Moon phase by progression, something in your life that has been building over the years comes to a point of culmination that you can see and define, and is probably quite visible to your world, as well, though others may not necessarily define what is going on in your life in the same way that you will. Very likely an origin of what is happening now is the fulfillment of something that germinated within you about fifteen years ago during your progressed New Moon. The seeds of it may have been sowed in the prior Balsamic years, but a significant beginning can likely be traced to New Moon. Now, what was within has manifested externally. There is a sense of completion—the idea that became a blueprint you set out to construct has become a visible structure. One question that has to be answered now is: do you want to continue with it, live in it? And if so, how? How will you embellish it, care for it? What did you build it for? Only if you can clearly see your purpose and are still strongly vested in that purpose, will you remain living there. If not, you may move on to create and build something else, while the older structure you previously built deteriorates through neglect or is taken over by someone else.

With the plant's life we've been following, the seed that sprouted grew stronger and formed buds that have now opened up into flowers. Whether you find the color, scent and usefulness of a flower to your liking or not depends a lot on how you tended it during its growth, but even more than that, whether you care enough about the flower to keep on nurturing it until it bears fruit. All depends on how you see this flower now, in comparison to others in your garden. If you neglect this one, it will wilt and wither.

These analogies, hopefully, will help you see the significance of the illumination that is an essential part of the Full Moon phase. Though I will show you a few examples of very problematic Full Moon progressed phases, in most cases what appears to the outside world, at least, is a time of notable success. If, however, you have made wrong choices along the way, this phase may have its areas of shadow. To use the analogies, if you've built a house that you now find you don't really like that much, or the flower has become unhealthy through neglect or mistakes you've made in its care, the results of these choices are likely to become visible, too. Also many, if not most of us, have more than one flower blooming in our gardens. More than one thing is coming to a place of fulfillment, and part of this phase may then involve recognizing that one activity (however it may be valued) should be dropped in favor of devotion to another one for which you feel a more compelling sense of purpose. So, a choice must be made of what will be your primary focus going forward. Or, it could be that a choice to focus on a secondary significant activity may come through dealing with disappointment over a critical setback in a favored activity.

James (not his real name) came to a realization at Full Moon that echoed the mythical young Sun God's Midsummer maturing recognition of his coming role as father/protector. He took very little seriously in the early phases of his current lunar cycle, even to the point of frequently playing with drugs. He'd met Annette at New Moon, his progressed Moon and Sun in Pisces, and eventually, during his Crescent phase, they moved in together, subsequently working on typical partnership issues of handling money and each other's families. It was not until he entered his Full Moon phase (Moon progressed into Libra) in 2001, that James took major steps toward assuming his responsibilities as a mature adult. Realizing that he wanted to show the world how much Annette meant to him, he stopped his drug use completely and then married Annette. They've since decided to buy a house and are expecting their first child.

This is a critical passage, the progressed Full Moon. Relish your successes, while accepting that it may be best to allow some things in your life to fade into the background. Do not neglect the inner work that must be done at this phase to move forward with the structures you've created that you most want to continue. Take a good objective look at them to understand why they bring you such a strong sense of fulfillment, what purpose you think they serve, what you intend them to serve going forward, and just what all this means in the whole scheme of your life. Moon is the form through which solar energy is reflected to Earth in stages that can be clearly and directly seen. Your progressed Full Moon, showing the full light of your Sun, reflects his message of vital purpose for your life. Your lunar Goddess speaks to you: "Let me serve you. I will mediate for you by showing you your Sun's full light message in softer hues that you can see directly and with objectivity. Look at me! I illuminate the purpose you are to fulfill. Through me you can understand the meaning of the flow of vital energy within you. Look at me, that your enlightenment in the Now may serve the future well!

Once you have received and understand the illumination of this phase, the purpose you carry forward is enriched with meaning and content. You'll build new and vital additions into your structure that will greatly enhance its usefulness. You'll nurture the life energy of your flowering plant so that it will bear healthy fruit.

## During Progressed Full Moon:

**President Clinton** faced scandal over his affair with Monica and through lying about it. The Starr report was sent to Congress just one month after his progressed Full Moon began (11, 1998) and articles of impeachment were approved by early 1999. He was acquitted but damaged the legacy he might have otherwise had, which contributed to the political shift to a Republican administration in the 2000 election. Clinton was subsequently disbarred in his home state of Arkansas, but remains widely popular.

**Neil F. Michelsen**, in progressed Full Moon from 11/'80 to 10/'84, considered those years to be the heyday of his business. Neil became internationally famous in these years, publishing many books, facilitating research and development in astrology, and speaking at many conferences. Astrologers all around the world looked to Neil and ACS as standard-setters for accuracy.

**Sybil Leek**, in her first Full Moon at age 16, married a well-known pianist conductor 24 years her senior and traveled extensively with him, but was widowed by age 18. During her second Full Moon in the 1960s, she moved to America in pursuit of media opportunities stemming from her career as astrologer and public Witch. She achieved considerable fame in the USA that continued building far beyond this phase.

**Carl Llewellyn Weschcke**, Full Moon born, bought Llewellyn Publishing Co. in 1960, during his first progressed Full Moon. An active leader in the Neopagan movement during his New Moon phase (early 70s), Carl juggled multiple activities—the highly popular bookstore and magazine of the same name, Gnostica, organizational leadership, festival organizer and more. During the subsequent phases, leading toward Full Moon, Carl had to confront the fact that his doing so many things was likely why his Llewellyn publishing business was stagnating. So, he sold Gnostica and put himself more in the background, albeit strongly so, with his focus squarely on Llewellyn's priorities. By his second Full Moon phase in the late 80s, Llewellyn was growing steadily, well on the way to becoming the largest and most successful publishing company of its genre.

**Adolph Hitler** joined the German army during his first Full Moon, winning medals for his bravery. Full Moon came around again 1943-46 during World War II. When millions of battlefield casualties led to an unsuccessful attempt to assassinate him in 1944, he had those responsible tortured brutally and put to death. In 1945, following the failure of his offensive, he married his mistress Eva Braun, and then the very next day, the two of them committed suicide.

**Mohandas Gandhi** left India to go to England to study law in 1888, during his first Full Moon, and it was during those years that his philosophy of non-violent protest developed through his studies of ancient Hindu and Christian scriptures. During his second Full Moon phase, 1918-21, he began his freedom movement in India. Long years later, the very month that Gandhi entered his third Full Moon phase, India finally broke from England (August, 1947), but just a few months later, January 30, 1948, he was assassinated, a martyr to the cause of non-violent protest who will live forever in the memory of countless people.

**Ronald Reagan** was elected President of Screen Actors Guild in 1947 at his Progressed Full Moon. At his next Progressed Full Moon, he was elected President of the USA.

**Senator John Kerry,** during his Progressed Full Moon, was the Democratic nominee for President (2004). His Full Moon period extends until early fall 2007. He announced his candidacy just one month after entering this phase.

To continue with the Waxing Moon examples of the story of famed entrepreneur and "domestic diva" **Martha Stewart:** her catering business that was the beginning of her phenomenal business career began in 1975 during the first Progressed Full Moon in her adult life. Now, at her subsequent Progressed Full Moon, the seeds of potential faulty judgment of her Progressed New Moon, and years later during Progressed Gibbous, have now come to full light as she experienced the public trauma on June 17, 2004, of her sentencing to five months in prison, five in house arrest. She announced plans to appeal. Her conviction had occurred on March 6, just two weeks before she would enter Full moon. Even though the action for which she was tried had nothing directly to do with her own highly successful business, her troubles have had serious repercussions on it. This is a prime example of the critical setbacks that can happen during this progressed phase when there are issues of imbalance that the soul needs to confront.

Martha's story is one to which I can empathize from having also lived through a humiliating (thankfully, not nearly so public) experience during the early part of a progressed Full Moon phase stemming partially from my own misjudgment. Though quite different from Martha's decisions of 15 years prior (see Progressed New Moon examples) my Full Moon problem, in retrospect, was also traceable to a lesson I should have learned from my prior New Moon experiences sufficiently well to avoid a mistaken judgment made years later during Gibbous phase. When we do not fully understand our patterns, we tend to repeat them. The solution, recommended for Martha and for any of you who confront a difficult challenge, is to be brutally honest with yourself. Don't blame the other guy. Own your part in the problem, accept the consequences, and repair the situation as best you can. Once past that painful part, my own Full Moon phase eventually brought a significantly rewarding culmination after all—and it all makes great sense, in retrospect.

There's always a personal lesson to learn in challenging experiences, and at Full Moon it has to do with balance, and with realizing it is not the "other" who has caused your problems. He, she or it is only a reflection of what you need to assimilate and change within self. It appears that Martha may have taken a hard look at this within herself, and that may be part of why she decided to serve her term in prison without waiting for the appeal. So, while still within her progressed Full Moon phase, Martha was released and resumed her career. She received a good deal of public empathy, as with a softer and warmer persona, she began two new TV shows.

## Disseminating Phase

*Ah, pray make no mistake,*
*We are not shy;*
*We're very wide awake,*
*The Moon and I!*

—Sir William Gilbert,
*The Mikado* (1885)

*In looking at objects of Nature while I am thinking, as at yonder Moon dim-glimmering through the dewy windowpane, I seem rather to be seeking, as it were asking for, a symbolical language for something within me that already and forever exists, than observing anything new.*

—Samuel Taylor Coleridge,
*Anima Peotae*, 1805

The Moon, still bright and full, illuminates the night with magic of her patterns of light and shadow…but is that a little dent, there on her right? Yes, she's beginning to lose a little of her roundness, to wane in light. That gradually increasing dent coincides with a gradual shift of energy and a sense of impending change. Comparing this phase to the solar year, visualize the "dog days" of summer in August, when although summer is still very evident, we get the first stirrings of approaching fall. The gardens and orchards are rich with ripening vegetables and fruits, the corn has grown tall with ears ready to pick and the Wheel of the Year turns to Lammas. This sixth phase of the eight-fold cycle, seen in the autumn festival of first harvest and in Disseminating Moon, is another cross-quarter point of great momentum and release of energy. This phase of the never-ending cycle of solar year is the one in which the first grain is harvested, and shared with celebration (and relief) that the harvest will be abundant. At Disseminating Moon phase, the full fruits of the lunar cycle are demonstrated and shared. Disseminate means to spread, to diffuse, to disperse. What has been created, built, learned, assimilated, must now be shown, taught, shared. We may perceive the waning light, but all the more reason to make the most of the light that remains. Don't waste it! Dance with the Moon and lead others to join you!

## Born in Disseminating Moon Phase

It is a very strong aspect of your purpose in life to demonstrate what you know, to share and disperse your knowledge, diffusing or scattering it about so that it reaches others, most hopefully to their benefit. You could be one who is described as a born teacher. You may have an innate sense of what the market—the world—needs or wants, and you know just how to sell it. Perhaps you've shown a natural talent from an early age for writing or speaking or performing.Certainly you're one who will let others know what is on your mind, and what opinions you hold. Likely you're a very effective communicator, able to publicize and promote whatever it is that is meaningful to you. You may become a true crusader for a cause that has strongly impressed you with a sense of truth and purpose. Sometimes Disseminating types become so caught up in a cause that they become fanatical about it, with little patience for anyone who doesn't see things the same way.

But, that is the extreme, and one you should seek to avoid, if this is your phase type, for hearts and minds are won more easily with example and gentle persuasion than by harassment. I remember taking a course in creative business communication skills in which it was emphasized that example was not just the best way to influence people, it was the only way. In propagating a cause, the most important thing that you can do is to be sure you unfailingly "walk your talk," for if you are caught saying one thing and doing the opposite, what you say to those who observe or hear of your behavior will no longer count for much, and will likely fall on deaf ears. For the most part, those born in this phase come into life showing early on an innate ability to define what they are doing and thinking and then effectively convey it to others. Perhaps it could be that they've come into the world to demonstrate wisdom acquired in a prior life, but did not live long enough to adequately disseminate then. It is a good idea to step back once and a while and monitor yourself, though, especially if you are by sign type inclined toward impatience. Your zeal for expressing yourself in whatever area in which you have expertise could be carried to the point of overbearing behavior or even anger if you feel crossed, "my way or the highway," and alienate those you want to impress.

You, who are born in this phase, need to have a purposeful and meaningful objective that you can demonstrate. You need to show—to display—what you know and what you can do. If somehow you are thwarted in that quest to express yourself, you could be inclined to withdraw into a disinterested state, failing to live up to your potential or even try for any significant advance, unless finally you happen across something that fires your interest and confidence again. I am thinking here of one Disseminating-born man whom I know who is highly intelligent. He had an early dream as he was growing up, but washed out when he finally was able to try to achieve it. It took him many years, working at menial jobs far beneath what he could have achieved and living somewhat as a loner, before he began to put his life back together again.

It is very unusual for Disseminating types to be loners, for defining a cause and propagating it, by very nature, involves interacting with groups of people. Most likely you readily associate yourself with groups that have purposes you want to support, and become an active participant, even a strong leader. In the process of sharing ideas, vision, ideals, causes and activities involved in promoting them with others of similar mind, you are bound to have your own ideas stimulated, challenged and enhanced through the interaction. It is to your benefit if you can be open to this. You may not change your views, but you will refine and develop them even more clearly if you are willing to adjust and adapt, and you'll become even more effective in your ability to articulate the core purpose of your activity.

## Public Figures Born During Disseminating Moon

Those born in Disseminating phase include **Tony Blair,** the highly articulate British Prime Minister; **Diana, Princess of Wales,** the "peoples' princess"; movie stars **Elizabeth Taylor, Marilyn Monroe** and **Cher;** genius **Albert Einstein; Tammy Faye Bakker** of TV evangelism fame whose forum to spread the word crumbled in scandal; **Jacqueline Kennedy Onassis,**who as First Lady exemplified refined glamour and grace, and who as grieving widow, inspired a nation; famed postimpressionist artist **Vincent Van Gogh**; **Buzz Aldrin**, astronaut who walked on the Moon and later found a new career as an published author; **O.J. Simpson**, football star who was accused and acquitted of murder; the highly articulate **President Bill Clinton** whose lies marred his message and caused scandal; Clinton's **VP Al Gore** whose earlier career as an environmentalist brought him recognition especially appropriate to his birth phase; **Dorothy Hamill** of figure skating fame; **Jane Fonda** whose younger days saw her champion her cause against the Vietnam war to the extreme, and **Adolph Hitler**, whose zeal and brutality in his cause threatened to take over the world until he was stopped by the USA and its allies in WWII.

## Disseminating Phase by Progression

When you enter Disseminating phase it is time for you to take the culminating experience of your Full Moon and the illumination that you hopefully received as a result of it, carry forward what you learned and demonstrate what you can do. Here you must use all your knowledge and skills to the very best of your ability as you build upon prior achievement, ready to develop it even further as, with feedback and new ideas you pick up from others, you refine your own technique and ideas into a lasting expertise and philosophy. You will most likely feel compelled to disseminate and spread what you are thinking and doing to a wider audience, to whomever will look and listen, and if you have something worthwhile to show and say, the audience will be there. Here you may be the proverbial teacher who appears when the students are ready.

It is of the utmost importance that you "practice what you preach" and "walk your talk," and that you do so for the basic principle and values that are at stake, certainly not just because others are likely to be watching. More significant than the opinion of others is your understanding of yourself and your conviction about what you have learned, along with the wisdom you've derived from it. What you have to say, in sharing your message with others, will sound hollow and insincere even to your own ears if you do not really believe it and behave accordingly. The fulfillment reached at Full Moon confers a certain power that you must now accept with a degree of humility so you will exercise your power with discretion and due consideration for the impact you could be having on those who are watching and listening and who may be influenced by you. You are an exemplar, for good or ill. Be aware of that and never forget it. If you do misstep, be honest about it to both yourself and anyone else affected by your words or actions, then fix it and get back on track. This is no time to waffle about the truth you've found; it's time to teach it, live it, be it. Like the plant in this season, your vision has manifested like the fruit ripening on vine or stalk, ready to harvest and nurture those who will feed on it. So teach and share, and the more you give, the more you will receive. Any good teacher will say that one learns as much or more from the students as they learn from he or she who teaches. So, pay attention to that, too, for it may come in handy in the Last Quarter "crisis of consciousness" you'll encounter with the next turn of the wheel.

Patricia (not her real name), as a young mother of three (the first born at New Moon) with no education beyond high school nor work record beyond waitressing, had some concerns about what her future might hold once her children no longer needed her so much. Then she faced a life-altering experience (Crescent to Gibbous phases) when her third child, at age five, had a sudden stroke and six month coma that later led to paralysis. The strength with which Patricia handled the obvious difficulties of her situation included the necessity to take on the school system multiple times to fight for the rights of handicapped children. Her own handicapped child, now 16 years old, is doing quite well and showing great determination to be as independent as possible. Patricia has met with the governor of her state with the result that he is working on a task force to explore the issues fully. She'll continue with this project, though she modestly says she still feels like "just a waitress," Patricia, in disseminating what she has learned, has found her "voice" and strength, and will make a significant difference for the benefit of others.

## During Progressed Disseminating Phase

**George H.W. Bush** fired the patriotism of his country and allies to the cause of Desert Storm, but due to subsequently widespread dismay over the decision not to continue to Baghdad and unseat Saddam, plus his raising taxes after having been emphatic he would not, lost his bid to be reelected.

His son, **George W. Bush**, who during his Progressed Full Moon was primarily and heavily active in Dad's political campaigns, purchased the Texas Rangers during his Progressed Disseminating phase. This move has been considered highly significant in setting the stage for his own future political career, as it moved him out of his father's shadow into an individual identity and made him independently wealthy.

**Jim Bakker,** who had found God at the age of 12 in his early Crescent phase, made major strides to spread the word as he went into his Disseminating phase, beginning the vastly lucrative Praise the Lord Foundation. Unfortunately he later fell away from "walking his talk," and that caught up with him much later, during his next second phase cycle (see progressed First Quarter.)

**Ollie North**, appointed to the National Security Council under Reagan, was fired a year later for allegedly setting up foreign bank accounts and diverting millions in profits from arms sales to Iran in order to fund the Nicaraguan Contra rebels. He was later acquitted (see Balsamic examples).

Former President **Bill Clinton's** book, *My Life*, written and published during progressed Disseminating Phase, became an instant bestseller, earning him millions, despite its being panned by some critics.

**Liberace,** who had achieved substantial career recognition by the time of his first Full Moon return, went on in Disseminating phase to make his film debut and then obtain a network TV show that ran on for five years and won two Emmy's, as the name of Liberace became a household word.

**Margaret Thatcher,** who had become Tory leader at Full Moon, ascended to Prime Minister during her Disseminating phase and served with distinction through three election victories, earning the nickname of The Iron Lady.

The **Dalai Lama** was called upon to show his mettle very early in life. Born at Crescent phase, he entered Disseminating phase at age 15 when Chinese communists invaded Tibet, and three years ahead of when it was intended, he was given the political and religious authority of his divine office to wield within a very difficult situation.

**Catherine Zeta-Jones** displayed versatile skill and talent in the movie Chicago, earned many accolades including an Oscar.

**Michael Jackson,** born at Full Moon, entered Disseminating phase as a tot and before the phase was over had skyrocketed to fame as the youngest and cutest of the Jackson Five. Deprived of any normal childhood, his development through continual fame became progressively eccentric, such that his second Disseminating phase was also marked by notoriety, from a 1993 media frenzy and investigation after a complaint of his sex abuse of a 13-year old boy through subsequent settlement of that, to another 1994 media frenzy over his marriage to Lisa Marie Presley.

# Last Quarter Moon Phase

*Art thou pale for weariness*
*Of climbing heaven and gazing on the earth,*
*Wandering companionless*
*Among the stars that have a different birth,*
*And ever changing, like a Joyless eye*
*That finds no object worth its constancy?*

—Percy Bysshe Shelley,
*To the Moon* (1792-1822)

*Of the brighter, cold moon,*
*' Mid planets her slaves,*
*Herself in the Heavens,*
*Her beam on the waves.*
*I gaz'd a while*
*On her cold smile;*
*Too cold—too cold for me…*

—Edgar Allen Poe, from *Evening Star* (1827)

The Last Quarter Moon in the night sky is half light and half dark once again, but now the light side is on the left, the dark on the right. Our culture has associated the light with consciousness and the dark with the murky depths of the unconscious. So, if dark is right, just what does that say about the meaning of "right?" Food for thought.

From a moment of equilibrium we are on the brink of increasing darkness. What will it mean? In the eternal Wheel of the Year the corresponding season marked by Fall Equinox is often called Harvest, for the time of full harvest is here. All fruits of Nature's abundance have ripened and must be brought in and used or preserved, or they will fall to the Earth and eventually disintegrate, as fall becomes winter. So, amidst the celebratory feasting from harvest abundance, much work is to be done, but with the realization of impending change. Though the time has passed, for most modern folk, when the survival of life through the winter may have depended on the success of autumn hunting, symbolically this is still the time when the Great Stag falls, in willing sacrifice to feed his grateful people.

Through stag and harvest and waning Moon, we can see both this pivotal autumn season and the Last Quarter phase of the Moon, as well, as the "crisis of consciousness." This is the phase of all cycles of experience in which you come to the realization that something must fall away in order to set the stage for something else to emerge. But, the mystery of what that might be is contemplated deep inside the soul. The crisis is experienced mostly in silence, the silence of the inner mind, which though resolute…perhaps…is not quite ready yet to make the life changes that are nonetheless already occurring inwardly, though not yet outwardly visible.

## Born in Last Quarter Moon Phase

Without thinking about the fact he was born in Last Quarter, Neil Michelsen described a basic nature of those born at this phase when he would often tell people, "I was always an iconoclast. I knew that somehow I just did not fit into the environment into which I was born and grew up." Though he had interests all through his childhood that would be deemed unusual to his Midwestern and conservatively religious family of origin, he fed those interests in fairly quiet ways by a love of reading countless books in the sci-fi and fantasy genre, and in later years with various private interests in the occult and then astrology. Until middle age, his life on the surface would have, for the most part, appeared conventional—college, marriage, children. Then, after 17-years with IBM as a systems engineer, he abruptly (as it must have seemed to colleagues) quit IBM in 1973 to focus fully on the fledgling Astro Computing Services he'd been developing quietly out of a spare room at home since '71, figuring out how to calculate astrological charts on the huge mainframe computer that was the only kind available back then. He pioneered computer technology for astrologers and in the process, set the standards for accuracy that would propel massive development of astrology in the modern world.

What does Neil's story tell you about you? Plenty. You know inside that you are different, even if you don't choose to show it or even tell anyone about it—that is, until you are fully good and ready to do so. Your soul has entered near the end of a cycle that began before you were born, suggesting that on a soul level you know it's harvest time. Though benefits from your past may sustain for awhile, it's time to prepare for change, to process an inner reorientation from what you've been in the past to something new that is developing inside. Silently and internally you're going through an analysis—the crisis of consciousness—of your present situation and your potential for the future. "Somehow I weary of what I am and what I'm doing...what else can I accomplish, explore? Though I do this well, so much of it has lost the zest it once had. Must I continue to do what I'm doing? What about my obligations? Isn't there anything more to life than this? There has to be...what if I...?

Before you are ready to show your new colors, to all outward appearances you'll continue to successfully do what you're doing well and behave just as the expectations of your environment dictate. Even when placid and apparently content on the outside, on the inside you are silently seething with a growing wish to rebel. Then, when one fine day you come out with it and make a decidedly visible change, it may come as a huge surprise to others around you (at least all those who do not know you very, very well). What?? You're doing what? Where did that come from?

With Last Quarter as your birth phase, such inner reorientations could happen continually. You may have a hard time with yourself in bouts of dissatisfaction and tensions that fester until you finally come to the place where you know you must make a change. Or you may go through only one or two major critical reorientations in your lifetime, but if so, they'll be zingers.

It is a significant part of your purpose in life, as well as your psychological and soul process, to question the status quo, to challenge it and perhaps even destroy some aspect of it, in order to clear the way for new ideas and structures to evolve. You see a future that others can't yet see, and perhaps through deep unconscious soul memory of seeds planted long before you were born, you are compelled toward transformative process, toward a future birthing the extent of which may even be far beyond what you are now able to imagine…but what you can see is a potential that sooner or later cannot and will not be denied.

## Public Figures Born During Last Quarter Moon

The **Last Quarter born** include popular and influential author-astrologers **Marion March, Zipporah Dobyns, Ph.D.** and **Marc Edmund Jones; George Washington**, first USA president; **Dame Margaret Thatcher,** highly influential "Iron Lady" British Prime Minister; **Mohandas Gandhi**, whose principles of non-violent disobedience won freedom for India; highly influential First Lady **Eleanor Roosevelt; Karl Gustav Jung**, the highly influential Swiss psychologist and author; **Oprah Winfrey,** popular talk show hostess; **Jim Bakker,** star of TV evangelism who fell hard in a scandal of fraudulent abuse of his trust; opera star **Maria Callas; Yoko Ono**, artist whose marriage to Beatle John Lennon brought her fame; **Mick Jagger,** superstar singer of the Rolling Stones, and **Walt Disney**, whose cartoon characters and movies will live forever.

## Last Quarter Phase by Progression

During this progressed phase, expect to experience an inner reorientation, even though on the surface others may see you as continuing to successfully do what you've been known for and expected to be doing for years.  In many ways, this phase is similar to the Harvest of autumn. With all the appearance of abundance and satisfaction over what has been accomplished, the work of reaping that harvest is now complete. But, then…now what? What next? A colloquial expression tags your feelings well: "Been there, done that." And inside, somewhere festering in silence is the question: "Isn't there something more to life than this?  I hope so!" Feeling restless, tired of what has become routine rather than charged with the excitement you once felt about it, you begin the process of change internally. You'll probably keep feelings of discontent inside because you're not all that comfortable with them yourself yet, so you're reluctant to upset the status quo and then maybe regret it, at least not before you're sure what you want to do. Keeping it within creates tension, though, so the "crisis of consciousness" begins to build. One fine day, perhaps toward the latter part of this phase or perhaps not until a later one, what was churning around inside you comes out and you make a change, perhaps surprising others around you, who had no idea you had anything like that in mind.

Alternatively, the "crisis of consciousness" may be precipitated by events not to your liking and perhaps beyond your control. This can cause you to regard this time as not a "harvest" period at all, but one in which the impending darkness is a primary theme and maybe a scary one. You could be trying to hang onto past glory in the face of challenge or competition, or feeling frustrated because your plans are not going the way you wanted. Or the loss of something or someone close to you might trigger the restlessness and dissatisfaction that will eventually lead to change. Whatever the reason might be, the theme and your experience corresponds to the half-light of Last Quarter Moon where from a temporal point of balance, what was light becomes slowly overtaken by darkness. You, like the Moon's waning light, turn away from the sunny beginnings that were so fresh years ago during your early waxing phases. Like it or not, there is naught to do but assimilate, accept and begin the work of moving on. Through introspection you may find a seedling of light that dropped from the harvest. Allow it to germinate within you for it may become the source of a new cycle. For now, though, it is time to harvest and store what is good and savor it, but also prepare for winter, knowing that in its proper season—during your next New Moon and waxing cycle—spring will come again.

At his second birth phase return, progressed Last Quarter, Neil Michelsen left this world for the next, after a highly successful iconoclastic two decade-long career. I've reflected on why this soul, the last man anyone who knew him would ever have expected to become ill, did so, at a time when to all appearances he was "on top of the world" enjoying life. His "crisis of consciousness" was complex, I think, with multiple facets. He was, by avocation, a wholistic healer who'd believed consciousness would heal. After an initial optimistic remission that failed, he had to come to terms with the reality that physical illness manifested didn't easily yield. Prior to the illness he'd complained that his successful business had become too much like the corporate life he'd left behind, demanding his time on everything but the creative programming he loved to do, though he wouldn't delegate the control that could free him. But, perhaps at the root of it all, Neil just couldn't imagine himself as old and infirm. A memorial quote sent to ACS by the board of United Astrology Congress on ACS' Founder's Day '96, when Neil would have been 65 expressed it: *For us Neil will never be 65 years old. In our memory he will forever be the fun-loving, imaginative, forward-looking, community-oriented man who was always ready to help, to dare and to do.*

Jim, dissatisfied with his current job in 1983, started a small business on the side in his home garage during his progressed Last Quarter phase. Two years later, with a divorce in process and no financial backing, he'd moved to New Hampshire and established his small business in an old mill building. The first few years were a struggle, but he persisted through his "crisis of consciousness" and subsequent Balsamic Phase, such that by the time his New Moon began at the end of 1989, his business had grown into a substantial corporation, and he was on his way toward acquiring his own large commercial building for it. Now, at his Full Moon, progressed Moon in Cancer, his business has two patents and is respected throughout its industry. Conventional astrological interpretation too often emphasizes the downside of waning cycles, such that people look upon them with dread, but what Jim says about them is a good lesson for all of us to keep in mind. He says, "It's the best time to start something new. You've got nowhere to go but up, and you try harder."

## During Progressed Last Quarter Phase

**Queen Elizabeth II** was in her Last Quarter phase during 2002 when she lost her beloved mother, the "Queen Mum" who died at the venerable age of 101, and also her sister, Princess Margaret.

**Diana, Princess of Wales,** divorced Prince Charles but died in an automobile accident a year later, both years part of her Last Quarter phase.

**John F. and Jacqueline Kennedy** were each in progressed Last Quarter when he became President and she First Lady.

**Ollie North** was indicted in 1989 by a Grand Jury over the Iran Contra affair, on a charge of conspiracy to defraud the government. He was eventually freed of that charge (see Balsamic).

**John Glenn** capped a distinguished career as the first American to orbit the Earth in 1962 and was celebrated with a New York tickertape parade. Surely something else was stirring inside though, for he resigned his commission and retired from the Marines in his next phase (see Balsamic).

**President Abraham Lincoln** issued the *Emancipation Proclamation.* Toward the end of the phase he was assassinated.

**Pope John Paul II** was in his Last Quarter phase when the priest sex scandal broke out.

**Vincent Van Gogh** went to Paris and began painting with impressionist brush strokes. In two years he became disillusioned with the Paris scene and went to live with his brother on whom he was financially dependent.

**Maria Callas** made her American operatic debut (1954) and became the world's most famous diva.

**John Kerry**, after earlier disappointments in running for political office, was elected to the Senate for the first time in 1984 during his Progressed Last Quarter, and then went on to win in three subsequent elections.

# Balsamic Moon

*And now, as the night was senescent*
*And star-dials pointed to morn—*
*As the star-dials hinted of morn—*
*At the end of our path a liquescent*
*And nebulous lustre was born,*
*Out of which a miraculous crescent*
*Arose with a duplicate horn—*
*Astarte's biadimonded crescent*
*Distinct with its duplicate horn.*

—Edgar Allen Poe, from *Ulalume—A Ballad* (1847)

*Moon, worn thin to the width of a quill,*
*In the dawn clouds flying,*
*How good to go, light into light, and still*
*Giving light, dying.*

— Sara Teasdale, *Moon's Ending*

Lighting the night sky to the east, not long before dawn, is the slender crescent of the Crone Goddess—or Astarte, of Poe's description, if you prefer. Her horns point toward the right, or sometimes upward, beautiful but seen all too briefly before she gives way to the rising Sun. The following night she's even thinner, until at last she can be seen no more at the end of the night just before dawning. Once again she's too near the Sun. The night sky returns to inky black, save for the distant stars.

In the corresponding season of the 8-fold solar cycle, the Wheel has turned to Samhain, secularly known as Halloween, when the veil between the worlds grows very thin and spirits pass through to walk among us. It is said that some pass out of this world, but others are coming back, seeking rebirth and another cycle of incarnation.

The plant we've been watching now nears the end of its cycle, too, withering in the increasing cold of days that grow ever shorter as sunlight wanes. It turns brown and dies, going back into the earth, but dropping seeds of potential for new life in the future, for all of Nature teaches us that nothing is ever completely lost. The Earth Mother receives back what has been born of her womb, and births it again, in a different form. The seeds that die are the seeds of rebirth, and the Wheel keeps turning.

She who sees beyond the veil, she from whose spiral cauldron life withdraws and is born again, knows that Crone's Crescent Moon will vanish for a while into the darkness. But, soon she'll return to grace the western sky as the lovely Maiden Crescent Moon…sooner than you may think! Dream and have faith! For a time, it may be dark, until that unseen moment within the darkness, when Moon and Sun conjoin—not seen, but known through mind and mathematics and instinct. This is a time of magic, from Balsamic to New Moon—and from Samhain to Yule of the solar eight-fold cycle—that we might call Chaos.

Do not fear the Crone, she who is Three-in-One. While Chaos may be descriptive of Balsamic phase, it is also well to hold an image of Clotho, Maiden of the Three Fates, who dances in Chaos, gathering the stuff of life to be spun into new forms.

**Born in Balsamic Moon Phase**

I've often heard the Balsamic born compared to the proverbial one who listens to the beat of a distant drummer that others cannot hear or yet imagine. At best such a person may be a visionary prophet, attuned to the future and drawn to it, pulled by soul tides that are known and felt to be much larger, stronger and more profound than self, but worth reaching out for, even if great personal sacrifice be the price. At worst, they may suffer through their feelings of being different, of being out-of-step and humiliated for it, feeling martyred and misunderstood. Most of you will be probably somewhere in between the two extremes. In a way you are pulled between having come into this world at the tail end of a long process of development that has imprinted your soul, but has run its course. Now here in a new environment, and needing to strike out anew, you have no clear idea yet of where you've come from or where you are going. That may not seem so unusual for a baby, but as you grow it becomes more complicated because you'll recognize that you are not exactly in sync with those around you, which may be problematic for them in a way that also creates a problem for you. How can you explain about your sense of destiny when you aren't really sure just what it is yet, only that you have one? The distant drumbeats beckon you to follow…

Part of your process will almost surely be the necessity to make clean breaks from situations or people who impede your ability to evolve. The Crone is the destroyer aspect of Goddess, and you will recognize and act on the understanding that sometimes destruction is necessary in order to allow the phoenix to rise from the ashes of what was, so that what might be…or will be…can arise within you.

Demetra George, Balsamic born, speaks of her own experience in her book, *Finding Our Way Through the Dark*, saying that the Balsamic born, in all areas of their life, become involved in short but intense short-term relationships. She feels they are meeting many people from past lives with whom they have unfinished business. The loose ends must be tied up, the problems healed and the differences resolved, so that old patterns of relating can be healed, creating the opportunity to move forward with kindness, decency and acceptance.[2] The effort to resolve relationship issues are not so much about the people themselves, but about the process and what was or can still be learned from it. Once that has been accomplished, the relationship ceases to be important, and can be released without regret.

Seeing yourself as ahead of your time releases you to be yourself and what you are becoming without the conflict of striving to fit in where you know you really don't. Experiment with possibilities and try them on for size, but if they don't fit, let them go. You are planting seeds that may take root for you in this lifetime, or even if they don't, perhaps they will mean something significant to some one else who nurtures the seedling into a sprout and then beyond. The important thing is for you to commit to the future, even if you haven't yet defined what course it will take for you. Trust that the Goddess within will guide your destiny so that your purpose will unfold as you progress through the phases. Flow with the currents that you feel within you, always keeping in mind that it is not the result but the process that you are here to serve, both for your own soul growth and as you may, by your example, assist the soul growth of others.

Allow your vision of something larger than yourself to move through you. Make a commitment to it, trusting that you will grow in understanding of it and of your full purpose as time goes on. You have come from the past to dedicate yourself to the future. Open yourself to channel your vision for the future into manifestation, either in your own time or beyond, through the work of others for whom your own work may represent a step along the way that they'll continue.

## Public Figures Born During Balsamic Moon

Well known people born in Balsamic Moon include **Dane Rudhyar,** the astrologer-philosopher who first defined the eight lunar phases; astrologer **Demetra George** who wrote two books unveiling Dark Moon mystery; **Alfred Witte,** founder of the Hamburg School of Astrology (Uranian), and his protégé, **Reinhold Ebertin,** who simplified the system into Cosmobiology; **Sydney Omarr,** popular author-astrologer and syndicated columnist; **Elizabeth Kubler-Ross,** psychiatrist and author whose research assisted transition for the dying as she revealed their images of life after death; **Karl Marx,** who developed the theory of socialism, author of *The Communist Manifesto;* **Abraham Lincoln,** Civil War president who declared *The Emancipation Proclamation*; **Betty Friedan,** who founded National Organization of Women and wrote *The Feminist Mystique*; movie actor **Marlon Brando**

## Balsamic Phase by Progression

During the years that you pass though Balsamic phase you'll be finishing and letting go of some things in your life, and quite likely experimenting with various new things, as well. This is a time of transition similar to Samhain myths, and to the last falling leaves that give way to the onset of winter— transition through the death that is change. At the crossroads of Hecate, the future waits, but which way will you go? Some aspect of you that has been at the core of your identity may have lost its luster and interest to the point that you are releasing it. The seed of what will one day become a highly significant new identity may be already known to you at some level of consciousness, its emergence just a short way down a crossroad path. You may not have consciously realized its potential yet, or even if it is something you've already begun, you've not yet defined its importance or decided on that path as your future direction.

The Balsamic phase, like all phases of ending, may be scary at times, confusing at others. You may experience bouts of feeling isolated, discouraged and maybe even depressed. But, chaos and discouraging things can happen within any phase, so do not look upon this phase with dread. Just accept the reality that something is ending. There may be significant successes and happy occasions with these years, as I remember from mine, and as I will show you in some of the examples of this progressed phase. As with all progressed phases, this one is likely to be marked by visible events that fit the phase theme, but may also be marked by events that seem, on the surface, to not fit at all. Events, alone, can be deceiving. It is not the events, but what is going on unseen inside you that is the most important expression of the phase. In the Balsamic period you are, in some way, retreating from and releasing core aspects of nearly thirty years of your life. This may be triggered by events outside your control, or it could be happening as a result of your own decision to change your direction, or it could stem from mistakes you've made that have come back to haunt you. Or, it is also possible that it could be none of these things, but only a slowly evolving dissatisfaction that seeks something else without yet knowing what "else" is.

Retreat and withdrawal from too much public exposure may be a real need for you during this time. You need to just be rather than do, to have time to reflect, perhaps to heal from the aftermath of the "crisis of consciousness" of the prior phase. You may especially benefit from activities that allow time for introspection and intuitive expression, such as being in Nature, working in art forms, journaling, spiritual practice and meditation. Rituals of symbolic banishing and letting go of what you feel is passing could evoke healing release, and help you open yourself to the seeds of the new that will soon germinate within you. At some point during this phase you will begin to have a stronger sense of the future that is ahead, of which path from the crossroads feels right to you. When you do, commit yourself to walk that path, even though what you may encounter on it is not yet seen and you do not yet know where it will ultimately take you. Trust that as in the cycles of Nature, nothing ever completely dies, but only changes to a different form. When one door closes there can always be found another to open. Death is only change to a future that is being born.

## During Progressed Balsamic Phase

**Patty Hearst** tried her wings as author and as actress, appearing in plays in 1990 and 1995.

**John F. Kennedy** was assassinated November 23, 1963, just two months into his Balsamic phase. His widow, **Jacqueline Kennedy,** also Progressed Balsamic, inspired a grieving nation and helped it to begin healing. Years later in her next Balsamic phase (1994), after seeing her children into adulthood and with a satisfying editorial career behind her, she passed over into the realm of Spirit.

**Ollie North** saw charges against him over the Iran-Contra affair dismissed in court, but he retired from the Marines as a Lt. Colonel. He published his memoirs, planting the seed that would become a new career as author and media personality.

**Hillary Clinton** became First Lady, with all the instant international fame that implies. After starting out with a concept of shared executive power, her attempt at a national health insurance program failed. In the face of widespread criticism, she was forced to redesign herself.

**Dorothy Hamill** started skating at age 8, in her first Balsamic phase. In her second, she and her husband bought the Ice Capades in Atlantic City. She then announced her retirement from professional skating, but divorced a year later, still in Balsamic.

**Muhammad Ali,** in his 1967-70 Balsamic phase, refused military service as a conscientious objector and had his heavyweight champion title taken away as a result. He took the case to the Supreme Court. His boxing license was restored in 1970.

**John Glenn** resigned from the Manned Space Center in 1964, was promoted to Colonel, but retired from the Marines the next year.

**Elizabeth Barrett Browning,** famed for her love poetry, was at age 40, a sickly reclusive spinster whose father had forbidden his children to marry. During this phase she began receiving letters from Robert Browning, left her sick bed and before the phase ended, the two were secretly married.

**Oprah Winfrey** debuted with great success *The Oprah Winfrey Show.*

Actor **Ronald Reagan,** who was once a New Deal Democrat, gradually changed his politics to more conservative ideas. In 1962, during his Progressed Balsamic phase, he switched to the Republican Party. Years later, in his subsequent Balsamic phase, **President Ronald Reagan** came to the end of his two terms in office and retired to his ranch in California.

## Endnotes

[1] Adapted from the *Dark Night of the Soul,* a poem of St. John of the Cross, that was adapted by Loreena McKinnit for her song by the same title, but with slightly different wording than I have used, for her CD, *The Mask and the Mirror.*

[2] Demetra George, *Finding Our Way Through the Dark,* pg 36

*Dance of the Forest*
pen and ink drawing by Maria Kay Simms

# Chapter Six

# *From Obscurity to Enlightenment*

## *Prenatal New Moon and Eclipses*

At New Moon, all is in darkness, but within the dark a seed of light is germinating and a new cycle is beginning, introducing a primary theme for the month ahead. You were born at one of eight lunar phases within a monthly New Moon cycle. Your specific birth phase with that cycle  has imprinted your soul with basic characteristics and also has determined the start time for the lifetime progressed phases covered in the previous chapters. Obviously it would be interesting and perhaps helpful to consider what New Moon theme you have entered to continue.

Your *Moon Tides* report lists the New Moon before you were born in the third line under the heading **Prenatal**. Note that both Moon and Sun are in exactly the same degree of the same sign. This is the moment of New Moon, the conjunction of Moon with Sun. Unless you were born at New Moon, the degree and sign position of your birth Moon will be different than your birth Sun. In most cases (but not all) your birth Sun will be in the same sign as it was in at **Prenatal New Moon**, though it most likely will be at least a few degrees later.

## How to Interpret Your Prenatal New Moon

To consider what your Prenatal New Moon may mean to you, reread the section in Chapter Three about its sign. This sign is the keynote for the phase cycle into which you were born. It has a message for you. Then review the material on New Moon and all other phases between New Moon and your birth phase. Think about this cyclical flow of phases in context of whatever you know from family history or world history about what was happening shortly before you entered the world. This is the environment into which your soul incarnated. Of course, you remember little detail, if anything, from your baby to toddler years. Still, others I've talked with, like myself, have a few flash pictures in their minds of things that happened at very young ages. These things that you may be able to recall from your birth phase or the one just after, along with what you generally know or have been told of your early environment, can be very important in your understanding of what you came to do and share in this life, and what lessons you came to learn. The people and events who influence us in those very young but formative years may be only dimly remembered, or not at all remembered in the conscious mind, but in the subconscious, their impact can be dynamite. The sign of your Prenatal New Moon may yield significant clues to those subconscious depths. Think about it.

# Eclipses

## Solar and Lunar Eclipses, and their Cycles in Your Life

*O dark, dark, dark, amid the blaze of noon,*
*Irrecoverably dark, total eclipse*
*Without all hope of day!*

—Milton, *Paradise Lost*

*The mortal moon hath her eclipse endur'd,*
*And the sad augurs mock their own presage;*
*Incertainties now crown themselves assur'd,*
*And peace proclaims olives of endless age.*

—Shakespeare, from *Sonnets* (1609)

Eclipse means obscurity—one celestial body is hidden, or partially hidden, from our view by another. To eclipse means to outshine or surpass something or someone else. To **be** eclipsed is to fail to appear, to be obscured, in the dark, hidden, or at the least unclear, indistinct and not understood. With these labels, it's little wonder that the ancients regarded eclipses as omens to be feared. Too often eclipses must have been seen to occur near some calamity, and consequently they came to be associated with significant events, dramatically bad events near that time—the death of a ruler, a critical battle, a natural disaster. Because they hoped to somehow avoid future disasters, the ancients devoted a good deal of time and effort in trying to predict just when eclipses might happen. So it was that after a good deal of patient observation, eclipse cycles were identified so that future eclipses could be anticipated. Robert Jansky, in his book, *Interpreting the Eclipses*, wrote that reliable records of eclipses have been kept since about 747 BC in ancient Babylonia. In the British museum are records, one carved on a stone tablet from Nineveh, that lists the lineage of kings and eclipses that occurred during their reigns.[1]

## Eclipse Cycles, and the Eclipse Tables in the Appendix

Gradually, eclipses were identified to occur in cycles. One of them, the Saros cycle, was the more reliable method for the ancients to predict eclipses, but it is more complex to explain or interpret than the scope of this book allows. The Jansky book, already mentioned, has quite a bit on this cycle. There is another cycle, though, the Metonic cycle, that was observed and identified by Greek astrologer Meton in 432 BC. This cycle is one that you may be able to identify at work in your life using only the information given in the *Moon Tides* report and the eclipse tables in the appendix of this book.

According to the Metonic cycle, phases of the Moon repeat after a period of 19 years. It is possible for a series of about four eclipses to occur on the same dates 19 years apart, and often a series of from 2 to 4 will occur in the same degree (or nearly, by minutes) of the zodiacal signs. You may find that the eclipses that occurred just prior to your birth will repeat when you are about 19, 38 or 57. Usually the degree pattern changes after a series of four.

The Metonic Cycle won't always work for you, but it's worth looking at. Of those people whose reports I checked against the eclipse tables, it appears that the Prenatal Lunar Eclipse may repeat less reliably than the solar, though this was based on a small sample that may not hold up if I checked more reports. Look at the Prenatal Solar Eclipse in your report and then find it within the **Solar Eclipse Table** in the Appendix. Count forward about 19 years to see if there's an eclipse in the table in the same sign and degree (give or take one degree). If so, count forward 19 years after that to see if perhaps it repeats again.  You may find the times of repeats coincide with significant events in your life. Do the same with your Prenatal Lunar Eclipse and the **Lunar Eclipse Table**.

The sign of your prenatal eclipses can also be interpreted in a spiritual sense for insight into your life purpose. There will be more about that soon. First, let's first dispel the old fearfulness about what eclipses mean, and then briefly understand just what is happening in the cosmos during an eclipse.

## Eclipses Symbolize Emphasis or Focus

In order to explain their fear of eclipses the ancients imagined stories of dragons and monsters and spirits to swallow the Moon. Solar eclipses were sometimes characterized as quarrels between Sun and Moon. Even into the earlier part of the last century, the idea that eclipses were always malefic ("bad") persisted, but with increased observation plus more accurate tools, most contemporary astrologers have steadily moved away from terms like malefic and benefic (beneficial, or "good"). We now know that eclipses are neither "good" nor "bad" but instead, denote strong emphasis. When an eclipse transits an important point in your birth chart, especially conjunct (in the same or nearly the same degree), there is usually something very important going on in your life. Often the eclipse coincides with a significant event and/or a critical turning point. But again, events are only on the surface of what is happening. I choose to believe that what is most significant, in the long run, is not the event itself, but how the experience of it influences the soul in the process of evolutionary growth.

Any eclipse has a potential message. The two, one solar, one lunar, that occurred prior to your birth have a lifelong message about what you are here for in this life, and what you came to learn. The degrees of your prenatal eclipses, both solar and lunar, should be considered as sensitive points in your birth chart. It has been observed that the degrees of these prenatal eclipses, when activated by transits, often symbolize important changes in life. I have found that the degree of my Prenatal Solar Eclipse, especially, has marked critical turning points for me when it was contacted by major outer planet transits. If you have your full birth chart and an ephemeris, check this out in your own life.[2]

Any post-birth eclipse that occurs conjunct or opposite[3] the degree of your birth Sun or Moon is also very important. Check the eclipse tables. You may find that those eclipses will also repeat 19 years apart, and if so, mark dramatic times for you. Try to identify what types of things were happening, and more significantly, what you were being called upon to learn at the time of any eclipse to your Sun or Moon. Then look 19 years ahead to see if anything of a similar nature was going on. If you see a pattern, likely it will involve development of the same area of personal growth. If so, it will be worth your while to count forward again to find out if and when the eclipse will repeat in the future. Anticipation offers the opportunity to plan how you can handle similar issues well, or at least better than the last time.

Whether events you associate with an eclipse are "good" or "bad" is largely a matter of how you define those terms and what choices you make at the time. Although a repeated pattern of the same eclipse may indicate a general issue and its development, the presence of an eclipse does not dictate what will happen or how you will respond to it. All it really does is offer a clue that whatever is happening in this time period is critical, emphasized and in strong focus. It may point to a challenging time, but it may as easily point to something wonderful that is taking place.

In looking for celebrity examples, one can often find eclipses near significant biographical events, but just as often the more important eclipses are **not** marked by the public events. They occur in years not mentioned by historians. What this tells us is that the event was not necessarily the most significant time of inner process. Again, it is what is going on inside you, your process of change and growth, that is most important. The most meaningful times may be the times of notable events, but not always. Keep this in mind when thinking about what was going on in your own life at the time of significant eclipses. At the end of this section you'll find examples of public figures whose biographical events were near (3° or less) eclipses to natal Sun, Moon or Prenatal Eclipse. Please note that I have deliberately chosen some examples where the eclipse marked events that we can imagine the person considered successful, while others were near events that were most likely seen as just the opposite. Again, eclipses are neither "good" nor "bad." Think in terms of emphasis and focus.

It is also worth looking at eclipses that are in the degrees opposite your Sun, Moon or prenatal eclipses, for these may be as significant as the conjunction. This is especially so with the lunar eclipse, which is an opposition in itself: Moon at one end of the polarity, Sun at the other. (Review opposition signs under Full Moon phase, Chapter Four.)

## Notable Events Occurring near Eclipses to Sun, Moon or Prenatal Eclipse Points:

**Diana, Princess of Wales**, met Prince Charles in 1980. A solar eclipse conjoined her natal Moon. Her Birth Moon is only one degree past her Prenatal Solar Eclipse, so this 1980 eclipse was its 19-year Metonic repetition. They were married in 1981; their children were born in 1982 and '84. A lunar eclipse exactly on the degree of her Cancer Sun in 1982 emphasized the importance of the births, but in the years following she was beset with turmoil over the sham her storybook marriage had become. In 1988 Diana's Prenatal Lunar Eclipse repeated and in 1989 another lunar eclipse conjoined her natal Moon. During these years she apparently adjusted, then emerged as the internationally famous "People's Princess," but the solar eclipse of 1992 conjunct birth Sun marked a public reflection of the very painful inner process that obviously continued. This was the year that her father died, the scandalous Andrew Morton book, *Diana— Her True Story*, was published, and hers and Charles' infidelities were confessed.

**Prince Charles'** report offers no similar examples during the earlier years of his marriage and the births of his sons, but in 1993, when his official separation from Diana was announced, a solar eclipse was conjunct his Sun. In 1995, the year before his and Diana's divorce was final, there was a solar eclipse exactly opposite his Prenatal Solar Eclipse, and another solar eclipse exactly opposite his natal Moon.

At the 19-year return of her Prenatal Lunar Eclipse **Dorothy Hamill** won a world skating title. The next year she would win the Olympic gold medal.

Boxer **Mike Tyson** became heavyweight champion at age 18, one month after a solar eclipse repeated the degree of his Prenatal Solar Eclipse. In 1992, imprisoned after his conviction for rape, the solar eclipse was conjunct the degree of his birth Sun.

Boxer **Cassius Clay** became the Olympic light-heavyweight champion in 1960, the year both his Prenatal Solar and Lunar Eclipses repeated. In 1963 we can speculate that great inner change was going on. A solar eclipse exactly opposed his natal Sun degree. In 1964 he won the heavyweight crown, but the event that may have been equally or more significant for him was his conversion to Islam and the changing of his name to **Muhammad Ali.**

President **Franklin D. Roosevelt** had a solar eclipse on his Sun in 1944, the year before he died in office. Roosevelt had served as state senator and assistant Secretary of the Navy prior to 1921 when he was paralyzed by polio. In 1929-33 he was Governor of New York, and was elected President in November 1932, obviously not allowing his paralysis to stop his political career. 1928, the year he was elected governor, a solar eclipse opposed his Prenatal Solar Eclipse, and a lunar eclipse conjoined his Prenatal Solar Eclipse. His Prenatal Solar Eclipse was repeated exactly by the solar eclipse of 1938, a time he must have felt extreme pressure as the Nazis moved rapidly to overrun Europe. Born with prenatal eclipse in the last degree of Scorpio, he would soon face an ultimate test of survival in leading the free world toward victory in World War II.

In 1959, the year **John Glenn** was selected to be an astronaut, his Prenatal Solar Eclipse was repeated. He was the first man to orbit Earth in 1962. In 1963, when he was still dealing with the impact of suddenly becoming an international celebrity, a lunar eclipse conjoined his Moon and a solar eclipse conjoined his Sun. In the early 1970s, a new career was in the making, heralded by a string of eclipses conjunct/opposite his Sun and Moon in 1971, 1972 and 1973. 1974 was his first year as a US Senator.

**Pope John Paul II**, according to the ancient prophecy of St. Malachi concerning the future line of the papacy, was to be characterized by the legend *De Laboris Solis* (of the labor of the Sun). This pope, with his great charisma, vitality and endurance, strongly exemplifies his solar legend. Born on the day of a solar eclipse, he was elected Pope in October of 1978 at the time of a solar eclipse. His Prenatal Solar Eclipse did not repeat after his birth, though the Prenatal Lunar Eclipse did, in 1939 when the then young actor would go to work as a stonecutter to avoid notice and possible imprisonment after the Germans invaded Poland. That lunar eclipse repeated in 1958 when he was named auxiliary bishop of Krakow. A solar eclipse conjunct birth sun coincided with his 1956 appointment as a professor at a Catholic university, and in 1966, the year prior to his becoming a Cardinal, a solar eclipse closely conjoined his natal Sun. 2003, his papal Jubilee year, had a lunar eclipse conjunct Sun and a solar eclipse opposite his Moon. And finally, the world watched the burial services of John Paul II during a solar eclipse on April 8, 2005!

## Personifying What We See in an Eclipse

The events demonstrated show emphasis and focus, but on what... really? Events are on the surface, but when studied for when they occur in the lives of public figures, we can only speculate on what may have been their soul process at the time. What is being expressed? What is being learned? Let's consider eclipses from physical and mythological perspectives.

All eclipses are formed by three entities in relationship to each other.

A **solar eclipse** occurs only at New Moon, which normally renders Moon invisible within the sunlight.

At the time of eclipse, **Moon** moves in between **Sun** and our vantage point on **Mother Earth**.

Though she isn't anywhere nearly as big as Sun, she is a lot closer to us, so she can cast a very big shadow.

Total Solar Eclipse

She might partially shadow the Sun, or in a total solar eclipse she might blot almost all of him out, making a big, very black round blot so that the only thing left to show is his fiery corona, sort of like a lion's mane with no face.

In a **lunar eclipse**, it is **Mother Earth** who casts the shadow. She moves directly in between **Sun** and **Moon** at Full Moon phase, so that Moon can't receive the full Sun's light. Because of Earth's shadow, Moon is obscured.

Sun

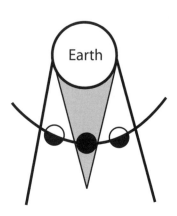

Lunar Eclipse

Just for fun, let's imagine what these three cosmic deities are doing and what message we might receive from observing their cosmic dance. We'll start from something Dane Rudhyar said, that in a solar eclipse, the present is blocked out by the past, while at a lunar eclipse the past is obscured by the present.[4] That has to be based on the concept of Moon as memory and subconscious, and Sun as consciousness. Lady Moon has a very long memory, encompassing the programming planted in your psyche when you were baby. You may not consciously remember such memories, but they prompt your emotional flow and moods. Memory may even go back before birth to lives lived long ago, impressed on the soul and brought forward into this life, again influencing your feelings. Perhaps, as well, memories of the distant past may offer reasons for inherent likes or dislikes, abilities or blockages, and help to explain why some talents or skills come so easily while others seem difficult or impossible.

# *A Solar Eclipse Myth*

*One fine day, the Moon Goddess was scheduled to have her monthly tryst with the Sun God. Shunning her New Moon guise as the shy Maiden who permitted his all consuming light to encompass her so that only his message could shine to Earth's children, our Lady became just a bit contrary. She slid herself right into the forefront. Small but mighty, she made sure that the earthlings could see her, too, even if only as a black shadow against the glaring Sun. Flaring and bristling behind her, Sun demanded, "Why do you shadow me, girl? Get out of my way!" "When I am good and ready," she retorted. "Don't you realize it is that time of year again—time to impress the souls of a whole new crop of Mother's babies with a message about what they came to Earth to do this time around?" Sun mused, "Well, I suppose so, my Lady, but get on with it. We have a lot of day left yet in which to shine…passionately, eh?" And so it was that the Moon Goddess passed before the Sun, shadowing him with her darkness, and the newest souls to incarnate through the Mother's womb received a message of ancient soul memory, a message of purpose. Each soul remembered, deep within the unconscious, the things that were well learned in the past. Seeds were planted that would one day germinate and sprout within each new little life being born, helping it to instinctively know how best to contribute to the world and share his or her talents and abilities with others. The Sun would shine through the new souls with a message of energy and purpose, but beneath that bright consciousness would be the lunar memory of something more, something important, that would emerge when the time was right.*

*For other souls on Earth, at later stages of growth in their bodies, Lady Moon's shadow on the sun served as a trigger. For them, the time was "right"—now. A significant phase in the process had come for these souls to realize, fulfill or demonstrate the purpose of the eclipse that had marked their birth. As Moon passed over the Sun and then away, again, his full light once more brightly shining, the souls awakened to a new sense of mission, calling them to use the special abilities and talents they had come to share with the world.*

## The Prenatal Solar Eclipse

Look to the **sign** of your Prenatal Solar Eclipse for insight into what you have come into the world to do, are inherently capable of doing well, and should develop ways to share with others as you fulfill your life purpose. If you have your full birth chart and know the house position of the solar eclipse before you were born, that too will contribute to your understanding, as can the theme of any planet conjunct or in very close aspect to the eclipse degree. Use the short interpretations below for clues about what the sign or house of your prenatal solar eclipse might mean.

## Prenatal Solar Eclipse in Aries (or in House 1)

Inherently strong in the ability to take initiative and assert yourself, starting projects or ideas comes naturally for you, and you may be noted for innovation. You've been an independent, take-charge person in past lives— competitive and liking to be the head of the pack in whatever you do. Now you'll have a natural impetus to move ahead first and fast, though unless other factors in your birth chart are significantly fixed in quality, you may lack the staying power and attention necessary to effectively build on what you started. If you've started a business enterprise, be wise enough to know whether you also have the patience to do the necessary follow-through, and if not, hire people who do, and be willing to listen to and consider their advice. Then you can happily go on being the inventor, the innovator and the sparkplug that provides the energy and courage to take the risks that most anything new always involves. You have a flair for the new, and most of the time, your instincts are worth trusting.

**Public Figures with Prenatal Solar Eclipse in Aries include:** Michael Jackson, John Glenn, Martha Stewart, Madonna, Sigmund Freud, Annie Besant, Krishnamurti, Neil F. Michelsen, Zipporah Dobyns, Ph.D

## Prenatal Solar Eclipse in Taurus (or in House 2)

You came into this world to demonstrate mastery of the physical world in some way. Whatever your career may be, you have an eye for what is practical, useful, comfortable and can be built toward stability and security. You have a clear idea as to what makes you comfortable and what does not. Depending on other more mutable factors in your chart, you may be willing to compromise up to a point, but you can be stubborn about seeing that your own needs are met. Your awareness of your senses may be expressed through your liking for the best of everything—good food, fine art, soft textures, beautiful music, and of course, sexuality. That sensuality and stubbornness can go awry, and sometimes drastically so, can be gleaned from the histories of just a few of the example public figures below. Remember, this position signifies what you have come to demonstrate and share to the benefit of yourself and the world. Reflect on how the individuals cited below, however varied their career lives have been, have expressed Taurus in their lives, most of them in a highly positive manner.

**Public Figures with Prenatal Solar Eclipse in Taurus include:** Lucille Ball, Jacqueline Kennedy Onassis, Hillary Clinton, Mike Tyson, Pope John Paul II, Sean Connery, Clint Eastwood, O.J. Simpson, Gloria Star, John Edwards


## Prenatal Solar Eclipse in Gemini (or in House 3)

You came from past abilities to use your mind with a level of detachment from feelings that will allow you to deal with analysis, logic, abstractions and complex intricacies, and make connections among them. Able to sort out a multitude of ideas in your head, sometimes like several voices speaking to you all at once, you'll pull it together, connect the dots, come up with what will work and then convey what you've figured out to others. Whether it be through mathematics, art, movement or anything else, at the core is a connecting link—your innate ability to analyze, connect, communicate. Versatile skills and talents make it possible for you to adapt readily when changes need to be made. You are tuned in to your environment, able to pick up clues whether you appear to be listening or not. Nearly always busy, you are likely to be one who can juggle several "balls" (projects) at once and keep them all in play.

**Public Figures with Prenatal Solar Eclipse in Gemini include:** Picasso, Dorothy Hamill, Elizabeth Kubler-Ross, Bill Gates

## Prenatal Solar Eclipse in Cancer (or in House 4)

With an inherently strong flow of emotional warmth and power you are able to generate supportive response from others and win them to your cause. They sense in you a protective quality that cares very deeply about whatever you say or do, and that you care about them personally. Cancer is the sign most closely associated with mother, or maternal nurturing instincts, and you express that, whether you are female or male. It's a big part of your purpose in life to take care of others, to protect them, to build a better and more secure world. Where you could go too far is in becoming such a source of strength to others that you elicit dependency, when what they really need is to sometimes stumble and have to pick themselves up without your help, in order to learn. Teach by example, but turn some of your strong empathy toward sensing when it may be best to let go.

**Public Figures with Prenatal Solar Eclipse in Cancer include:** George W. Bush, Bill Clinton, Dalai Lama, Indira Gandhi, Sydney Omarr, Margaret Thatcher, Susan Sarandon, Demetra George, Stephanie Clement

## Prenatal Solar Eclipse in Leo (or in House 5)

Coming from a past of confidence, you likely were a precocious tot, boldly inserting yourself into the center of attention. If you got good feedback, you stayed in the center and achieved success in life that enabled you to benefit others and feel good about yourself, too; if you were squelched, you didn't give up but may have developed a façade until you could find another venue where you could freely shine. In a few cases (known through private examples rather than the public ones presented here), those with this prenatal eclipse sign who've not found a way to shine or lead to win approval have, instead, bid for negative attention. Coming from past lives of leadership positions, you've come prepared to be a leader in this life, too. Through whatever signs and phases you've chosen for your present life expression, you'll want to convey a sense of pride and showmanship. You approach what interests you with passion, are easily assertive in going after what you want, and can be magnanimously generous when you feel like it.

**Public Figures with Prenatal Solar Eclipse in Leo include:** Woody Allen, Oliver North, Mohandas Gandhi, Louisa May Alcott, Marc Edmund Jones, Lucianno Pavarotti

## Prenatal Solar Eclipse in Virgo (or in House 6)

You come from past lives that gave you a storehouse of well-developed skills and also a sense of perfectionism about them, such that when any of them emerge in this life, you'll be adept from early on. Not that you'll be satisfied, of course, because there's always a higher level of refinement toward which you'll strive. You've got a head for detail and analysis, but it is not the airy logic of Gemini. For you it's down-to-earth pragmatism. You want to find out how whatever interests you works and how you can use it to make things better for yourself and others. It is important to find practical uses for your time and energy. Theory alone just won't do; it has to be useful to be worth your while. You've come to demonstrate how what you do can be developed to a high level of perfection. Whether your aim is to help, heal, organize, inspire or entertain, you will want to be of useful service, creating a positive impact on your world.

**Public Figures with Prenatal Solar Eclipse in Virgo include:** Catherine Zeta-Jones, Tammy Faye Bakker, Evangeline Adams, Clara Barton, Muhammad Ali, Yoko Ono, Patsy Cline, Charlton Heston, Giacomo Puccini, Marion March, Rob Hand

## Prenatal Solar Eclipse in Libra (or in House 7)

You've arrived in this life with an innate sense of balance, and a need to maintain it. The art of tact and compromise long learned through past relating carries over to a natural charm that appeals, often enabling you to get your ideas across effectively. You prefer peace and diplomacy, if at all possible, but if you find yourself in a relationship or situation where charm doesn't work and compromise sincerely tried doesn't either, you will fight— and if that doesn't work, you may just flee. Balance, fairness and niceness, are as necessary to you as breathing. A natural negotiator, shrewd but fair, you have a highly developed sense of cooperative enterprise and a strong ability to relate to others one-to-one. Able to see multiple facets of any situation, you can find the point of connection that will often resolve the issue so all concerned will be satisfied. You may also have a strongly innate sense of beauty, of aesthetic balance and visual harmony. In some manner you can be a significant role model for others in the art of balance.

**Public Figures with Prenatal Solar Eclipse in Libra include:** Dane Rudhyar, Jimmy Hoffa, John Lennon, Elizabeth Taylor, Michelangelo

### Prenatal Solar Eclipse in Scorpio (or in House 8)

Your past lives forged strong survival instincts formed through a myriad of challenging past life experiences and most likely some major power struggles. There is an innate and intense sense of passionate persistence in you that won't allow you to give up completely, no matter what, even when you meet resistance or disappointment. Your emotional depth enables you to learn (or re-learn) how to see through others and how to understand yourself, as well. Instinctively you know the importance of self-mastery, so usually you are self-contained and in control of yourself, though you are capable of expressing with intensity and impact. You can be inscrutable when it suits your purpose—few, if any, will ever know all that you are thinking and feeling. On the other hand, when you need to know something, you'll probe until you figure it out. Little, if anything, can be kept from you for long if you decide you want to know it. You can inspire others to know that they, too, can handle just about anything, if they persist in trying. When you come from a place of deep conviction it will draw others to your cause.

**Public Figures with Prenatal Solar Eclipse in Scorpio include:** Prince Charles, Ronald Reagan, Buzz Aldrin, Al Gore, Reinhold Ebertin, Betty Friedan, Abraham Lincoln, Walt Disney, Franklin Delano Roosevelt

## Prenatal Solar Eclipse in Sagittarius (or in House 9)

You come in with the background of idealist or ideologue. The nuance of which will predominate in this life may depend on how you apply what you believe, and on the varied opinions of your audience. Naturally enthusiastic and optimistic, you have an innate need to seek Truth, spread the word and convince whoever will listen. As the selfless idealist, philosopher or romantic you can be highly inspirational, raising others to new truths and growth in spirit.  By contrast, an ideologue conjures an image of leadership power that can be abused. What begins as visionary idealism becomes an advocacy where what identifies and benefits the group blurs into what identifies and benefits you, until finally the latter goal becomes dominant. At your best, you will inspire others to fearlessly seek their highest truth and be a role model for all who seek to follow their highest ideals, whether or not they are the same as yours, recognizing that freedom and independence are essential to their quest.

**Public Figures with Prenatal Solar Eclipse in Sagittarius include:** Vincent Van Gogh, Liberace, Abdal Gamal Nasser, Jim Bakker, Elizabeth Barrett Browning, Jack Nicholson, John Kerry

## Prenatal Solar Eclipse in Capricorn (or in House 10)

The sense of responsibility and aura of authority you brought to this life may be evident when as a small child, you seem mature beyond your years. You'll probably want and expect some level of authority in this life, and will work with dogged determination to achieve it. Self-absorbed and even zealous in going after what you want, you're a realist who sets goals and then works hard to achieve them. Behind the façade of even the most flamboyant entertainer can be one who takes what he or she does very seriously. You view both process and results pragmatically, and strive for the highest possible level of expertise so you will be well worthy of the recognition and status you expect to gain. Tradition and formality may be important. As the exemplar of the tradition of your field of expertise or your culture, you can be impeccable, playing your role to the hilt.

**Public Figures with Prenatal Solar Eclipse in Capricorn include:** Adolph Hitler, Rudolph Steiner, Patty Hearst, Elvis Presley, Shirley Temple Black, Elizabeth II, George Washington, Cher, Oprah Winfrey, John Travolta

## Prenatal Solar Eclipse in Aquarius (or in House 11)

Even if other factors in your horoscope point to emotional or earthy themes, there is something within you carried over from the past that sets your mind on the future and how you can change it for the better. Innovator and a reformer, you're unafraid to tread an uncharted path and blaze a trail for others who come after you. If you break time-honored traditions in the process, so be it. You'll refuse to be bound by them if they fail to measure up to your detached and objective perspective of how you think things should be. As you envision a more interesting and better future for yourself and for others, you may dedicate your life to it. You'll have a life-long interest in the new, innate tolerance for all kinds of people, and perhaps even an advocacy of those who are different or less fortunate.

**Public Figures with Prenatal Solar Eclipse in Aquarius include:** Diana, Princess of Wales, Albert Einstein, Sybil Leek, Alfred Witte, Shirley MacLaine, John Fitzgerald Kennedy, Mick Jagger, Nicolai Lenin, Tony Blair

## Prenatal Solar Eclipse in Pisces (or in House 12)

There is a highly visionary aspect to what you bring into this lifetime, and it will somehow be expressed in whatever work you choose to do. Vision emerges from your sensitivity to thoughts and feelings from mystical hidden realms. Some of your best ideas may seem to come from nowhere, and you are capable of transmitting them in a way that inspires aesthetic appreciation, idealism, spirituality or patriotism in others. You strive to create harmony and healing wherever you can. You develop high ideals and strive to express them honorably. There is a sense of synthesis and unity within you that you'll find a way to express. You may be able to sense connections that others wouldn't see—unless you point them out—and that may be a significant talent you have come to teach and to share with the world.

**Public Figures with Prenatal Solar Eclipse in Pisces include:** George H.W. Bush, Mary Baker Eddy, Sir Francis Burton, Willem de Kooning, Ralph Waldo Emerson, Marlon Brando, Charles Emerson

## *A Lunar Eclipse Myth*

*Now, as you know, on one night in each lunar cycle Lady Moon reaches a point full opposite the blazing Sun King, so that when he travels below the distant western horizon, she rises up in the east. On these nights, of all nights, her full round face illuminates sky and earth with mystery and magical beauty. Unlike the bright Sun whose face cannot be looked upon directly without damage to earthling eyes, Luna can be gazed upon by all. She conjures all the brightness of the sleeping Sun, and now as she rises high in the sky, she casts that light to Mother Earth's children. She shows them Sun's light message in a softer and more approachable version. Her message continues his theme for the cycle when she last conjoined him, but she speaks in a different tone, a counterpoint theme, contrasting but complementary, much needed for harmony, balance and full understanding. Each earthly month without fail, this pattern repeats…except for those occasional nights when Mother Earth has a message of her own to deliver! This is such a night, a significant one, indeed.*

*Mother Earth moves herself right in between Lady Moon and Lord Sun so that his light is blocked, even by Moon's attempt to reflect it. Earth's shadow falls over Luna, who protests, "Mother, you are hiding his light from me! Move aside, else your children will fail to receive our full cosmic message."*

*"They need a different lesson this time," retorts Mother. "The vibrant light of Lord Sun sends some of the answers my children seek in fulfillment of their lives, but not all, not even within your most nurturing translation. His wisdom cannot provide all they need, and neither can yours. After all, it is within my realm—here! now!— that their souls are born and must live out their appointed time. By casting my shadow upon you, I show the newborn babes the lesson they most need to learn in this earthly incarnation in order to grow strong in soul and spirit."*

*And so the shadow of the Mother passed slowly over the Full Moon's bright full face, causing the earthlings below to watch in wonder, and some with fear, as to what the portent might be. The souls of many choosing to incarnate near this time became marked by this moment. Their life path would cause them to encounter the Mother's lesson, again and again in endless variation, until through experience, they would confront her shadow message and banish it. Through this they would grow in wisdom and in strength.*

*For other earthling souls, at later stages of growth in their bodies, the shadow of Mother Earth on the Moon this night served as a trigger. Another phase of her lesson was at hand. How would they handle it this time? Would they see their need? Become aware? Change old patterns that had previously blocked their growth? Banish the shadow that just passed over them? Another focal phase in their soul process had come. As Mother Earth passed over the Moon, her shadow lifted and Full Moon shined brightly once again. What would Earth's children do this time? Only through time will the outcome be revealed.*

## The Prenatal Lunar Eclipse

Unless you are Full Moon born at the time of a Lunar Eclipse, it is most likely your Prenatal Lunar Eclipse will be in a different sign than birth Moon or Sun, perhaps different than either one of them. Always consider the Lunar Eclipse as an axis of two signs in opposition to each other, rather than as one sign alone. Like Full Moon, the lunar eclipse should always be understood as the relationship between two contrasting themes that are best resolved when considered as complementary opposites to be balanced, neither overwhelming the other and each appreciated for its value to the whole. In the headings below, the first sign to appear is the Moon, the second the Sun, as in Aries-Moon/Libra-Sun. Within the lunar eclipse polarity, the Sun (energy) symbolizes the area that probably feels more comfortable of the two, but the Moon has the theme that your soul has agreed to emphasize as an area of growth, something you need to learn and bring into better balance with the Sun theme of the eclipse polarity. In the public figure examples that follow each interpretation, you'll probably think that some learned well, while others did not, and that may be. Of these people we only know what is published about them. Public events and private process sometimes mesh, but other times do not. My interpretations, here as elsewhere in this book, tend to be more derived from what I've learned by observing and talking with private individuals.

## Prenatal Lunar Eclipse in Aries/Libra (or in Houses 1/7)

Though it likely feels most comfortable and right for you to work and live in harmony, cooperation and compromise with significant others, there is a deep need for you to learn to stand on your own two feet and take charge of yourself and your life. Whether or not you have a partner, life will present challenges where you must manage alone, for that is an important aspect of what your soul has agreed to learn. When first confronted with this prospect, it may seem as though your sense of security is severely threatened, but as you rise to the occasion—and you can—you'll begin to learn that what felt like security was really more like dependency. You find that you *can* depend on yourself and your own resources, and your inner core of strength will build in the process. Relationships and teamwork, when that is what you choose (and you will), can become more balanced and equitable as you grow through the experience of independent initiative.

## Public Figures with Prenatal Lunar Eclipse in Aries/Libra include:
Jimmy Hoffa, Catherine Zeta-Jones, Michelangelo, Prince Charles, Elizabeth Taylor

## Prenatal Lunar Eclipse in Taurus/Scorpio (or in Houses 2/8)

Probably you are inherently strong in your capacity for self-control, tenacity and the ability to pick yourself up after a crisis and survive, though you are capable of testing the limits of deep waters from time to time. Now you must learn how to turn that strength and intensity toward the building of stability and material security and to experience the ease and comfort that can thereby be created. This presents a more challenging balancing act for some than for others, depending on relative lure of sensation, but if you apply yourself with discipline, integrity and persistence, you will build substance, perhaps beyond what you originally envisioned. You will also learn the lessons of balance of this very strong polarity: when to hold on and when to release, how and when to acquire but when to let go, and how to properly manage what's yours vs. what you share with others.

**Public Figures with Prenatal Lunar Eclipse in Taurus/Scorpio include:** Jim Bakker, Walt Disney, Betty Friedan, Abraham Lincoln, Ronald Reagan

## Prenatal Lunar Eclipse in Gemini/Sagittarius (or in Houses 3/9)

With an easy inborn type of faith, your quest for higher truth leads you to adopt ideals, perhaps to the point of overly confident optimism that all will be well if you can only convince others to believe as you do. Life challenges force you to learn to balance the impulse to latch onto ideas as revealed Truth with the nitty-gritty of checking things out first, logically and systematically. Where your impulse was too dogmatic, you'll learn to be adaptable, to look at an idea from all possible sides and to consider other points of view. In this way you gain the knowledge that serves wisdom, while at the same time understanding that inherent wisdom can be valid, but is nevertheless more convincing if it is supported by reason. The Truth that you seek can be best found and conveyed through a balanced approach.

**Public Figures with Prenatal Lunar Eclipse in Gemini/Sagittarius include:** George Washington, Reinhold Ebertin, Al Gore, Shirley Temple Black, Cher

## Prenatal Lunar Eclipse in Cancer/Capricorn (or in Houses 4/10)

Comfortable with handling power and control, your soul has chosen lessons in this life about how to express close, caring relationships within home and family life. This may be especially so if you come from a past of power for the sake of power. If you attain in this life in a leadership role that influences large numbers of people whom you cannot know personally, your greatest point of balance may be through adopting them all, in your soul, as family by walking the path of compassionate and sensitive understanding. When you balance your realistic pragmatism with a sincere opening of your sensitivity to the flow of feeling and spirit, you can find a way to feed those needs in others while still achieving much for yourself, not the least of which will be your own spiritual growth.

**Public Figures with Prenatal Lunar Eclipse in Cancer/Capricorn include:** Vincent Van Gogh, Lenin, Adolph Hitler, Elizabeth Barrett Browning, Patty Hearst, John Fitzgerald Kennedy, Nasser, Sybil Leek, Dalai Lama, Oprah Winfrey, Jack Nicholson, John Travolta

## Prenatal Lunar Eclipse in Leo/Aquarius (or in Houses 5/11)

Comfortable with detached emotions, you may prefer to remain relatively free of closeness. You may find it easier, perhaps even safer, to identify with a group expression or cause than to stand in the spotlight alone. Your inclinations may be very individualistic, but in work with like-minded others you'd prefer blend in, even if in the lead. But, this life you've agreed to experience taking center stage alone, opening yourself to the vulnerability that the generous sharing of yourself must involve. Find a way to express your own personal creativity, your warmth and your solo individuality. Take a chance on yourself and do so with enthusiasm, allowing the experience of personal pride to grow, and you may find that you'll also have a positive effect on larger social changes and humanitarian reforms that balance this polarity within your soul.

**Public Figures with Prenatal Lunar Eclipse in Leo/Aquarius include:** Yoko Ono, Alfred Witte, Albert Einstein, Rudolph Steiner, Evangeline Adams, Shirley MacLaine, Elizabeth II, Tony Blair, John Edwards

## Prenatal Lunar Eclipse in Virgo/Pisces (or in Houses 6/12)

You who may find it most inherently comfortable to dream in the clouds of a quest for beauty, mysticism and high idealism have chosen to enter this life so you can also find the method and develop the skills to turn your ideals into practical forms of service to society. You are to learn discernment, attention to details and competency an area that will be of service. Be willing to do the hard work necessary to build worthwhile skills, and then find a venue where your abilities are needed. Adherence to a high ethical standard as well as a selfless attitude becomes necessary for the balance of this polarity. What you do must feel right within your soul. Like the Maiden goddess you've danced out of chaos into this life, and are here to gather the stuff of life and somehow organize it to serve humanity in a practical and healthy manner.

186 Moon Tides, Soul Passages

**Public Figures with Prenatal Lunar Eclipse in Virgo/Pisces include:**
Mick Jagger, Tammy Faye Bakker, Mary Baker Eddy, Sir Francis Burton, Krishnamurti, Reinhold Ebertin, Martha Stewart, George H. W. Bush, Ralph Waldo Emerson, Marlon Brando

## Prenatal Lunar Eclipse in Libra/Aries (or in Houses 7/1)

Charging into this life with a competitive "get there first and fast" spirit, you've agreed to accept and experience lessons of cooperation and compromise. Where you might prefer to be selfish, you'll learn to share. Where you may feel like making war, you must seek peace. If you have rough edges or an inclination to crudity, you should develop refinement and grace. Rather than making demands, discover the art of diplomacy to achieve the ends you seek. The Moon of your Prenatal Lunar Eclipse is the very symbol of the Scales of Balance, so balance you must seek, that delicate point where your own interests and those of whomever else has become involved with you can be resolved in a manner that squelches neither, is fair to both and lifts your spirits in harmony.

**Public Figures with Prenatal Lunar Eclipse in Libra/Aries include:**
Annie Besant, Wilhelm de Kooning, Sean Connery, Patsy Cline, Clint Eastwood

## Prenatal Lunar Eclipse in Scorpio/Taurus (or in Houses 8/2)

From past lives where you've built substance and learned well how to feel comfortable, you bring an inherent sense of inner security. While this is extremely good to have, in this life you've chosen to challenge that residue of complacency by learning survival skills. That could pit you against some traumatic odds. You may experience the temporal quality of material structures, even of traditions you thought so inviolate as to be set in stone, by learning how all can crumble in a flash, leaving only your inner resources to pull you through. In a big way or perhaps many times in smaller ways, you'll learn that true security cannot be found outside the self, for it lies within. Call it Goddess within, or merely inner fortitude. Whatever it is, you must discover it, and in doing so, revitalize and renew yourself and the structures of your life.

**Public Figures with Prenatal Lunar Eclipse in Scorpio/Taurus include:** Pope John Paul II, Karl Marx, Coco Chanel, Michael Jackson, Liberace, John Glenn, Mike Tyson, Timothy Leary, John Lennon, Sigmund Freud, Nancy Reagan, Lucille Ball, Prince Charles, Madonna

## Prenatal Lunar Eclipse in Sagittarius/Gemini (or in Houses 9/3)

Your comfort zone stems from a past where your quick mind stored a zillion collected bits of knowledge that sometimes pulls together or sometimes doesn't. You could be an intellectual wizard, or scattered and fickle or somewhere in between. The point is you need to learn, in this life, how to develop the wisdom that, balanced with your knowledge, can bring your soul growth to a higher level. For this you will need to develop high ideals that you can advocate honestly —"walk your talk". You have the capacity to inspire, but in order for your message to ring true, you can't just talk about it, you have to **be** it—an exemplar of what you believe. This takes a clear head and personal integrity, as you collect the facts and state the reasons, balanced with the higher wisdom and convincing power that can only come through practicing what you preach.

**Public Figures with Prenatal Lunar Eclipse in Sagittarius/Gemini include:** George W. Bush, Bill Clinton, Jacqueline Kennedy Onassis, Dorothy Hamill, Hillary Clinton, Picasso, Bill Gates, Susan Sarandon, O.J. Simpson

## Prenatal Lunar Eclipse in Capricorn/Cancer (or in Houses 10/4)

You have an innate emotional, maternal quality that can bring tears to your eyes in a moment of sentiment. You want to love unconditionally. This enables you to conjure a romantic flow or compassionate empathy, and that may be helpful to you in your work. What you have agreed to learn in this life, however, has a harder edge and a serious overtone of figuring out what will work for you in the material world and then applying it purposefully. Though not by nature ambitious, you are challenged to forge a professional life that makes a mark on your world. Though still caring of home and family, stretch to shoulder responsibility for an area of public life that interests you—business, politics, education, welfare, medicine, culture, the arts—the possibilities are many. In whatever area of endeavor you choose, your lesson is to demonstrate practical initiative, stability and ethics in the advance of your cause.

**Public Figures with Prenatal Lunar Eclipse in Capricorn/Cancer include:** Elizabeth Kubler-Ross, Indira Gandhi, Woody Allen, Lucianno Pavarotti

## Prenatal Lunar Eclipse in Aquarius/Leo (or in Houses 11/5)

You've probably basked in the spotlight in lives before, holding positions of authority and even dominance. This time, while you may again shine with creativity or leadership, you've also chosen lessons about blending in with a group and putting its goals, values and identity ahead of your own personal expression. It won't always be easy for you to detach from your need to stand out as an individual, but the larger cause will call to you, and you'll come to see how much more effective a group working together can be to effect real changes of far-reaching benefit. Learn to step outside yourself and view the world with an objective eye Develop an openness and tolerance for those who are different from you, and look for opportunities to contribute to progress in humanitarian concerns and social reform.

**Public Figures with Prenatal Lunar Eclipse in Aquarius/Leo include:** Mohandas Gandhi, Margaret Thatcher, Sydney Omarr, Oliver North, Goethe, Elvis Presley, Louisa May Alcott, Marc Edmund Jones, John Kerry

## Prenatal Lunar Eclipse in Pisces/Virgo (or in Houses 12/6)

From a practical, real world place of comfortable security you have chosen to open yourself to seek and experience mystical transcendence. Others won't always understand you, and more practical types may try to dissuade you into a more realistic choice of what you should do. Your life quest to follow your dream is as necessary as breathing, food or shelter. At best you'll find a way to make a living in support of your dream, never compromising the quest for in the process. What matters is your devotion to a larger quest—to create beauty, to heal, to inspire, to (as is sung in *The Impossible Dream*) "right the unspeakable wrong." Nothing else will feed your soul and spirit, and for you that is the priority. Keep to your highest ideals and let nothing dissuade you from them, for through them the spirit flows.

**Public Figures with Prenatal Lunar Eclipse in Pisces/Virgo include:**
Clara Barton, Muhammad Ali, Charlton Heston, Giacomo Puccini

## Endnotes

[1] Jansky, Robert Carl, *Interpreting the Eclipses*, San Diego, CA: ACS Publications, 1979.

[2] An ephemeris (tables of planetary positions) can be scanned to find out when major outer planets contacted your Sun, Moon or prenatal eclipse degrees. The term "transits" refers to the current positions of the planets compared to the planets and houses of your birth chart. It is fascinating to study this, and looking back on your own life is one of the best ways to learn to understand how the transits work. There are books that interpret transiting planets to birth planets, including one of mine, *Future Signs*.

[3] "Conjunct" or "conjunction" means in the same degree, or very close to the same degree. "Opposite" or "opposition" means in the opposite degree, or very close to it. Though most references will say 5° or less is "close," I find that the closer to exactly the same degree it is, the stronger it is.

[4] I do not know which Rudhyar book this concept comes from. It is related by Demetra George in *Finding Our Way Through the Dark*, pg. 161.

## Moon Tides, Soul Passages
for
### Eleanor Roosevelt
October 11, 1884
11:00:00 am EST
New York, New York, New York

### At Time of Birth
Phase of Moon ◑ Last quarter
Sign of Moon    Cancer
House of Moon    8

### Lunar Phases

| Pre-natal | Date | Time | Moon Position | Sun Position |
|---|---|---|---|---|
| ☌ *Solar Eclipse* | *Apr 25, 1884* | *9:46 am EST* | *05 Taurus 40* | *05 Taurus 46* |
| ● New | Sep 19, 1884 | 4:37 am EST | 26 Virgo 50 | 26 Virgo 50 |
| ☊ *Lunar Eclipse* | *Oct 4, 1884* | *5:02 pm EST* | *12 Aries 05* | *12 Libra 04* |

| Birth Phase | Date | Time | Moon Position | Sun Position |
|---|---|---|---|---|
| ◑ Last quarter | October 11, 1884 | 11:00:00 am EST | 19 Cancer 34 | 18 Libra 44 |

| Progressed Phase | Date in Lifetime | Ephemeris Date | Moon Position | Sun Position |
|---|---|---|---|---|
| ☾ Balsamic | Apr 16, 1888 | 23:20 Oct 14, 1884 | 07 Virgo 14 | 22 Libra 14 |
| ● New | Feb 18, 1892 | 19:31 Oct 18, 1884 | 26 Libra 03 | 26 Libra 03 |
| ☽ Crescent | Mar 16, 1896 | 21:19 Oct 22, 1884 | 15 Sagittarius 06 | 00 Scorpio 06 |
| ◐ First quarter | Apr 25, 1900 | 23:54 Oct 26, 1884 | 04 Aquarius 12 | 04 Scorpio 12 |
| ○ Gibbous | Feb 6, 1904 | 18:45 Oct 30, 1884 | 22 Pisces 59 | 07 Scorpio 59 |
| ○ Full | Jun 20, 1907 | 3:37 Nov 3, 1884 | 11 Taurus 22 | 11 Scorpio 22 |
| ○ Disseminating | Sep 6, 1910 | 8:43 Nov 6, 1884 | 29 Gemini 35 | 14 Scorpio 35 |
| ◑ Last quarter | Jan 28, 1914 | 18:13 Nov 9, 1884 | 17 Leo 60 | 17 Scorpio 60 |
| ☾ Balsamic | Nov 1, 1917 | 12:22 Nov 13, 1884 | 06 Libra 47 | 21 Scorpio 47 |
| ● New | Nov 13, 1921 | 13:12 Nov 17, 1884 | 25 Scorpio 51 | 25 Scorpio 51 |
| ☽ Crescent | Jan 4, 1926 | 16:38 Nov 21, 1884 | 15 Capricorn 02 | 00 Sagittarius 02 |
| ◐ First quarter | Jan 14, 1930 | 17:16 Nov 25, 1884 | 04 Pisces 07 | 04 Sagittarius 07 |
| ○ Gibbous | Aug 31, 1933 | 8:17 Nov 29, 1884 | 22 Aries 47 | 07 Sagittarius 47 |
| ○ Full | Nov 25, 1936 | 14:00 Dec 2, 1884 | 11 Gemini 04 | 11 Sagittarius 04 |
| ○ Disseminating | Jan 31, 1940 | 18:23 Dec 5, 1884 | 29 Cancer 18 | 14 Sagittarius 18 |
| ◑ Last quarter | Aug 3, 1943 | 6:31 Dec 9, 1884 | 17 Virgo 52 | 17 Sagittarius 52 |
| ☾ Balsamic | Jul 13, 1947 | 5:05 Dec 13, 1884 | 06 Scorpio 52 | 21 Sagittarius 52 |
| ● New | Sep 1, 1951 | 8:25 Dec 17, 1884 | 26 Sagittarius 05 | 26 Sagittarius 05 |
| ☽ Crescent | Oct 10, 1955 | 10:58 Dec 21, 1884 | 15 Aquarius 16 | 00 Capricorn 16 |
| ◐ First quarter | Sep 1, 1959 | 8:21 Dec 25, 1884 | 04 Aries 14 | 04 Capricorn 14 |
| ○ Gibbous | Feb 25, 1963 | 20:01 Dec 28, 1884 | 22 Taurus 47 | 07 Capricorn 47 |
| ○ Full | May 3, 1966 | 0:26 Jan 1, 1885 | 11 Cancer 02 | 11 Capricorn 02 |
| ○ Disseminating | Aug 3, 1969 | 6:30 Jan 4, 1885 | 29 Leo 21 | 14 Capricorn 21 |
| ◑ Last quarter | Apr 5, 1973 | 22:37 Jan 7, 1885 | 18 Libra 05 | 18 Capricorn 05 |
| ☾ Balsamic | May 3, 1977 | 0:27 Jan 12, 1885 | 07 Sagittarius 15 | 22 Capricorn 15 |

### Progressed Moon Ingress Dates

| | | | | | |
|---|---|---|---|---|---|
| ♌ Leo | Jul 12, 1885 | ♎ Libra | Apr 17, 1917 | ♐ Sagittarius | Jun 20, 1949 |
| ♍ Virgo | Sep 28, 1887 | ♏ Scorpio | Sep 20, 1919 | ♑ Capricorn | Dec 31, 1951 |
| ♎ Libra | Jan 19, 1890 | ♐ Sagittarius | Mar 20, 1922 | ♒ Aquarius | Jul 6, 1954 |
| ♏ Scorpio | Jun 14, 1892 | ♑ Capricorn | Sep 29, 1924 | ♓ Pisces | Dec 23, 1956 |
| ♐ Sagittarius | Dec 8, 1894 | ♒ Aquarius | Apr 6, 1927 | ♈ Aries | May 6, 1959 |
| ♑ Capricorn | Jun 19, 1897 | ♓ Pisces | Sep 17, 1929 | ♉ Taurus | Jul 26, 1961 |
| ♒ Aquarius | Dec 20, 1899 | ♈ Aries | Jan 8, 1932 | ♊ Gemini | Aug 22, 1963 |
| ♓ Pisces | May 15, 1902 | ♉ Taurus | Mar 1, 1934 | ♋ Cancer | Aug 14, 1965 |
| ♈ Aries | Aug 10, 1904 | ♊ Gemini | Mar 5, 1936 | ♌ Leo | Aug 1, 1967 |
| ♉ Taurus | Sep 14, 1906 | ♋ Cancer | Feb 19, 1938 | ♍ Virgo | Aug 20, 1969 |
| ♊ Gemini | Sep 16, 1908 | ♌ Leo | Feb 18, 1940 | ♎ Libra | Nov 4, 1971 |
| ♋ Cancer | Sep 16, 1910 | ♍ Virgo | Apr 2, 1942 | ♏ Scorpio | Mar 23, 1974 |
| ♌ Leo | Oct 12, 1912 | ♎ Libra | Jul 14, 1944 | ♐ Sagittarius | Sep 22, 1976 |
| ♍ Virgo | Dec 20, 1914 | ♏ Scorpio | Dec 17, 1946 | | |

## Sample of Page One of a *Moon Tides* Software Report

Eleanor Roosevelt is the subject of a *Lunar Life Flow* story in Chapter Seven. To assist you in learning to work with your own and other's reports, Eleanor's story will refer to specific lines within her report, as shown above, by phase and date.

# Chapter Seven

# *Lunar Life Stories*
## *Seeing the Theory in the Flow of Life*

You've now had the chance to read interpretations of your sign, house, phase and prenatal eclipses with a sprinkling of isolated examples of how each has expressed in various lives. But, unless you've been reading **all** of the text while thinking about how each interpretation applied and making notes about how it all fits your own current and past life experiences, as I advised, you've not yet seen an example of the evolutionary flow through one full 29-1/2 year phase, let alone successive phases. In this chapter I hope to bring that flow alive for you through biographical sketches of elders who have lived long and well through three complete cycles, or at least two complete cycles plus part of a third. These life stories have been chosen for contrast, to demonstrate various ways each progressed phase might manifest within different people, as well as for one person within a successive cycle. It is important that you know this, in applying the theory to yourself.

There is no factor in astrology for which there is only one interpretation. For each separate symbol there is a general theme with countless variations. Synthesizing all that into an understanding of the whole person at any given time in his/her life is the most challenging task of the astrologer.

Still, awareness of the themes, even if imperfectly understood, offers understanding and validation of what **is** and the opportunity to plan for **what might be**, or that perhaps with foresight **can be changed—IF you choose**.

It is beyond the scope of this book to synthesize its myriad of separate sign, house, phase and eclipse interpretations for you. By showing you the flow of lives as seen primarily through the powerful pattern of progressed phases, with other factors mentioned when they are notably related to the phase cycle, I hope to set you on the path toward weaving together the separate interpretations you've read into a deeper and evolutionary understanding of your own soul passages as they are reflected in the phases of your Moon.

## *Moon Tides, Soul Passages* for Connie

### Born in Gibbous Phase,
### Moon in Scorpio, Sun in Taurus

I am fortunate to know an interesting and spirited 90-year old lady with whom I like to converse. She was willing to give me an extended interview about what was happening in her life as each progressed phase flowed into the next, and after reviewing what I wrote, has given me permission to share it with you, providing I do not use her real name. Here you have an example of the phase pattern within the life of a private individual who has lived almost her entire life within one locale.

Connie was born in May of 1913, but doesn't know her birth time. This also allows me to point out that, unlike some other astrological techniques, most of the *Moon Tides* report works quite well even if birth time is not known. Though Moon sign and house vary with birth time, the phase changes are not that time sensitive, since they flow from one to another without sharp demarcation, even though the pattern, itself, is evident. Connie's Moon, set for noon EST on her birthday, is near the middle of its sign, so would be in Scorpio no matter what time of day she was born.

Of all the Gibbous phase people I've known, Connie fits the traditional description as well as any and better than most. Even now, at age 90, she is as eager to learn as she's always been. She reads avidly, questioning anything and everything. Recently, in response to her questions about a book she was reading and a cookbook she's writing, I showed her how to do an Internet search through Google, and we downloaded pertinent information. The computer is a new thing for her this year. She'd mentioned that writing her cookbook on a typewriter was hard on her hands, so my husband found her a used computer at his office and set her up with it. She's now working on her cookbook with a word processor and communicating with some distant friends via email. She and I have often discussed comparative religion when we've been together. She's skeptical, but interested in my spiritual path and its Goddess concepts. For years she's subscribed to secular humanist publications, and often marks an article for me to read.

My friend has no children of her own, but in a very real sense she fits the Mother Goddess image of her Scorpio Moon, as well as its fixed, watery power. She has mothered family and community, without a doubt, and does so still. She's approached her life with intensity, passion, strength and determination, and I believe she has confronted darkness within herself and infused it with light, achieving a self-mastery that makes her an incredible role model for this Scorpio Sun grandmother, as I approach an age that, to Connie, probably seems still pretty young.

**Progressed Last Quarter 1921**
Eight-year old Connie was sent home from Catholic catechism because she kept questioning what she was being taught, making her teachers very impatient. he was told not to come back until she had "faith." Enough of that! She turned against religion. "After that," she cheerfully confided, "when my parents forced me to go to catechism, I would leave and then pick up skates I'd hidden in a tree and go skating for the hour I should have been at church." The significance of this early memory on the development of Connie's thinking is emphasized by the 1921 solar eclipse on the degree of her birth Sun.

**Balsamic Phase**
At age 15, a solar eclipse occurred near her natal Moon. Connie met a friend who was Unitarian, visited her church and liked it. She became active as a Unitarian and remained so until ... (we'll pick that up later).

Also at 15, Connie left home to stay with a married sister after her father threatened to send her to a Catholic boarding school. Her mother, a practical nurse, was away on a temporary home care position. After a "meeting of the clan" it was decided that Connie should be boarded with an older woman until her mother was back at home again. Connie remarks, "I was somewhat of a juvenile delinquent, I guess."

**New Moon into Crescent Phase**
Connie entered college at age 17, graduated and taught in a local high school for one year. "I quit after that because I was starving," she said. "Pay for teachers was very poor, and a woman who lived at home was thought to need less than a man. I had to work part time as a waitress to survive."

At age 21, Connie worked the summer as a waitress, then took off for Mexico in the fall, traveling with two girl friends in an old car they'd bought together. They lived with a Mexican family and explored the culture until New Year's 1936, when they returned to Texas. Connie and one friend got jobs, while the other friend returned to New Hampshire.

**First Quarter, spring of 1936, into Gibbous Phase**
Precipitated by her friend's wish to return home, Connie went back to college in her home state and obtained her master's degree in history and English literature in 1937. She made good money through this and through her **Gibbous** phase working as a head waitress, then for a construction company—a job she says she enjoyed very much. When the company moved out of the USA, she went to work for the state soil conservation department.

**Full Moon, beginning spring 1943**
Connie, who at 31, was considered a spinster by the standards of her generation, met Bill, two years older than she and a farmer. The two fell in love. "Bill was bright and well educated," Connie told me. He had a college degree in accounting and banking, but when his father became ill in 1937, he went back to the family farm. He liked to work outdoors, but his father expected him to work for barely any wage at all. Still, Bill didn't mind because as the only son, he expected to inherit the family farm.

Bill's father did not approve of independent Connie, and he was accustomed to being in charge of his family. Connie's prior friendship with Bill's sister cooled after Connie's relationship with Bill was known. Connie's "new fangled" ideas did not by any stretch fit the mold of father's expectations for a proper farm wife for his son, and sister was reluctant to defy him.

Changes in Bill after he and Connie began dating annoyed his father so much that he opposed their 1944 wedding. Nobody from Bill's family attended. Still, Connie and Bill were invited to move into the house of an aunt within the family complex. Bill's aunt spent little time in her house but forbade Connie to use any of its 16 rooms other than the kitchen and their own bedroom. Forced to put almost all her own furniture in storage because she had no room to put it anywhere, Connie began to rearrange a few things in the house, which angered the aunt to the point that the couple moved out.

Once Connie and Bill had married, Bill's mother softened toward Connie and the sister also became friendly again, but Bill's father remained firmly opposed to the marriage. Finally, the last straw came when Connie, who had money saved from her years of work, purchased a plot of land that was for sale, but which Bill's father had leased to grow potatoes. This gave Bill land of his own to farm, but rankled Dad. Just one year after their marriage a confrontation between Bill and his father resulted in the couple leaving the family farm. They built a camp on their new land. "Just a two room shack," Connie told me, "but we ended up living in it for eight years."

Connie was now 33, an age marked by two solar eclipses, one conjunct her Sun, the other her Moon. This was also the time that she left the Unitarian Church because it was too involved with political activism for her liking. She has not been active in any church since.

### Disseminating Phase
Connie worked with Bill to run the farm for four years and they steadily progressed, acquiring a tractor and a truck. With Connie's encouragement, Bill joined community organizations, eventually becoming a major leader.

### Last Quarter Phase
Connie, who by 1953 was restless to have her own independent earnings

again, began to work at a bank, and was sent by her employer for further schooling in banking. By 1955 she'd been moved to the consumer loan dept. Before the end of the phase she was promoted to Vice President of the bank, becoming the first woman in the state to hold such a position.

**Balsamic Phase**
Our newly successful bank VP encountered personal sadness on the home front as her mother passed away, and her father's health declined.

**New Moon Phase, Second Progressed Cycle**
Connie's parental home was sold, and Connie and Bill built their own new home. Her father came to live with them, and later an elderly uncle, too. Connie continued as Vice-President at the bank, but with added duties as caregiver. The uncle died.

**Crescent Phase**
Connie's care of her father became increasingly difficult, and he was not to live out this year. Connie says that once both her parents were gone she felt like an iceberg in the middle of the ocean all alone.

**First Quarter and Gibbous phases (1965-72)**
Connie continued at the bank. She enjoyed helping people with the responsible handling of loans that enabled them to have homes and manage small businesses. Her bank became known as the "friendly bank" and often people were lined up waiting to talk with her. This very successful time of Connie's life was marked in 1966 by two solar eclipses, one conjunct Sun, the other conjunct Moon. In 1970 an agricultural museum she'd been helping establish was incorporated in 1970, with Connie as Trustee. She also found time to be active in the local drama society, appearing in a few shows and directing others.

**Full Moon Phase through Disseminating Phase**
Connie and Bill were now in their 60s. During these years they both retired, he from farming, she from the bank, but they were far from inactive. Connie turned her very considerable energies even more heavily than before to community projects. Still active as trustee and officer of the museum for twelve years now, she stepped into the background of that, urging Bill to step forward. He became president and served in that capacity for many

years. Connie and Bill were active in Democratic politics on both state and national campaigns, often traveling to various conventions having to do with environmental concerns or election campaigns.

## Last Quarter Phase
In 1983, they sold their farm at a good price, then bought the home where Connie still lives. The "crisis of consciousness" came as this always very active woman had to deal with the slowdown of a health condition that required a hip replacement.

## Balsamic Phase
Connie's health condition persisted, requiring the other hip to be replaced, as well. In between, on car trips with Bill who didn't like to talk while driving, Connie's active mind silently constructed a new project.

## New Moon, Third Progressed Cycle
In 1991, Connie self-published her first cookbook, dedicated to the preservation of regional agrarian history, a goal of the museum in which she and Bill had been so active. In Connie's own words,  here is an excerpt from her Introduction:

> *These recipes or "receipts" plus word of mouth "rules" passed down from generation to generation, form the basis for this cookbook.  You may find some recipes lip-smacking, others may make you cringe. They are all authentic.*

What follows is an amazing collection including everything from (as she said) the lip-smacking (delectable sounding desserts) to the cringe ("Calf's Head and Pluck" or "Hag Maw" (with details of how to clean the pig's stomach, plus pages of home remedies covering a variety of concerns from chiliblains to foreign bodies children might push in their noses. (Over a decade later, the cookbook continues to occupy a prominent place in the museum's gift shop, where at a recent event, Connie presided to sign autographed copies.)

## Crescent Phase
Connie required another surgery.   On the plus side, in 1994 Connie and Bill had a very big anniversary party.  They were much admired leaders in a

community they'd both served long and well, so this party was attended by a great many townspeople—a far cry from their wedding fifty years earlier, attended only by members of Connie's family.

## First Quarter Phase
Bill became ill and kept up "a good front," Connie remembers, but he died in 1997. His passing was very hard for Connie. In addition to handling the loss of her husband, leg ulcers stemming from earlier surgeries formed.

## Gibbous Phase
The leg ulcers led to yet another surgery and ongoing related recovery issues—not that any of them appeared to keep her down or dampen her spirits. Connie continued her active community life, including book clubs, support for the local library, work for the farm museum and being a neighborhood and community source of the regional history.

## Full Moon
Now, at 90, it's Connie's fourth **Full Moon** in this life. She lives with her large, gentle dog, and petite yellow cat. She has help once a day with food for supper and shopping, but otherwise takes care of herself. Still mentally sharp and active in community organizations, she's working on that new cookbook. This great lady's story illustrates beautifully her three+ complete lunar phase cycles, and I'm very grateful to her for sharing it with me, and with you.

## A First Lady to Remember

The next story of the lifetime flow of *Moon Tides, Soul Passages* profiles a very famous woman, Eleanor Roosevelt, who as First Lady of the United States, had enormous influence. In understanding her experience of some of her phases, we have the added advantage, over published biographical material, of her own thoughts, as she expressed them in a syndicated column she wrote for many years.

# Moon Tides, Soul Passages
# for Eleanor Roosevelt

## Born in Last Quarter Phase,
## Moon in Cancer, Sun in Libra

Eleanor Roosevelt[1] was a woman who made a difference, well beyond the fact that she revolutionized the entire concept of First Lady that before her time had been a largely social/ceremonial role. She became an activist for social causes, particularly for desegregation and women's rights. Declining to call herself a feminist, she nevertheless was an exemplar for any woman who wants an identity of her own separate from spouse and children, as well as for any woman, who faced with the insecurities and depression of loss and pain, can look them squarely in the eye and go forward, transmuting her pain into indomitable strength. Eleanor was ahead of her time. She lived a long and productive life of 78 years, during which she became one of the most greatly admired and respected—but by a few, one of the most hated—women of her generation. Her **prenatal Solar Eclipse** was in Taurus—she came into the world to demonstrate how to persist against all odds and to build substance. Her **prenatal Lunar Eclipse** was in Aries. She would have to learn how to stand on her own and fight for what she thought right.

*As orientation on how to use the Moon Tides report, the personal data page for Eleanor's report is reproduced on page 190. Throughout Eleanor's life story, specific references to lines within her report will be inserted. Also, if you compare this report and story with dated events within other published biographies of Eleanor Roosevelt, you may receive additional insight into how her report corresponds to her life flow. This is how I wrote her story and most of my other examples! When you study your own report, look for references to the phases or signs and then think about how those basic themes have manifested for you.*

**First Progressed New Moon** *(Look at Progressed Phase column and date column, 2nd line, New Moon from Feb.18, 1892 through Mar. 15, 1896 )*
Eleanor, who was born in New York City to a prominent family, lost both her parents before she was 10—her mother to diphtheria in 1892 and her father to alcoholism in 1894. A shy, awkward and plain child, Eleanor

had been a disappointment to her beautiful mother, and obviously received little counter to her insecurities from an alcoholic father.

**Progressed Crescent** *(look at the lines for Mar. 16, 1896 through Apr. 24, 1900)* Eleanor was educated at an English school

**Progressed First Quarter** *(Apr. 24, 1900–Feb. 5, 1904)*
Theodore Roosevelt, her father's older brother, became President. Shortly after that Eleanor returned to New York and made her debut into New York society. She also worked for improved conditions of the immigrant poor via the Junior League and the Consumers' League, gaining confidence in herself in the process.

About a year later, in 1903, when her prenatal **Lunar Eclipse** repeated (the Solar did not), she became engaged to Franklin D. Roosevelt, who was her fifth cousin, once removed. (*See Pre-Natal Lunar Eclipse, column 1, line 3, under Lunar Phases at top of report. Read across for Moon sign and degree and note that Eleanor's Prenatal Lunar Eclipse is 12 degrees of Aries. Now, scan the Lunar Eclipse Table, App. II, for another lunar eclipse at 12 Aries.*)

**Progressed Gibbous** *(Feb. 6, 1904–June 19, 1907)*
It was her uncle, the President who, in the absence of her father, gave her in marriage in March of 1905. A challenge of this phase was likely that the fragile confidence gained through her independent work was nipped in the bud as her life became totally subsumed into her new role as wife and mother.

**Progressed Full and Disseminating** *(June 20, 1907–Jan. 27, 1914)*
Eleanor was busy having children, her fourth sadly dying in infancy of influenza. During the Disseminating years, Eleanor attended her first Democratic Party Convention and FDR became Secretary of the Navy.

**Progressed Last Quarter** *(Jan. 28, 1914–Oct. 31, 1917)*
The Roosevelt's fifth child was born just as Eleanor's **Last Quarter** phase began. It was 1914 and World War I had just broken out in Europe. In 1916, Eleanor gave birth to their sixth and last child. The next year the United States entered the war.

**Progressed Balsamic Phase** (*Nov. 1, 1917–Nov. 12, 1921*)
With this phase came a devastating emotional crisis: Eleanor's discovery that her husband and her social secretary, Lucy Mercer, were having an affair. Perhaps there could be some symbolism for Eleanor that this was also the year that the House of Representatives passed the women's suffrage amendment. A *Time* magazine article profiling Eleanor, by Doris Kearns Goodwin, quoted her remembrance of that time: *"The bottom dropped out of my own particular world. I faced myself, my surroundings, my world, honestly for the first time."* Eleanor and Franklin talked of divorce, but he promised to end the affair, so she stayed. But, this had to have been a time when she confronted the darkness and committed herself to a future that would be quite different, one where, even though remaining within her marriage, she would also maintain her own space, blazing her own trails and forging her own individual identity. She would accept the challenge of her Prenatal Lunar Eclipse in Aries and learn to stand alone.

In 1921, in the last months of Eleanor's Balsamic period, her husband became paralyzed from polio, another major crisis, but one that, in its way, could be considered a seed of the New Moon phase she would enter just two months later. Her **progressed Moon** was by now at 25 **Scorpio**. (*Go to line 2, columns 3 & 4 at the foot of the report: Scorpio Sept. 20, 1919–Mar. 19, 1922.*) She'd been facing the necessity for the Scorpion's survival skills. Now she would be called upon to use them in her new cycle.

**Second Progressed New Moon through Progressed Crescent**
(*Progressed Phase; scan for 2nd New Moon: Nov. 13, 1921—Jan. 13, 1930*)
Eleanor became her husband's "eyes and ears," traveling when he could not to gather information he needed for his political career, and at the same time, she became increasingly active in her own interests. She was active in a variety of programs for social reform, and collaborated in purchasing a school where she later taught history and government. By 1928, the Democratic National Committee had appointed Eleanor its director of Women's Activities, and FDR was elected Governor of New York. In 1929 the Stock Market Crashed, and within the next two years…

**Progressed First Quarter** (*Jan. 14, 1930–Aug. 30, 1933*)
FDR, with his ideas for a "New Deal" formulating, was elected President of the United States in 1932. The new First Lady's "crisis of action" had begun

in full force. She would use it to the hilt, forging ahead and making her own mark on history. She became the first wife of a president to hold her own all-female press conferences—an ulterior motive, that, for it encouraged newspapers to hire female reporters in order to keep up with her news. Her Moon progressed into Aries, as she pioneered a new style of First Lady.

**Progressed Gibbous Phase** (*Aug. 31, 1933–Nov. 24, 1936*)
Eleanor became increasingly active and influential in the desegregation movement and for women's rights. She began her syndicated column, *My Day*, in which she comments on her reflections, opinions and experiences of a variety of topics of current interest. For a sense of Eleanor in her own words, on the topic of *Women in War* (October 15, 1943):

> *"If I were young enough, I would rather be a nurse in the Army or Navy, for they are allowed to share more nearly the men's existence...* [military life] *is hard and uncomfortable, but I think women can stand up under that kind of living just as well as men."*

**Progressed Full Moon** (*Nov. 25, 1936–Jan. 30, 1940*)
This phase began in 1936, progressed Moon in Gemini. FDR won re-election.Eleanor's outreach grew. At Southern Conference for Human Welfare in Alabama, she defied segregation laws by refusing to sit with the whites. She sat between them and her black friends. She called attention to her cause in Washington, D.C. by arranging for Marion Anderson to sing at the Lincoln Memorial on Easter Sunday of 1939, the same year that Hitler invaded Poland. A **Solar Eclipse was conjunct Eleanor's Sun** when the Daughters of American Revolution (DAR) barred Marion Anderson from their auditorium. Eleanor resigned, quite publicly. In her February 27, 1939, *My Day* column, she reflected that in times past when she'd disapproved of an action of a group to which she belonged, she usually stayed until she'd at least *"made a fight and had been defeated."* In accepting defeat, she'd decided that perhaps she was *"a little too far ahead of the thinking of the majority."* This time, though, she concluded, *"To remain as a member implies approval of that action, and therefore I am resigning."*

**Progressed Disseminating** (*Jan. 31, 1940–Aug. 2, 1943*)
Two **eclipses**, a Solar and a Lunar, both in Aries closely opposite her Sun, marked 1940, the year that Eleanor made an impromptu speech at the

Democratic National Convention that helped FDR win his unprecedented third term in office. The next year was Pearl Harbor, and during the war years, Eleanor toured the South Pacific to boost military morale. *(Birth phase line, Sun position col. 5, 18 Libra. Scan Eclipse Tables for 18 Libra or Aries, give or take a degree.)*

**Progressed Last Quarter** *(Aug. 3, 1943–July 12, 1947)*
By 1945, Eleanor had influenced the Army Nurse Corps to open its membership to black women, and she joined the NAACP board of directors. This was the year that FDR died in April, and was succeeded by his Vice-President Harry Truman who led the nation to the end of World War II.

On April 21, 1945, Eleanor wrote about leaving the White House : *There is always … emotional strain about the last time for anything… I have spent my last night in the White House…I wonder if others have been thinking, as I have, of the rather remarkable way in which our people and our government have passed through this major period of change.* Continuing on to muse on this and about how much it is a tribute to the people of the USA as a whole, Eleanor reaffirmed her confidence in the future.

In 1946 Eleanor was elected head of the United Nations Human Rights Commission, and she initiated the creation of Americans for Democratic Action, a group that focused on domestic social reform and resistance to the developing Cold War.

**Progressed Balsamic**  *(July 13, 1947–Aug. 31, 1951)*
In 1948, Eleanor spoke at the Sorbonne on "The Struggles for the Rights of Man" during a meeting of the UN General Assembly. When Truman delayed recognizing the State of Israel, she threatened to quit the UN. In December 1948, the UN passed the Human Rights Declaration.  Eleanor and her children promoted her causes with radio and TV appearances.

**Third Progressed New Moon**  *(July 13, 1947–Aug. 31, 1951)*
In 1952, Eleanor resigned from the UN and campaigned for Stevenson for president.  In 1953  (**Solar Eclipse conjunct Eleanor's Moon**), the Women's division of the Democratic National Committee was abolished with the women integrated into existing party structure.  Segregation was outlawed in the public schools.   Eleanor was seeing her causes manifest into changes for which she'd long worked.

**Progressed Crescent** (*Oct. 10, 1955–Aug. 30, 1959*)
In 1957, Eleanor visited the Soviet Union as a representative of *New York Post* and met Khrushchev. This was also the year that Congress passed the Civil Rights Act. Eleanor's activism had generated admiration from many, but had also made serious enemies along the way. One of them was FBI Director Hoover, who apparently threatened by her affiliation with liberal groups and her outspoken support of desegregation, caused extensive investigation of her activities and associates from when she was First Lady right up until she died, amassing one of the largest single files in the entire FBI collection. The Klu Klux Klan went so far as to threaten her life when she spoke at a 1958 civil rights workshop at Highlander Folk School Tennessee. One FBI file, according to the huge collection of documentation on the *pbs.org* web site, includes a copy of the $100 check she sent the school, press coverage of the event and a document relating to the Klan's threat on her life.

**Progressed First Quarter** (*Aug. 31, 1959–Feb. 24, 1963*)
1960 saw Eleanor again active in the presidential campaign, this time working for the election of John F. Kennedy. After he became President, JFK re-appointed Eleanor to the United Nations and named her chair of the President's Commission on the Status of Women.

In 1962, Eleanor died of tuberculosis. She'd been active to the end. In this final year she spearheaded a Commission of Inquiry, reporting on the efforts and progress of the fight for Civil Rights.

Of what we might learn from Eleanor Roosevelt, in how she lived her life and defined herself from shy and insecure girl to a woman of confidence and strength who could make a positive difference in her world, I can think of no better conclusion than her own words, from her 1960 writing *You Learn by Living*, as quoted within *Bartlett's Familiar Quotations*:

> *"You gain strength, courage and confidence by every experience in which you really stop to look fear in the face. You are able to say to yourself, "I lived through this horror. I can take the next thing that comes along...You must do the thing you think you cannot do."*[2]

# Moon Tides, Soul Passages for Don

## Born during Full Moon,
## Moon in Virgo, Sun in Pisces

Don, born in 1932 and a business associate of my husband's, is a retired executive who "keeps his hand in" by consulting. On a recent trip here, he agreed to tell me about his life in relation to his lunar phases. He expressed considerable surprise throughout our con-versation at how well the phase themes worked with his life events.

Don's early memories of his childhood were mostly happy ones (**Full** and **Disseminating** phases). Though he grew up during the depression, he felt little of the effects. His father lost his job, as so many did, but got a job driving a Good Humor truck and Don remembers liking that—Dad would bring home the leftovers!

### Progressed Last Quarter
By 1938, the shift of energy of the waning phases was felt.  Don remembers listening to the war news on the radio, his mother sometimes crying with worry that his Dad would have to go to war. Then came Pearl Harbor, and the worries increased. Mother became quite strict. Don recalls building a crystal set so he could secretly listen to the war news under the covers after bedtime. He and his brother collected tinfoil for the war effort. He still fights to this day a residue of fear that war might push us back into the depression of not having enough of anything, realizing that he tends to put a price on things and even though he is affluent, wonders always whether or not he should spend money on this or that.

### Progressed Balsamic Phase
Teenager Don was looking for "something else" other than the sports that most boys pursued. Through an after school job at a gas station, he found that he was very good at mechanical things.

### First Progressed New Moon
Don's  growing expertise with cars enabled him to make friends and get the girls to notice him.

## Progressed Crescent Phase

Don was off to to UCLA, and while there (in late 1951) experienced **the first of a series of three Solar Eclipses closely conjunct his natal Moon** that would coincide with significant shifts in his thinking. Realizing that he was about to be drafted anyway, Don left college before finishing his degree, joined the Navy and became a pilot. He served in the Korean War for about a year, says he was not in "major battles," but valued the "major bonding" that occurred within the squadron. He finished college by correspondence and was granted his degree in engineering in 1955.

## Progressed Full Moon

During this first return of his birth phase, Don was discharged from the Navy in 1960, and then went to work at an engineering company where his father was already employed in management. Don describes himself as "a planner." *"I got that from my Dad; didn't let anything just happen."* Don's job was in Operations at a different company location than his father's, and Dad's boss was Don's mentor.

> *"He apparently saw management potential in me. At my young age, he put me in charge of about 25 people—a life-changing event. These were workers of all ages, a serious management situation. It was unheard of to be recognized in that capacity at such an early age."*

In 1962-63 (still Full Moon), the bosses wanted Don to move to the New York City headquarters. This seemed a good career move, but it met with a lot of opposition from his Dad. Dad apparently was right, for New York was not a pleasant experience for Don. It was a harsh environment with a boss who was *"a donkey."* The upshot was that Don quit his job, a move that almost broke his Dad. But Don got another job in San Francisco; a different company.

## Progressed Disseminating Phase

Don met Karen and they married in 1966. He did very well with the new company, remaining with them for almost ten years.

## Progressed Last Quarter

Don recalls a significant shift in consciousness at this phase toward wanting a senior management position. In 1968, Karen gave birth to their daughter.

Don was traveling nearly 70% of his time as the 1970s began. His life was increasingly compartmentalized, with regrets at having to be away from his family so much. At the end of August 1970, the **19 year eclipse cycle brought another solar eclipse conjunct his natal Moon.**

## Progressed Balsamic Phase
In 1972. Don was offered a Vice Presidential position with a Chicago firm. This would cut his travel to about 20%, so the family moved to Chicago.

## Progressed New Moon
Nearly four years after the move to Chicago, Don was offered the position of Executive Vice President at the London office of his firm. He moved his family there for two years after which he was sent to Oklahoma to open a new branch there.

## Progressed Crescent Phase
Living was difficult in Oklahoma, bringing many frustrations. Since the parent corporation headquarters was in London, Don found himself constantly fighting the London office. He also found himself back in the mode where frequent travel was necessary.

## Progressed First Quarter
The ongoing corporate fight was getting to be just too much. *"Either I go back to the London office,"* he thought, *"Or I leave the company completely."* It was at this time that Don made a decisive move to pave his way toward being able to quit the corporation when he felt like it. He bought a business in California with his younger brother. Within his existing corporate position, he made moves that would lead to his being transferred to a California office. Though he continued in his position, his attitude shifted. He was no longer striving to "make it to the top." Now he was biding his time until he was ready to leave. Another significant element in his decision was the wish to avoid having his daughter constantly obliged to change schools and with her father so frequently traveling. When the move to California came, Don's and Karen's primary decision on where to live was where the best possible high school was located.

## Progressed Full Moon, Second Return to Birth Phase
Just a few months after the **19-year repeat of the solar eclipse conjunct**

**natal Moon**, Don chose to retire from his senior management position with the big corporation. He had planned ahead wisely, and could now *"leave and do what I want."*

### Progressed Disseminating Phase
Almost immediately as this phase began, Don met my husband through another business associate. Don enjoys consulting for Jim's business.

> *"I can keep my hand in and have fun at the same time. This is so different from a big corporation. It's much easier without the constant political pressure, and without the pressure of having to work. No work environment can intimidate when one does not **have to** work!"*

Will there be another major move? Nothing is planned, though if there ever were, it would be to allow he and Karen to be closer to their daughter's growing family. Don is in **Progressed Balsamic Phase** again, but appears quite relaxed and at peace with himself. He feels the potential of a shift of energy toward something new that is as yet undefined. Likely it will involve the business enterprise he has with his brother. They bought a tiny little town that sounds like it could become an interesting tourist attraction. We'll see…on Don's last trip here he was researching where he could buy a stagecoach!

# Moon Tides, Soul Passages for Lucille Ball

### Born in Gibbous Phase,
### Moon in Capricorn, Sun in Leo

While I was writing this book, a movie of Lucy's life was on TV. I'd just run her *Moon Tides* report as one of my selections from *AstroDatabank* of AA data on public figures whose names are well known. So, of course I watched the movie with interest, and enjoyed the recreations of some *I Love Lucy* shows I remembered having watched years ago. I also made some notes, her report in hand, and with those plus the biographical info from *AstroDatabank*, could see that this was quite a remarkable woman whose career spanned quite a bit more than the work as a comedienne for which she is best known. What was even better, for my purposes, is that it was easy to see how her life and career changes flowed right in sync with her lunar phase changes. Then, I discovered on an Internet search that she'd written her own autobiography, *Love, Lucy*. Even better! I bought the book and enjoyed it very much—I recommend it![3]

From the opening of *Love, Lucy*:

*I'm a Leo. I was born on a Sunday, August 6, 1911. Unfortunately, everybody knows my birth date because I told the truth when I first came to Hollywood.*

**Progressed Full Moon**
Lucy, as an only child at age three, was showered with affection by her parents, a life at center stage. She was soon to have her first very major relationship challenges. Her father died of typhoid when she was four, and her mother was pregnant. Not only did Lucy lose a loving father, but also soon had a new little brother to compel Mom's attention. Lucy was ignored and jealous. Mother, obviously desperate to keep track of her lively older child, hitched her with a dog leash. Lucy begged to be set free, and was, quite a lot. Finally, her mother arranged to have a kindly grocer watch her. Lucy would prance up and down his counter, reciting little verses her parents had taught her and gleefully accept candy from customers—her first paid performances!

**Progressed Disseminating Phase**

Lucy's mother remarried. Lucy and her brother were sent to live with an aunt and uncle while her mother and new stepfather went to California to find jobs. Aunt and Uncle were strict fundamentalists, very dour. Nothing had prepared Lucy for how hard this new life would be. She escaped as best she could by developing an imaginary life with imaginary identities and friends. The chicken coop became her palace, the chickens her armies. She was Sassafrassa, a great queen, or at other times Madeline, a beautiful cowgirl. In her autobiography, Lucy offers the opinion that the drive and dedication necessary to succeed in show business, or most any field, is often rooted in a disturbed childhood. Though she felt neither unloved nor unwanted, her childhood was filled with many moves, deaths of people close to her and other "cruel circumstances" that brought painful separations.

**Progressed Last Quarter**

Lucy recalled a stormy adolescence in which she ran away a lot—"I'd leave the classroom for a drink of water and never come back." She said her main need was for someone to talk with. She found it with a school principal and missed him so much that one of her flights was to hitchhike to his new home fifty miles away after a job change had taken him away from her home town. Her restlessness stemmed from a multiplicity of things that weren't going well within her family during what would have been the years of her **Last Quarter** phase, the crisis of consciousness.

**Progressed Balsamic Phase**

As a freshman in high school, Lucy had a bright spot when she and a girl friend put on an amateur production of *Charlie's Aunt*. With that she learned to know "for the first time that wonderful feeling that comes from getting real laughs on a stage." After that, she got into dramatic productions at every opportunity, though family problems such as the divorce of her mother and stepfather and an accident leading to extreme legal problems for her grandfather contributed to more attempts to flee

Toward the end of Lucy's **Balsamic** phase, her mother decided that if she was so determined to run away it would be best to guide her. So at age 17, aided by a loan from her mother to attend drama school, Lucy left for New York, terrified but with the hope that somehow there she could make her dreams into reality. It was not an easy start. She failed out of the drama school. Not able to face the "sneers and snickers" that would await her back home, she decided to become a showgirl. Lonely, homesick and so poor she once panhandled for a pennies to get subway fare to the theater district, Lucy didn't give up. She was hired for a show, then fired after a few weeks, then found work as a model. Though she didn't realize it at the time, she learned a great deal modeling. But, then she came down with rheumatic fever. Not able to manage alone with her illness in New York, she went home to convalesce.

**Progressed New Moon**
Back on her feet in 1930, Lucy got a good part in a play that opened locally and then later played at Chautauqua. She was a great success in it, playing a hard-boiled confidence woman who could also pass, when she chose, for a debutante. This was also the first time, due to the necessity, that she dyed her hair for the performance, dark with a reddish cast, recalling in her biography that this was the first time she began to wonder if she might have a redheaded personality. Back in New York the following year, modeling again, Lucy won a small movie role as a slave girl in a flashy 1933 musical called *Roman Scandals*.

**Progressed Crescent Phase**
Off to Hollywood, Lucy was determined to stand out and succeed. At some point after she began working for RKO, she dyed her hair reddish gold, and also applied herself with great discipline. Soon there were other roles, in which she usually played the brash friend of the leading lady. A notable film came in the beginning of **First Quarter** phase (1937) when she played a major role in *Stage Door* with Katherine Hepburn and Ginger Rogers.

**Progressed First Quarter**
Lucy met Cuban bandleader Desi Arnaz on the set of the film *Too Many Girls*. *"It was not love at first sight,"* she said. *"It took five minutes."* The film's title would prove to be prophetic, though Lucy didn't recognize it at that time. The couple married only six months after they met.

**First Progressed Gibbous Phase**
Newlywed as this phase began, husband Desi went on the road frequently with his band, and often played with one of his "too many girls" on the side. Hollywood acquaintances gave the marriage six weeks, but as we

have already seen, Lucy was a determined woman. She and Desi were both jealous and the relationship was fiery.

In 1942, Lucy left RKO for a new contract with MGM. It was then that her hair was changed to the bright red "for Technicolor" that became her trademark. *"Every time I glanced in the mirror, I reared back, it was so startling...I hated it, but I went along with it...I wouldn't now."*

**Second Progressed Full Moon**
Lucy's growing tension with Desi had, for a time, been averted by his service in World War II, and as her own successes grew, she was rushed from *"one extravagant musical to the next with the full star treatment."* In 1944, though, her marriage *"crashing fast"* due to Desi's night life and drinking, Lucy filed for divorce, but then was persuaded by him that he would change, so she never filed the papers. Desi did change for a while, though Lucy no longer expected to be as happy as she'd been as a bride. She dreamed of having a child, and of somehow finding a way to co-star with Desi so they could work side-by-side and hopefully improve their marriage. Though he had his successes, Lucy's career was far more so, leaving him often depressed. His drinking and carousing continued as he returned to civilian status and was often away on the road with his band.

**Second Progressed Disseminating Phase**
Lucy began a CBS radio show that became quite popular called *My Favorite Husband*. She took Catholic instruction, as part of her hope "to become a better wife," and in 1949, she and Desi renewed their vows in a Catholic Church. She later said that she had seriously intended to become a Catholic, but lost interest when she realized that Catholicism didn't seem to help Desi with his life.

Numerous attempts to get herself somehow cast with Desi failed, until in 1950 they decided that since nobody else saw them as a team, they'd form their own company to make it happen. Desilu Productions later proved to have been a very shrewd business move. The two put together a vaudeville type act and launched it at various army camps. When word got around that it was liked, theater contracts followed. During all this, Lucy became pregnant, but miscarried. She was then offered a part in DeMille's *Greatest Show on Earth*, and feuded with her existing contract to be allowed to do the movie, which was with a different studio. She succeeded, but then found out she was pregnant again. She wanted very much to do the movie, but even more, being still childless and approaching 40, to have the baby. Tearfully, with Desi at her side, she broke the news to DeMille, who paused for a moment and then said, *"Congratulations, Desi, you are the only person in the world to screw Harry Cohn, Columbia Pictures, Paramount Pictures, Cecil B. DeMille and your wife, all at the same time."*

Lucy cancelled everything for a time, determined that nothing would interfere with her pregnancy…until her fourth month, when suddenly an offer from CBS gave her what she'd long hoped for, the chance to co-star with Desi. The radio show idea would now become a TV show. Lucy's autobiography credits Desi with the suggestion for filming the show live in front of an audience. The studio screamed, due to the extra expense that would involve, so Desi cut a deal that would later prove to be a shrewd one. In return for a salary cut for them, Desilu got complete ownership of the show that would become *I Love Lucy*. The result is history, and it was media magic.

### Second Progressed Last Quarter
From the debut of *I Love Lucy* on 10-15-1951, just a few months into this phase, and for six years following, the show was immensely popular, making Lucy and Desi (called on TV, Ricky Ricardo) household names. Lucy became known as one of the world's greatest comediennes.

Daughter Luci was born in 1951, shortly before the TV show debuted. The birth of Desi, Jr. in 1953 (still **Last Quarter** phase for Lucy) also became the birth of little Ricky on the TV show. On the show, Lucy secretly sent a song request to her Ricky as he performed at his club, a song for a couple in the audience who were having a baby. While a huge and rapt national TV audience watched, Ricky sang until he spotted Lucy at a table and it finally dawned on him that the song request was from her for him. His eyes filled up, she started to cry and even the hardened stagehands cried. When the director wanted retakes after the show ended, the studio audience stood up and shouted, "No, no!"

That was a "banner year" for Lucy and Desi. Besides the happy birth, the show won two Emmy awards, they became TV's highest paid stars, and were named Husband and Wife of the Year.

A difficult challenge of **Last Quarter** came when Lucy was accused of being a Communist. She had registered that way once in 1936, at the request of a relative who wanted to run for a local office under that ticket, but had never thought any more about it or participated in any way at all. Still, in the climate of the time, any accusation of Communism could be ruinous. She went through hearings with the FBI and the Un-American Activities Committee and was cleared, but a Walter Winchell broadcast still had the potential of great damage. Finally, the chairman of the committee held a press conference and publicly cleared her. But would that clear her with her audiences?

Desi welcomed the studio audience for the filming of their first show of the 1953 fall season, then told them he had something serious to discuss. With deep emotion, he told them Lucy had never been a Communist, they despised everything about it, and the only thing red about Lucy was her hair.

The audience cheered, and Lucy came out, speechless with emotion. Her years of self-discipline paid off that night in a great performance without a sign of strain. At the end, she told the studio audience, "God bless you for being so kind." In her dressing room, she gave way to the tears she'd been holding back.

The next night Winchell apologized for his inaccurate broadcast, just one week after he'd caused the furor that nearly brought down the show, a collapse that would have affected thousands and cost millions. In the following months, Lucy was chosen television's Woman of the Year, and President Eisenhower invited she and Desi to dinner at the White House.

## Second Progressed Balsamic Phase
Despite the couple's vast success, off-screen their marriage remained tempestuous and troubled. Desi, who also president of the increasingly successful Desilu, which had now acquired RKO, dealt with the pressures

of his life in part by gambling, alcoholism and womanizing. Through Lucy's **Balsamic** phase, the situation deteriorated.

## Second Progressed New Moon

Just into this phase, Lucy called it quits on her marriage. The final episode of their show aired in 1960. Because of the success of Desilu, Lucy and Desi were very rich indeed. Lucy was beginning a new phase of her life. It did not began as she may have wanted, but she handled it very well, indeed. The couple divorced in 1960, and Lucy married Gary Morton in 1961.

## Second Progressed Crescent Phase

In, 1962, the first year she entered **Crescent** phase, Lucy bought out Desi's share of Desilu. She had been Vice-President, and now she became the first woman to head a major production studio, and proved to be a very shrewd and competent executive.

## Second Progressed First Quarter Phase

In 1967, Lucy sold Desilu for $17 million. Later she and her husband formed Lucille Ball Productions. She continued to do TV and also movies.

## Second Progressed Gibbous Phase

A new show, *Here's Lucy*, ran from 1968-1974, and launched the careers of her two children

## Third Progressed Full Moon Phase

In 1974, Lucy played the title role in the movie version of the popular Broadway musical *Mame*.

## Third Progressed Balsamic Phase

Well past her Progressed Full Moon, and now in her late 60s, Lucy's age began show, as it eventually must, and she began to slow down, though she certainly did not quit. A final 1986 ABC series *Life with Lucy* lasted only 13 weeks. But, she was considered brilliant in the 1985 made-for-TV movie *Stone Pillow*.

Lucy's **Prenatal New Moon** was Leo, a theme she played to the hilt. Her prenatal solar eclipse had been in Taurus, and certainly she came to demonstrate persistence and real mastery of the material world with her brilliantly successful career. She also had ample opportunity in her life to accept and master the survival challenges of her prenatal lunar eclipse in Scorpio.

But all things eventually come to a point of inescapable transition from this life to the next. Lucille Ball died in 1989 at the age of 78, following complications after open-heart surgery. She was still within her **Third Progressed New Moon** of this life.

## Endnotes

[1] My sources for information and dates for Eleanor Roosevelt are from three web sites: *www.pbs.org*, where I found a detailed time line and copies of her syndicated columns, *www.time.com* where I found an archived article about her (cited within my text), and *www.whitehouse.gov/history/firstladies* where one can find biographies of all First Ladies.

[2] Bartlett, John, *Bartlett's Familiar Quotations*, 16th Edition, Boston: Little, Brown and Company, 1992.

[3] The quotes and most of the information in this biographical sketch comes from Lucy's own book, *Love, Lucy*, published by Berkley Boulevard Books, mass market edition, Oct. 1997.

# Chapter Eight

# *Living with the Moon in Daily Life*
## *Timing by the Moon*

This is about Moon in "real time," the transiting Moon that you can walk right out and see in the night sky above you. Her sign and phase changes are fleeting, certainly compared to the lifetime natal and progressed lunar phenomena that are the primary focus of this book. Still, by directly experiencing the Moon from day to day, you'll see her, feel her, know her, draw down her energy and become attuned to her cyclical changes within yourself and those around you. Besides enhancing your appreciation of the beauty of Nature, you'll find that following the changes of the Moon have practical value.

Admittedly, sometimes it helps to have modern assists to looking at the sky—like clocks and calendars! If it's the dark of the Moon and you want to be sure when Balsamic phase changes to New, or if the sky is very cloudy, our modern tools give us the advantage of being able to find out exactly where the Moon is with a quick look at our handy computer generated guides to the sky, our ephemeris, our astrological calendar or a quick full chart of the day on our computer screen, plus of course, our clock. None of these, however, provide an easy method of finding what day and time all eight transiting lunar phases occur each month in your exact location. Now, you have that, too, with your *Moon Tides* report.

Your easiest resource for transiting Moon signs, all eight lunar phase changes, current eclipses (both lunar and solar) plus the bonus of exact start times for all eight corresponding seasonal phases of Sun and Earth (the eight Wiccan/Pagan Sabbats) is provided on pages 2 and 3 of the *Moon Tides* report. You only need to print those two pages once for one full year in your home location. With these pages, you'll always be able to know at a glance exactly where you are in the lunar phase cycle, no matter what the weather may be outside. If you are going to spend time traveling, you can easily adjust the location of the report so that it will print the transiting lunar phase pages for any other location, in any country of the world in its proper time zone. You can also set these two transit pages to begin with any start date you choose. (If you do not specify start time, the report will begin with the date you run it.

## Moon, Queen of Timing

Of all astrological factors one might use to determine the best time to carry out any anticipated action, the Moon reigns as queen. The sign and phase of the Moon are the most basic factors to consider, the ones you look at first when deciding, "is this the best time" for whatever you plan to do. This chapter deals with two facets of the Moon that can help you with timing decisions: her signs and her phases. Beyond this are other timing techniques that involve relating Moon to the other planets that are not included in the *Moon Tides* report. If you are serious about using astrology to elect when to do things, you'll need further study and resources, and I'll suggest some of those later in the chapter. First of all, let's see what we can do with the *Moon Tides* report alone. That, in itself, is quite a lot. It's easy enough for anyone with minimal astrological knowledge, and it is basic to other more complex techniques. First, let's consider the signs.

**Transiting Lunar phases, Eclipses and Solar Seasonal Phases**
**For One Year Starting January 9, 2006 US Eastern (+5) Time**

| Phase | | Date | Time | Moon Position | Sun Position |
|---|---|---|---|---|---|
| ◐ | Gibbous | Jan 10, 2006 | 6:28 am EST | 05 Gemini 05 | 20 Capricorn 05 |
| ○ | Full | Jan 14, 2006 | 4:48 am EST | 24 Cancer 05 | 24 Capricorn 05 |
| ◑ | Disseminating | Jan 18, 2006 | 7:51 am EST | 13 Virgo 17 | 28 Capricorn 17 |
| ◑ | Last quarter | Jan 22, 2006 | 10:14 am EST | 02 Scorpio 27 | 02 Aquarius 27 |
| ☾ | Balsamic | Jan 26, 2006 | 2:43 am EST | 21 Sagittarius 12 | 06 Aquarius 12 |
| ● | New | Jan 29, 2006 | 9:15 am EST | 09 Aquarius 32 | 09 Aquarius 32 |
| ☽ | Crescent | Feb 1, 2006 | 2:08 pm EST | 27 Pisces 47 | 12 Aquarius 47 |
| | *Imbolc* | Feb 3, 2006 | 6:27 pm EST | 28 Aries 49 | 15 Aquarius 00 |
| ◐ | First quarter | Feb 5, 2006 | 1:29 am EST | 16 Taurus 19 | 16 Aquarius 19 |
| ◐ | Gibbous | Feb 8, 2006 | 9:41 pm EST | 05 Cancer 12 | 20 Aquarius 12 |
| ○ | Full | Feb 12, 2006 | 11:44 pm EST | 24 Leo 20 | 24 Aquarius 20 |
| ◑ | Disseminating | Feb 17, 2006 | 3:26 am EST | 13 Libra 32 | 28 Aquarius 32 |
| ◑ | Last quarter | Feb 21, 2006 | 2:17 am EST | 02 Sagittarius 31 | 02 Pisces 31 |
| ☾ | Balsamic | Feb 24, 2006 | 2:39 pm EST | 21 Capricorn 03 | 06 Pisces 03 |
| ● | New | Feb 27, 2006 | 7:31 pm EST | 09 Pisces 16 | 09 Pisces 16 |
| ☽ | Crescent | Mar 3, 2006 | 1:13 am EST | 27 Aries 31 | 12 Pisces 31 |
| ◐ | First quarter | Mar 6, 2006 | 3:16 pm EST | 16 Gemini 07 | 16 Pisces 07 |
| ◐ | Gibbous | Mar 10, 2006 | 2:58 pm EST | 05 Leo 06 | 20 Pisces 06 |
| ☌ | *Lunar Eclipse* | *Mar 14, 2006* | *6:46 pm EST* | *24 Virgo 20* | *24 Pisces 15* |
| ○ | Full | Mar 14, 2006 | 6:35 pm EST | 24 Virgo 15 | 24 Pisces 15 |
| ◑ | Disseminating | Mar 18, 2006 | 7:51 pm EST | 13 Scorpio 17 | 28 Pisces 17 |
| | *Spring Equinox* | Mar 20, 2006 | 1:26 pm EST | 05 Sagittarius 11 | 00 Aries 00 |
| ◑ | Last quarter | Mar 22, 2006 | 2:10 pm EST | 02 Capricorn 01 | 02 Aries 01 |
| ☾ | Balsamic | Mar 26, 2006 | 12:00 am EST | 20 Aquarius 24 | 05 Aries 24 |
| ☀ | *Solar Eclipse* | *Mar 29, 2006* | *5:10 am EST* | *08 Aries 32* | *08 Aries 35* |
| ● | New | Mar 29, 2006 | 5:15 am EST | 08 Aries 35 | 08 Aries 35 |
| ☽ | Crescent | Apr 1, 2006 | 1:23 pm EST | 26 Taurus 53 | 11 Aries 53 |
| ◐ | First quarter | Apr 5, 2006 | 8:01 am EDT | 15 Cancer 34 | 15 Aries 34 |
| ◐ | Gibbous | Apr 9, 2006 | 10:19 am EDT | 04 Virgo 36 | 19 Aries 36 |
| ○ | Full | Apr 13, 2006 | 12:40 pm EDT | 23 Libra 37 | 23 Aries 37 |
| ◑ | Disseminating | Apr 17, 2006 | 9:16 am EDT | 12 Sagittarius 23 | 27 Aries 23 |
| ◑ | Last quarter | Apr 20, 2006 | 11:28 pm EDT | 00 Aquarius 54 | 00 Taurus 54 |
| ☾ | Balsamic | Apr 24, 2006 | 8:28 am EDT | 19 Pisces 11 | 04 Taurus 11 |
| ● | New | Apr 27, 2006 | 3:44 pm EDT | 07 Taurus 24 | 07 Taurus 24 |
| ☽ | Crescent | May 1, 2006 | 3:36 am EDT | 25 Gemini 48 | 10 Taurus 48 |
| ◐ | First quarter | May 5, 2006 | 1:13 am EDT | 14 Leo 35 | 14 Taurus 35 |
| | *Beltane* | May 5, 2006 | 11:31 am EDT | 19 Leo 42 | 15 Taurus 00 |
| ◐ | Gibbous | May 9, 2006 | 4:22 am EDT | 03 Libra 35 | 18 Taurus 35 |
| ○ | Full | May 13, 2006 | 2:51 am EDT | 22 Scorpio 23 | 22 Taurus 23 |
| ◑ | Disseminating | May 16, 2006 | 6:08 pm EDT | 10 Capricorn 54 | 25 Taurus 54 |
| ◑ | Last quarter | May 20, 2006 | 5:20 am EDT | 29 Aquarius 14 | 29 Taurus 14 |
| ☾ | Balsamic | May 23, 2006 | 2:54 pm EDT | 17 Aries 30 | 02 Gemini 30 |
| ● | New | May 27, 2006 | 1:26 am EDT | 05 Gemini 48 | 05 Gemini 48 |
| ☽ | Crescent | May 30, 2006 | 5:59 pm EDT | 24 Cancer 21 | 09 Gemini 21 |
| ◐ | First quarter | Jun 3, 2006 | 7:06 pm EDT | 13 Virgo 13 | 13 Gemini 13 |
| ◐ | Gibbous | Jun 7, 2006 | 8:47 pm EDT | 02 Scorpio 07 | 17 Gemini 07 |
| ○ | Full | Jun 11, 2006 | 2:03 pm EDT | 20 Sagittarius 41 | 20 Gemini 41 |
| ◑ | Disseminating | Jun 15, 2006 | 12:39 am EDT | 08 Aquarius 58 | 23 Gemini 58 |
| ◑ | Last quarter | Jun 18, 2006 | 10:08 am EDT | 27 Pisces 12 | 27 Gemini 12 |
| ☾ | Balsamic | Jun 21, 2006 | 9:21 pm EDT | 15 Taurus 31 | 00 Cancer 31 |
| | *Summer Solstice* | Jun 21, 2006 | 8:26 am EDT | 08 Taurus 06 | 00 Cancer 00 |
| ● | New | Jun 25, 2006 | 12:05 pm EDT | 03 Cancer 58 | 03 Cancer 58 |
| ☽ | Crescent | Jun 29, 2006 | 9:36 am EDT | 22 Leo 41 | 07 Cancer 41 |
| ◐ | First quarter | Jul 3, 2006 | 12:37 pm EDT | 11 Libra 37 | 11 Cancer 37 |
| ◐ | Gibbous | Jul 7, 2006 | 10:53 am EDT | 00 Sagittarius 22 | 15 Cancer 22 |
| ○ | Full | Jul 10, 2006 | 11:02 pm EDT | 18 Capricorn 42 | 18 Cancer 42 |
| ◑ | Disseminating | Jul 14, 2006 | 6:14 am EDT | 06 Pisces 51 | 21 Cancer 51 |

# Sample Page 2 of a *Moon Tides* Report

Shown above is an example of the first of two pages listing the transiting lunar phases and eclipses for one year, plus the astrologically correct times for the Wheel of the Year solar-seasonal festivals, in the order they occur. You can select the Start Date and location, and clock times are listed in the time zone for that location.

# Signs of the Transiting Moon
## General Mood of the Day

Each month, the Moon travels through all of the signs of the zodiac. She joins the Sun (called conjunction) at New Moon, and the signs of Moon and Sun are the same. From our perspective here on Earth, Moon then races ahead of Sun until she catches up with him again. Sun takes a full year to pass by all the signs of our zodiac circle, while Moon runs through twelve complete cycles and part of another one. Whenever she's passing through a sign, it seems that she takes on its mood and style, and we reflect that mood with her.

Moon changes signs quickly, entering a new one about every third day. If you're very busy and especially if you're working alone, you may not notice when the Moon changes signs. Also, your own mood and the situation will vary according to your individual temperament. Still, in some way, if you take the time to step back and "tune in" on your environment, observing both your own reactions and those of others, the daily Moon sign may become apparent to you, like a barometer of astrological weather. There's a general mood in the atmosphere that takes on some of the characteristics of the sign. It follows, then, that if you choose to blend your mood with that of the Moon and choose to do things that are in sync with lunar sign correspondences, you'll feel in the flow of her tidal current, rather than fighting to swim against it.

Each sign heading is followed by a list of keywords, some that you might consider favorable and others challenging or difficult. Keyword lists focus sign characteristics and themes in your mind, so that you can more easily see that the interpretations that follow are nothing more than elaborations of the same key ideas. If you then review the mythological treatment of the natal Moon signs in Chapter Two, you'll see that the same basic themes apply there, as well. This is important—that you see how just a few basic ideas can be expanded into many words, while the basic concept remains much the same. If you are aware of that, you can much more easily learn to expand on anything an astrological writer says, and also critically evaluate how it does or doesn't apply to your experience. The keywords come from the basics of our common tradition. They are followed by short sentences to illustrate ways they reflect general mood and types of activity, offering a flavor of what you might expect or plan for when Moon is in each sign.

# When the Moon is in Aries

**Keywords:** *energetic, fiery, impulsive, rash, assertive, impatient, courageous, initiating, adventurous, pioneering, direct, forceful, instinctive, competitive, eager, "me first," now oriented*

**General mood:** Energetic, in the mood to act. Activity motivated by impulse. Slowness or resistance causes temperaments to flare. "Me first" attitudes, assertive energies and impatience prevail.

**General Activity:** Good sign to initiate activity, especially if Moon is waxing, but not if you want it quiet and sedate. Make it upbeat, adventurous and now-oriented.

**Buying:** Tendencies toward impulse buying increase. If budget is a problem, make a list before you go and stick to it.

**Selling:** Close sales with a positive upbeat attitude that emphasizes what's exciting or innovative.

**Depart for Trip:** Expect adventure. If you want to relax, pick a different sign to leave.

**Food:** Spicy and zesty—how about Mexican tonight? Chili? Thai?

**Dos and Don'ts:** Take a deep breath and count to at least three to avoid reacting rashly. Others don't want to be idle. Encourage participation if you can. If you're edgy, impatient or not in the mood to be with others, work or play alone. Get off the couch and do something energetic.

# When the Moon is in Taurus

*Keywords:* stable, calm, practical, sensual, possessive, security oriented, patient, stubborn, persistent, wants comfort, holds on, loyal, placid, thorough, down-to-earth, builder, saver

**General Mood:** Energy mellows and slows. Caution and stubbornness prevail. Comfort and security needs dominate. Sensuality appeals. Tone is calm, soothing, easy.

**General Activity:** Build on projects already started. Take steps to improve financial condition. Not a good time to clean your closet—you won't want to let go of anything.

**Buying:** Quality matters, along with cost. Feel it, look it over carefully, smell it, taste it, listen to it, before you spend. Buyers err on the side of caution.

**Selling:** Emphasize quality reliability and comfort features of products or services. Plenty of patience wins. Take your time with customers.

**Depart for trip:** Choose a destination where you can be comfortable, leisurely and eat well, but not overspend.

**Food:** Comfort food, of course—warm, hearty and filling. Not a sign that aids dieting.

**Dos and Don'ts:** Expect to exercise extra patience in dealing with others. People won't move as fast; will be slower to decide or downright stubborn. If they **have** decided, don't bother to argue. Gardeners: put in perennials and let the earth energy soothe you.

# When the Moon is in Gemini

*Keywords:* busy, communicative, scattered, restless, spontaneous, indecisive, nervous, high stress, distracting, chatty, clever, adaptable, changeable, indecisive, logical, rational, rationalizing, quick, curious

**General Mood:** Busy, busy, busy. Talkative, scattered, nervous, restless. Phone may seem to ring constantly; interruptions abound. Attention spans are short.

**General Activity:** Good sign to initiate communication activities, though consider the phase, too. Waning Moon can be good for clearing your desk of things that need response.

**Buying:** Variety and novelty appeal, a problem if impulse buying breaks budgets, but then indecisiveness increases, too, so you may just try but not buy.

**Selling:** Emphasize variety and novelty—it might work! Also versatility, reason, logic. Offer choices. Be upbeat and friendly.

**Depart for trip:** Plans should feed curiosity and the urge to learn something new, perhaps also make friends, chat, network.

**Food:** Go out or order carryout tonight. Everyone can choose what he/she wants, or be indecisive all together!

**Dos and Don'ts:** Keep communications very clear and curb tendencies to be distracted. Expect to be busy and ready to move from one place to another. It's a good day to run all those errands. Thinking prevails over feeling, but underlying feeling could mean rational is actually rationalization.

## When the Moon in Cancer

**Keywords:** *emotional, sensitive, protective, moody, nurturing, sentimental, easily hurt, security oriented, sympathetic, empathic, instinctive, vulnerable, dependent, retentive, protective*

**General Mood:** Feeling prevails over thinking. Responses are emotional and subjective. People act on instinct, may be vulnerable, needy, easily offended, extra sentimental.

**General Activity:** Good sign to buy real estate or initiate home improvement project, if Moon waxing. Waning Moon is better for repairs or continuance of projects in progress.

**Buying:** Shop for home and family needs. House hunt, if you're in the market. Security concerns may increase budget consciousness.

**Selling:** Appeal to comfort and sentiment. Use a nurturing approach.

**Depart for trip:** Staying home may feel more right now. If you go, choose a place where you'll feel comfortable, safe and pampered.

**Food:** Mom's fried chicken and mashed potatoes with apple pie.

**Dos and Don'ts:** Empathy flows. If you're naturally empathic, you need extra psychic shielding, or avoid places where you'll pick up tension like a sponge. Hugs feel extra good.

# When the Moon in Leo

**Keywords:** *creative, risk-taking, charismatic, egocentric, needs applause, fun-loving, generous, proud, honest, exciting, dramatic, magnanimous, proud, childish, needs attention, arrogant, self-conscious*

**General Mood:** Egos are expansive; feelings on the line. Minor issues become major dramas. Upside: energies run toward romance, spontaneity, generosity and fun.

**General Activity:** Initiate creative projects. Give a party. Do something special for one you love.

**Buying:** Luxury and dramatic flair appeal. But rather than shop for things, how about tickets to a favorite entertainment or game?

**Selling:** Treat customers like royalty, give plenty of attention, point out creative aspects of what you're selling. Curb any tendency toward arrogance on your part.

**Depart for trip:** Go where you can expect to have fun, however you define that.

**Food:** Show off with your best gourmet recipe and attractive setting, or visit a romantic restaurant.

**Dos and Don'ts:** Be warm and friendly. If you take the lead in giving attention, you'll likely get more in return. Curb tendencies toward arrogance, or overt reactions on your part to arrogance expressed by others

## When the Moon in Virgo

**Keywords:** *efficient, pragmatic, discreet, modest, precise, work-oriented, attentive to detail, critical, discerning, health-conscious, methodical, careful, perfectionist, neatnik, earthy, fussy, fastidious, discriminating*

**General Mood:** Moods become subdued, egotism is replaced with modesty, critical tendencies are emphasized. People are more willing to help.

**General Activity:** Good day to scrub, scour, mop, dust, polish, sort, fix, repair, troubleshoot, schedule, weed, prune—whatever tasks need doing. Initiate activities to improve health.

**Buying:** Emphasis is on what's practical, useful and offers good follow-up service.

**Selling:** Emphasize the usefulness, technical support, follow-up service, quality control. Appeal to customers' intellect and to their technical skills.

**Depart for trip:** Go to a workshop, or perhaps a health spa retreat. Even if on a vacation, you'll likely take along that laptop and cell phone so you can work, too.

**Food:** Health food, of course! Practical, nutritious dishes that pay due attention to special diets or allergies and can be efficiently prepared.

**Dos and Don'ts:** Skimming the surface of a project just won't do. If it is worth doing, it is worth doing right. Curb tendencies to be picky with yourself and others. Nobody's perfect. Lend a hand to someone who needs it, and feel good to be of service.

# When the Moon in Libra

**Keywords:** *cooperative, fair, diplomatic, tactful, charming, sociable, refined, peace-oriented, compromising, aesthetically inclined, balanced, egalitarian, fence-sitting, wants to relate, tolerant*

**General Mood**: Being with others takes on importance. Romantic with refinement. Friendly and sociable. Compromise preferred; conflict if unfairness perceived. Charm and sincerity appeal.

**General Activity:** Initiative restores harmony to troubled relationships. Difficulty in deciding between two options—tendency to fence-sit. Increased interest in appearances. home. Tact and diplomacy wins; crudity or dissonance annoys.

**Buying:** Shop to improve appearance of self or surroundings— a beauty makeover, annuals for your garden, art or crafts supplies, home accessories, fashionable attire.

**Selling:** Friendliness and sociability appeal. Emphasize beauty, balance, harmony and aesthetic appeal. Perception of fairness is important.

**Depart for trip:** Take along lover, spouse or friend. If going alone, choose where new friends can be found. Go where there's refinement, art or cultural events.

**Food:** Try a gourmet meal at home or out, with friends and perhaps an array of appetizers or salads to share. Sweets appeal, so don't skip dessert.

**Dos and Don'ts:** Centering and balance meditation starts the day off right. Look your best. Turn on charm, but with sincerity. Be scrupulously fair.

Emphasize teamwork, and express appreciation for the contributions of each to the whole.

## When the Moon in Scorpio

**Keywords:** *intense, penetrating, powerful, resourceful, compulsive, jealous, secretive, inscrutable, controlling, manipulative, eliminating, determined, passionate, suspicious, shrewd, mysterious, deep, probing*

**General Mood:** Moods are intense, passionate, brooding; may be obsessive, jealous. Superficialities or hesitation breed impatience. Perceived insult provokes overreaction. Compulsive behaviors are stressed; may be manipulative.

**General Activity:** Secrets or mysteries unveiled with persistent probing. Intensity and determination prevail. Issues of sharing may be stressed. Sensuality heightens.

**Buying:** Scrutinize carefully. Make sure you know what you're getting before you buy. Ask questions. Probe. Insist on answers.

**Selling:** Pat answers to questions about the product or service won't do. Go into depth when asked to explain. Show respect for your customer's knowledge and perceptions.

**Depart for trip:** Trips begun today will have something intense about them. Go where you can research and explore, perhaps a place of mystery and mysticism. Nothing frivolous will do.

**Food:** Sensual and hearty, like pasta with savory red sauce and garlic bread or a full course Mexican dinner.

**Dos and Don'ts:** Avoid walking into a problem, but if you do mitigate it by remaining calm. Forgive and forget. Avoid brooding. You may be exaggerating beyond proportion. Empower others. Assist their process.

# When the Moon in Sagittarius

**Keywords:** *restless, adventurous, optimistic, enthusiastic, idealistic, philosophical, extravagant, superficial, acts on faith, blunt, inspired, confident, freedom-loving, restless, independent, goal-oriented, benevolent*

**General Mood:** Optimism soars. People are warm, outgoing, enthusiastic and ready for adventure. Friendly benevolence and openness prevail. Confidence rises. Strong opinions are freely, enthusiastically, and sometimes dogmatically, expressed.

**General Activity:** Extravagant moods feed quests for adventure, independence, freedom, opportunity and idealistic faith. Energetic, perhaps competitive activities spark enthusiasm.

**Buying:** Expansiveness can be extravagance so if you're on a strict budget or dieting, watch out! Shop for sporting equipment for the athletic; books for the philosophical Sag.

**Selling:** Novelty appeals. Emphasize what's different, exotic, upbeat and fun.

**Depart for trip:** Anticipate adventure. Casual, low budget and not too scheduled works. Feed interest for foreign travel though doing it, or visiting highly ethnic shopping areas you've not yet visited in your own country. Go on a philosophical or spiritual quest.

**Food:** Ethnic food of any variety appeals. Throw a party to enjoy it with friends.

**Dos and Don'ts:** Words may be bluntly expressed, before brain is in gear. If you're the target, avoid taking it too seriously. Direct energy to sports or other competitions, or turn enthusiasm toward idealistic goals. Explore the new.

# When the Moon in Capricorn

**Keywords:** *responsible, pragmatic, conventional, traditional, authoritative, career/business-oriented, cautious, serious, pessimistic, disciplined, organized, ambitious, conscientious, economical, realistic*

**General Mood:** Serious, traditional, conservative, pragmatic attitudes gain respect. Practical considerations rule the day. Realism may lean toward pessimism.

**General Activity:** Good day to get organized on most anything. Attend diligently to obligations. Focus on career and ambitions. Business issues are prominent.

**Buying:** Shoppers take a no-nonsense, business-like approach, status-conscious with an eye to quality, but also expect a good buy. Look for good workmanship. Status-conscious demands quality.

**Selling:** Emphasize dependability and good workmanship in your product. Your integrity, plus guarantees of consistency and reliability of your service impresses.

**Depart for trip:** Make it a business trip. If not originally planned so, it could still end up having a business aspect.

**Food:** Traditional and economical no-bother meals—try an easy but hearty soup or stew in a crockpot, made in the morning and kept hot for pauses from work.

**Dos and Don'ts:** Avoid falling into negative thinking. Turn pessimistic moods into constructive planning. Work within the established structure and rules, knowing that authorities may be in less benevolent moods now. This is not a time to flout convention.

## When the Moon in Aquarius

**Keywords:** *Independent, innovative, inventive, objective, intellectual, eccentric, unpredictable, rebellious, future-oriented, emotionally detached, impersonal, group conscious, broad-minded, tolerant, humanitarian*

**General Mood:** Gregarious, open and friendly…but not too chummy. Moods are emotionally detached—intellectual, curious, open-minded, not particularly serious and motivated more by airy and objective thought than by feelings.

**General Activity:** Eccentricity may be on display. Interests in technology and internet communication heightened. Humanitarian instincts rise. Freedom urges need outlet.

**Buying:** Look for the unusual. Check out the latest electronic devices. Try on an outfit with stand-out flair.

**Selling:** Emphasize the most cutting edge features of your offerings. Social or environmental causes appeal—call attention to products or service that assist the cause.

**Depart for trip:** Leave today and expect the unexpected. How about an astrology conference? Or, if you're into causes, join a protest rally.

**Food:** How about a fondue pot or two to share with friends? It's fun and makes dinner last longer, with plenty of time to converse.

**Dos and Don'ts:** Humor and a light touch are appreciated. Humanitarian concerns get extra attention. Express your individuality, but if you're part of a group, see what you can contribute to it. It's a good time to work cohesively together for reform.

## When the Moon in Pisces

**Keywords:** *Sensitive, dreamy, compassionate, impressionable, empathic, imaginative, visionary, mystical, confused, escapist, sacrificing, charitable, artistic, impractical, spiritual, indecisive, vulnerable, intuitive*

**General Mood:** Passive, quiet, gentler and kinder. Compassion and sensitivity heighten. Empathic people soak up moods of others and may need to shield. Impressionability and vulnerability increase.

**General Activity:** For artists, musicians, dancers and writers, imagination and inspiration soar. Seek spiritual and mystical experience. Charitable and helping/healing impulses increase.

**Buying:** People may not be in the mood to shop today—or if they do, are indecisive. Beauty appeals—flowing, romantic, mystical.

**Selling:** Keep background music calm and soothing. Sales appeal comes through tuning in on the dreams of others and appreciating them sensitively.

**Depart for trip:** Go where the soul is fed and inspired. Wade into the sea— take in the majesty of the womb from which all life emerges. Be inspired by great art, or choose a spiritual retreat.

**Food:** Fresh fish, of course. How about a fruit and yogurt smoothie?

**Dos and Don'ts:** If others are down, respond with empathy and reassurance. Don't push yourself if don't feel like it, especially with logical, intellectual work. Focus on what inspires creative flow. Seek spiritual growth through ritual, charitable work, quiet walks in nature.

## Phases of the Transiting Moon

Each month the Moon passes through all eight phases, and except for 29-day February, part of a second cycle. Once every 2 or 3 years, we have the very obvious phase repeat of two Full Moons within one month, and the newscasters will point out the "Blue Moon." Though various songs and folklore have cast the idea of "blue moon" as a romantically sad mood, I've never noticed any particular mood or occurrence that sets a Blue Moon apart from other Full Moons. It's nothing more than an artifice of a calendar that changed over time from lunar to solar as a means of measurement. The period from New Moon to New Moon (called synodic cycle) is about 29-1/2 days. Because our calendar has been varied over the centuries for various astronomical, political and religious reasons, the months (really moon-ths) of ancient calendars were replaced with a solar cycle calendar based on the time it takes for Earth to make a complete orbit around Sun.

Because the Moon moves so fast from day to day, the breakdown into eight phases, which works so well in natal and progressed symbolism, is perhaps overly detailed for short-term timing decisions. Even most astrological calendars show only four phases: New Moon, First Quarter, Full Moon and Last Quarter. Actually, the most important phase themes for transits can be reduced to the two most significant in energy shift: waxing Moon (New to Full) and waning Moon (Full to New). During the waxing period, energy builds. After the Full Moon, it wanes—winds down. You can sense this building or winding down mood going on around you, if you tune in. You'll also feel it within yourself and can use it to plan ahead.

With the basic idea of waxing and waning in mind, consider the First Quarter and Last Quarter phase beginnings that mark halfway points between New and Full Moons. Rudhyar dubbed them "crisis" points. Why? Because they are momentary points of balance between two opposing forces. From the moment they occur, light wins over dark within the waxing cycle, and dark wins over light in the waning cycle. First Quarter is a surge of light, or forward action. Last quarter is the realization and acceptance that light once brightly shining is passing away. Substitute "light" for "goal" or "dream" and you see the symbolic basis for interpretation of these quarter phases.

The intermediate points, halfway between each quarter of the lunar cycle, are half-square aspects most descriptively called octiles. Within the eight-fold cycle of the Wheel of the Year, they are often called cross-quarters. These phases, Crescent, Gibbous, Disseminating and Balsamic, do not appear on most astrological calendars, but the dates and times they occur do appear in your *Moon Tides* report. Rudhyar defined these in-between phases as being points of great momentum when energy is released. That is important, and worthwhile to consider even in quickly passing "real time." Think about how often your decision to anticipate a need in advance and act upon it provided just what enabled you to avoid or minimize a crisis? The distinction between these phases and the four that appear on calendars is a nuance, to be sure, but why wait for the "crisis of action" or the "crisis of consciousness"? When you are aware that a trend is changing, it makes sense to do what will more smoothly prepare you for the change of energy to come. Following are ideas and suggestions for what to expect of each transiting phase, and for appropriate activities to do during it.

## During New Moon Phase

New Moon until First Quarter is the best time to start things. If your choice is to begin at New Moon, first be sure it is actually new. Since the night sky is dark now with no Moon to be seen, you need to look at your *Moon Tides* transit pages or an astrological calendar to find out what time in your time zone New Moon actually occurs. You do not want to make a deliberate new beginning on a project only to find out later that you jumped the gun and actually started during Balsamic phase! Assuming you have checked the time, then, let's begin.

New Moon ideas often emerge instinctively and unbidden, as if out of nowhere. Don't ignore these intuitive flashes or hunches; they can be valuable. Don't necessarily trust them blindly, either. If in doubt, let them jell for a few days into the next phase or two to see how they develop. New Moon is a time to be spontaneous, give rein to your impulses, and let mood and the inspiration of the moment influence how you will spend your time, whether at work or play. Mental or creative block? Change your routine. Go for a walk and, observe what's going on around you. Chat with people. Be open to the moment. It's a good time to brainstorm. If you're involved in a group project, a lively brainstorming session can benefit all. Have one person take notes, preferably on a chalk or white board all can see, and make it clear that everyone is to call out whatever comes to mind on the topic at hand, no matter how silly or "far out." Put logical mind and second thoughts away for the moment, and let the creative thinking flow. I have been amazed at how effective such sessions I've been in or led have revived group energy and sparked good ideas.

Spontaneity aside, of course you can also advantageously launch well planned new things at New Moon, too. It is a very good time for that. Likely, though, this launch announces to a larger audience a project or a decision that had its initial inception in a previous cycle, maybe even several cycles ago. By now it has been evaluated, edited, revised and is ready to enter a new phase of public launch. Give it the energy boost of sending it forth with waxing light. Your decision of just what day to launch should consider both the phase and which Moon sign within the waxing phases is most appropriate to the project being launched. So, take another look at the sign symbolism, too.

If you're launching a very important project, or making a major life or career change such as marriage or starting a business, then it is best to also consider astrological factors not covered within this book. If you are an intermediate astrology student, you'll want to look at planetary aspects of the day and also how they relate to your own chart. Advanced astrologers will want to do an Election Chart, a full horoscope (birth chart) of the moment of proposed new beginning—and then make very sure the event actually happens at that time! If you are a beginner who is not yet skilled at either of these levels, you would do well to consult with an astrologer who is. If you are an advanced astrologer who is emotionally involved in the situation for which you are doing an Election Chart, you would do well to consult another astrologer who can view it more objectively. No matter what level of expertise you have, you can increase the energy of your intent through ritual that expands and projects it into astral and spiritual planes, along with the physical. See the next chapter.

## During Crescent Moon Phase

This is still a good time to start new things, in fact you might prefer the visual accent of actually seeing that pretty Crescent Moon appear in the night sky. It's real, it's tangible, it's a new thing you can **see**! It's a little less spontaneous than what emerged out of the dark of imagination, but it's still a newly waxing energy. What you instinctively began at New Moon may be showing signs of development. Things started now may take off a little faster…but then, it may be that either within yourself or from the outer world, a step backward proves necessary. The cross-quarter phases are semi-squares, challenging aspects that can be downright irritating at times. The irritant may come from outside you or from within. Perhaps that instinctive, impulsive new idea of New Moon conjures second thoughts. Maybe your enthusiasm has waned, or other things distract you, or someone dumped cold water on your little seed that was struggling to sprout.

The challenge with this phase is to avoid getting discouraged when you encounter resistance. If what you've begun is important to you, then you must accept the challenge of getting past your own self-doubts or feelings of lethargy. Keep the naysayers in proper perspective and persist in nudging forward toward your goal. It's always easiest to blame a naysayer—a person who expresses doubt or disagreement, or a difficult circumstance, but your most dangerous naysayer is you! If you can't tough it out now and keep moving forward on what you want to do, it's not going to get any easier. The Moon is waxing and she urges you to forward action, but you can't leave it entirely up to her. It's your dream, your intent, and only you can create that momentum and release of energy. The momentum that will propel you forward must come from within you. If you don't believe in it, how can you expect others to support you? Worthwhile results are unlikely to happen overnight, even within a "real time" phase. Good things take time, but this is not rest time. If the first day or so of this phase finds you taking a step backward, don't allow yourself to get stuck there. Do something about it. Clear out the clutter in your brain and maybe on your desk. Tune out the doubters. Take two steps forward and get back on track. The next little moment of lethargy or the next little obstacle will be easier to handle. Onward! This is your challenge. Accept it, learn from it and that, in itself, is a successful passage through this phase.

## During First Quarter Moon Phase

Crisis of action! Decision time! Time to get that project off the drawing board and into action mode. Pick up your plans and run with them. Confront obstacles and clear them away. Organize your tools and your forces.Be assertive in going after what you need to move forward. You've arrived at the waxing square. Squares are challenging. Some would say conflicting, but I've always preferred challenging. Challenges can be overcome, and when they are the result can be powerfully productive. They are like the grain of irritating sand that makes an oyster grow a pearl. At this point there is really no time left for the patience of that Crescent dance of step one back, step two forward. A goal has become clear and its direction is forward. To accept otherwise is a ticket to frustration or anger, and that can erupt in ways you wouldn't choose.

This is still a good time to start a new thing, and it's a good—or even better—time to decisively take whatever actions will best allow you to progress with what has already begun. The idea that had to jell is now nicely set into "jello," but you have to get it out of the mold and onto a presentation plate before anyone can eat it.

Remember that others are in action mode, too, so authoritarian attitudes may be in the air. If you encounter conflicts with others, some give and take may be necessary, but this is not the time to give too much. Stick up for yourself and your plans. Take charge and be willing take a few chances to make your point and accomplish what you want to do. Risk is worthwhile if there's a decent chance you can advance as a result. Very few people ever get anywhere in life—certainly not far—without being willing to expose themselves to the chance of getting a few figurative skinned knees in the process. This phase demands the courage of your convictions and the will to move ahead. Don't expect everything to come together right now, though. It's not culmination time yet, nor a time of finishing, but neither of these can come to pass without the groundwork you're laying right now.

Bless resistance you encounter rather than blaming it. Challenge is there to teach you something you need to know. Once you have met the challenge, momentum increases. This is where dreaming becomes doing, so take charge of yourself and your dream. From this point on, Moon is racing ahead of the Sun to reach her culminating light. Don't let her leave you in the dust. This is the best time this month to take a giant step forward. Go for it!

## During Gibbous Moon Phase

The light is still waxing but not yet full. It's still an appropriate time for beginnings and initiative, though a better time to develop what you began a few days ago, or for continued developmental activity within a longer-range goal. This phase is another cross-quarter, an octile aspect of momentum and release of energy—that is, if you move in sync with its energy as you are challenged to do. In one sense it can be tougher than Crescent, because it can be considerably harder to back down or give up on something that is on the upswing from the very visible "crisis of action" phase you've just passed through. It could even be rather embarrassing to quit now. Certainly, if you've vested strong energy in something, it can feel rotten inside to drop it before you've seen it through. Think those thoughts when you have a discouraging moment, take a deep breath and then renew your visualization of the end goal you've had in mind.

The resistance you'll encounter at this phase is somewhat different than before. Here you may be running along smoothly, effectively working on a goal and building your energy to achieve it. You can see the culmination of it in your mind—it's clear and bright like the brass ring on the next turn of the merry-go-round—but you are not quite there yet. Then the motor conks out and the horse stops, with the brass ring barely beyond your reach. Your goal hits a snag you didn't expect. Now what? It may be that you find out you just don't know everything you need to know to continue, so further research must be done. Or you need some tool you don't yet have, or have to repair one you do have before you can proceed. Maybe the software has to be updated and there is no way you can avoid taking the time to do it. An interruption of one kind or another temporarily distracts you, or perhaps the editor or the committee decides you have to change something you've done.

Again, a major challenge of all this is first of all to resist getting discouraged. Realize that this is all part of the process. Your job is to evaluate, revise if necessary, acquire what you need, manage the distraction, and by all means keep plugging forward. Persistence is the key here. Patience helps, too. It helps to realize that in resistance and challenge there is opportunity. If you're alert to that, it can be very creative opportunity. What you must discover, learn and do to meet the challenge can make your end result better. This is an optimum time in the month to learn and build your skills. Develop strategies and techniques, take a critical look at what has happened so far, consider what has to happen to keep you going forward, and then do it. Keep firmly focused on your goal. Culmination of the waxing light is just ahead.

## During Full Moon Phase

At Full Moon, results of things begun earlier should be evident. If new ideas that emerged at New Moon look to be winners, this is the time to make sure they are shining fully, visible to all those who ought to see them. This is a high time for accomplishment, and for enjoying what you've achieved. It is also a magical time that has inspired zillions to romance, art, music and poetry. By all means, take advantage of it! Whether you feel wild, tense or dreamy, get outdoors and be with the Moon. Draw down her energy. Experience her.

There are potential downsides to the monthly Full Moon phase. I found a *National Geographic* article showing research that links Full Moon with volcanic eruptions.[1] Well, that may be extreme…but Full Moon (and to a lesser extent New Moon) are associated with the crazies that we think of when we hear the term "lunacy." This most pivotal point of the monthly lunation cycle is widely known for extra high tides, an extra charge of tension within a lot of souls, bloodier flow for everything from female cycles to surgeries to accidents to violence, and an upsurge in police actions to curb wildness. Scientific types may dispute, and I know of no study that absolutely proves the phenomenon, but ask most anyone on the street and they'll more than likely agree that there's something to the lunacy factor. How much of this is folklore and how much is truth, I do not know. But, what masses of people believe tends to be projected out onto the world and made true, whether or not the statisticians give it support. So, expect that you may encounter—or feel within—some extra tension at Full Moon (and perhaps at New Moon, too).

Full Moon, more pointedly than any of the phases, is an aspect of relationship, an encounter of polar opposites. It is a complementary opposition, meaning that each provides something the other doesn't have. If you find yourself in a confrontation or conflict now, or even in the throes of an unusually magnetic attraction, try to step back and view what is happening with some objectivity. This is not war, and it may not be love either. It could be a mirror, though. There is something within the "other" that you need to look at within yourself. In resolving a conflict, there is a balance point to be reached, a place of compromise where the best of both and the good of the whole can be reconciled. Do your part to find that balance. Do this for your own sake internally, as well as for the outer situation. This is another example of the **illumination** that I've told you about repeatedly in previous chapters. True fulfillment does not come from winning over or even merging with another. It is found within, in completeness within one's own soul as you grow in wisdom and in spirit. The "other" in your life is not there to complete you, but because your soul needs to learn from the relationship. Even in the minor sense of quickly passing transits, this is true. Try to step back mentally from a tense encounter and think what it has to teach you. To learn is to become enlightened—another degree of illumination is received within your soul.

When illumination occurs within a monthly phase, it may be only a nuance about your current state of mind or activity a bit beyond what you'd thought of before. That could spur you on with additional energy, or it could provoke the beginnings of reevaluation about you want to happen next. From now until Last Quarter is a time when you can effectively consolidate what you've gained and build on it. If more development time seems to be needed that can realistically occur within this cycle, you may wind down a bit as the moonlight wanes, reevaluate where you are and begin to tie up loose ends. Remember we are only talking about one monthly cycle here. Many projects and goals require considerably more time and thought to bring to ultimate culmination.

## During Disseminating Moon Phase

At Full Moon phase your goal became objectified, fully conscious and in that sense, fulfilled. Now that you understand it, what do you do with it? That is a lot of what Disseminating phase is about. At this point you should be feeling pretty clear on what you are doing, what culminated at Full Moon, what it meant to you and what you want from it going forward, but in order to keep it going, you'll almost certainly have to reach out to others and communicate—to share what you've learned, demonstrate what you know. This phase is the beginning of waning light, but the Moon is still bright from her fullness, only very slightly dented with the shadow that will grow. The night is still very much alive with light—and shadow. All the fulfillment in the world won't give much satisfaction if you're like Midas counting your gold pieces, all alone with nobody knowing or caring about what you have. During the first half of the cycle, you built and acquired. Now the light is waning, and that means letting go. The first stage of letting go involves giving back to the Universe from what you have gained, and that means sharing it with others. You can continue to expand upon your Full Moon culmination, but in order to do so, you have to get outside yourself. This phase involves telling others about what you've learned, demonstrating it, enlisting support in your cause, presenting your project, promoting your idea. In short, it is time for disseminating your message. To disseminate is to spread—spread the word!

This phase is heralded by another octile aspect, the first of the waning cross-quarter phases. If you're still riding the wave of a successful Full Moon culmination, it may not seem as challenging as the previous cross-quarter phases, but it can be. A potential downside to this phase is that the truth of what has been accomplished (or failed to be accomplished) in the previous two weeks is now being clearly seen by others. (Or, remember, this monthly cycle may be just one disseminating phase within a much longer phase of your life and, as such, apply more to that cycle's theme, rather than this month alone.) If there are flaws in your demonstration or presentation, they'll show, and someone is bound to spot them. If there are holes in your theory or anything to question, someone is going to ask, and you'll have to answer. You can be on the "hot seat" to defend your position with others, who are now clearly hearing it for the first time and disagree. In transit time, you may be also playing a questioning and critical role for others—in "real time" we are **all** living through this phase. A wave of teaching—even preaching!—goes on now. It's a time of learning, evaluating, promoting and maybe demoting—and everyone may be talking at once!

Avoid feeling emotionally on the defensive if others call you to task. Again, don't blame, and even more importantly at this waning phase, look toward the challenge and bless it as an opportunity to learn. Events in our lives are superficial to the real process that happens within our souls. There, in order to grow, we need to understand. While likely a very active time, this phase is the first one of those that calls us to turn more introspective. Examine your feelings if you find you're not getting your point across as you'd like. It's not the other guy's fault if you're uncomfortable. What are you missing? What can you learn from the experience? Try again to speak your truth and hold your own with determined spirit and good grace. Smile. It helps.

## During Last Quarter Moon Phase

Last Quarter to New Moon, the waning quarter, is the best time of the month for reflection and revision. Moon has now caught up with the Sun to the point of waning square. Squares are aspects of challenge where some kind of change tends to be demanded. This time the change is not so likely to be a clearly visible action. It may not be visible at all because it is primarily going on internally, the "crisis of consciousness." Everybody is in it, so even though you may feel like it's only you experiencing this crisis, in some way everyone else is, too, so cut a little slack with others who interrupt your inner process. They may also need some introspective time.

What may be happening with you now? A short-term project could have come to fruition, and now that it's successfully handled, you're beginning to wonder what's next. Thinking seriously about delegating? If you can turn the project over to someone else, you can move on. Is something not working out as you once hoped it would? Face up to it and think about where to go from here. The project that had real potential may yet be reincarnated with some introspection and revised plans…maybe. A long-term project could benefit from a little down time for some serious thinking about revision?  Or you may need to interrupt it because other neglected obligations have to be dealt with sometime, like it or not. Or maybe, you've just "had it." You're bored and want to be done with it: "There's gotta be something more interesting and meaningful than **this** to do!" Last Quarter phase can be stressful, but the tension is not so visible or out in the open as First Quarter. More likely it is repressed, but when action is scrunched inside you and resisted, for whatever reason, it can sometimes come out in ways we wouldn't consciously choose, and that, to our regret.

Some months you may move along with a longer-term interest, generally happy, and just continue right through the waning phases. The most you'll need from this one could be a little respite, maybe some leisure time, a temporary change of pace. You may clear up one aspect of what you're doing to pave the way toward an anticipated next step. On the other hand, if you are feeling psychologically or spiritually uncomfortable, the best way to deal with this phase may be  to cut yourself a little slack. You need time to get inside yourself. Do the routine chores you need to do, but allow yourself the down time to reflect on what ought to be changed in your life.

Do some serious thinking about where you are now, what is working and what isn't. This is a time to begin letting go of whatever is detrimental to your well being. Is there a bad habit, too much fat, not enough exercise, or an attitude that deep down you know is causing you problems? From now through Balsamic phase the flow of the Universe aids your commitment to bring yourself in line and do what you need to do to stop what is bad for you and open the door to improvement. Is it someone, or more than one person, in your life that is draining your energy rather than contributing to it? This may be the time to minimize or put an end to those relationships. Nobody can impose upon you unless you give him or her permission by putting up with it.

This phase is one of the least of those you can really plan because so much of it stems from how you feel. It is about confronting your own inner truth, of reorienting yourself to let go of what conflicts with that truth, and for gaining a deeper understanding of your process.

## During Balsamic Moon Phase

Now the Moon shrinks from the waning crescent to a dark sky again, as one cycle ends and melds into the next in darkness. Again, as at New Moon, if you want to be very sure when Balsamic ends and New Moon begins, you'll have to check the exact time on your *Moon Tides* transit pages or an astrological calendar. A deliberate banishing act does not belong at New Moon, and you should be sure to wait until after New Moon occurs before initiating a new activity.

Balsamic phase can be a productive time to dream. Dream? Productive? Of course. Creative activity doesn't happen without some inner work, conscious or not. This is the best phase of the month to give your overworked, logical-thinking, practical and productive left-brain a rest and give your intuitive, imaginative, creative, even slightly loony (that's a Moon derivative, too) right brain free rein—hey, that rhymes: *right brain—free rein, right brain—free rein*. I could make a ritual chant out of that one! Back to business—what do you do with this phase? Sleep longer, if you feel like it. Most of our culture is sleep-deprived, so I've heard on the news. Meditate. Take time to read that fantasy or romance novel you've been putting off because you don't have time. Walk on a beach and pick up shells, or anywhere in Nature. Listen to the birds, smell the flowers, feel the snowflakes on your face, shuffle your feet in the falling leaves—anything the season offers. Do nothing useful? Not exactly, I don't mean that. There are some useful, worthwhile, even productive things to do in this phase, but here we are talking about just a few days out of a month, for heaven's sake. Everyone needs some time to just **be**, and this is a time when you may need it most. So, what I am saying is, if you need that, give in to it. It can restore your soul.

Now, if we must deal with the practical side, here are some things that are good to do during Balsamic phase: cut back on things you'd prefer to cut back on for a while, such as your hair, if you'd like it to not require cutting again quite so soon. (On the other hand, if you want a trim followed by fast growth, don't do it now. Have it cut during waxing Moon.) If you'd like to try for a little slow down on future garden chores, pull weeds and prune now. (Llewellyn's annual *Moon Sign Book* is a useful reference for more detail on what little things are good to do in waxing or waning phases.) Clean your closet and get rid of the stuff you haven't worn for years and aren't likely to wear again. Go on a diet. Make your peace with someone with whom you've been estranged, or bring a painful relationship to a final ending. I think you should get the idea from these few examples. In short, let go, banish, eliminate, bring to closure.

Can nothing new be tried? Of course it can, but you should recognize that it may be only an experiment. Things begun now are not likely to be lasting, or if they are, they'll probably undergo very large revisions. If there is something new you want to both begin and continue building to a significant longer-term culmination, then it is best to avoid beginning it now. Wait until after the Moon is new and waxing again. It is only few days from now. Imagine, visualize, fantasize, dream, experiment, but do so in that spirit of timelessness. Perhaps a thought you have will become the seed that will sprout in the next cycle, but don't invest in it now. Just let yourself dream a while…

## Timing Techniques Beyond Moon's Sign and Phases

First, notice the sign of the eclipses in your one-year Transiting Lunar Phase Report. The degree is the number shown to the left of the sign. In the example report shown on page 219, notice the Lunar Eclipse on March 14. Read across the line and see that Moon is 24 degrees of Virgo. A little further down on the list, see a Solar Eclipse on March 29, with Moon and Sun at 8 degrees of Aries. If either of those degrees are in close contact with planets in your own chart, particularly your Sun or Moon, then the eclipse is especially significant for you. We could think of eclipses as super New Moons or Full Moons. While New Moon themes are signficant for the month, and Full Moon themes for the two weeks until next New Moon, it often seems as though an eclipse is spotlighting important changes in life that have impact over periods of a year or more. If the sign of an eclipse matches that of your Sun or Moon, and if the degree number is within 5 degrees or less of the same degree as your Sun or Moon, pay special attention to it. It points to this time period as one of high importance for you. The sign of the eclipse may suggest what within your own life is being brought into strong focus now. Think about how you can use the energy of the eclipse sign theme to best advantage.

If you celebrate the Wheel of the Year festivals, remember (from Chapter One, page 39) that the traditional dates for the Greater Sabbats are not accurate astrologically. They should be exactly halfway between the equinoxes and solstices, when the Sun comes to the 15th degree of each fixed sign. Note on page 219 that Beltane for 2006, with Sun at 15 Taurus, is on May 5. Rudhyar called these "cross-quarter" degrees points of critical release of energy and maximum momentum. So, if energy is of particular importance to you, it's worth paying attention to these dates and times! Your *Moon Tides* transit pages provide one of the easiest ways to see exactly when the maximum power points for the Greater Sabbats occur.

There are many additonal things you can use for astrological timing that are not part of the *Moon Tides* report—positions of other planets, how they aspect each other and are aspected by the fast-moving Moon, for example. Electional astrology (electing or selecting propitious times to begin actions) is a technique with many layers of complexity. A beginner can effectively handle worthwhile facets of it, but you have to be at least able to read astrological glyphs and know the basic meanings of planets, signs and houses.

If you know the basics, and want to pursue astrological timing to a greater extent than the scope of this book/report combination is designed to cover, then I recommend you begin by acquiring an astrological calendar and my book, *A Time for Magick*. The book has careful instruction designed to show beginners how to use both an astsrological calendar and the planetary hour system. Planetary hours are especially easy and effective for quick timing decisions. My book *Future Signs* is a beginner's guide to working with transits, the comparison of the planet's positions in current time with the planets in an individual's birth chart. *Future Signs* teaches how to use an ephemeris and an astrological calendar, and it has interpretive paragraphs for the aspects of transiting planets (Sun, Moon, Mercury, Venus, Mars, Jupiter, Saturn, Uranus, Neptune and Pluto) to birth chart planets and through the houses of the birth chart, including transiting New Moons, Full Moons and eclipses.

My astrological calendar and my planetary hour list are my best tools for daily timing choices. I always have a big calendar on the wall beside my computer desk and a miniature one to carry in my purse. For planetary hours I have a software program from which I print daily listings for several weeks at a time.[2] On the National Council for Geocosmic Research website, there's a free daily planetary hour listing.[3] Of course, if I have a very important reason for wanting to begin an action at the best time, I do full charts and study them in detail, but there are many times when that kind of effort is just not practical. "Quick and dirty" timing is useful for the myriads of minor choices you might make that could benefit from a quick look at whether this time or that would be better, like for example, when you're on the phone and have to make an appointment right that moment to do something important.

Bottom line, though, it's not astrological technique that primarily determines the "right" time to do whatever good things you might choose to manifest what destiny has in store for you. It is your attitude! Actually, I believe it much more likely that you had a major hand in choosing that, too—your destiny—by your choice of the moment you entered this life. It is that moment of birth that determines not just your natal horoscope alone, but also both your progressed cycle and the cyclical pattern that all of the transiting planets follow throughout your entire life and beyond. **Believe** that you had a good reason for choosing that pattern. It's a healthier attitude to claim that power of choice—even if you wonder in some of your down times just what moment of craziness caused you to choose it! If you then consider, "I must have had a good reason for this, so what is the Universe trying to teach me, and what should I do about it now?" you have taken the first and most important step toward turning challenge into opportunity to make changes for the better, and to attain soul growth in the process.

Somebody said in my presence once—I don't remember who or when—that it is a real shame that we usually spend the very largest percentage of our day doing and thinking about very mundane things and only a few minutes most days (if any minutes at all) thinking about the state of our soul and spirit. After all, that is what we primarily incarnated to work on—our soul, our spiritual growth.

Regardless of what I have done in technical astrology, I have always thought that the highest calling of the art is its use in the service of Spirit. Though I philosophized about that idea in the past, while busily working with technique and astrological business, it was only after I began regularly working with astrology in sacred rite that I began to fully understand the concept on an intuitive, energy level. This is what I will share with you in the next and final chapter of *Moon Tides, Soul Passages*.

## Endnotes

[1] *www.news.nationalgeographic.com*   Article by Brian Handwerk, February 15, 2002, is entitled "Are Volcanic Eruptions Tied to Lunar Cycle?" The text discusses research pointing to the greatest spikes in volcanic activities falling just between Full Moon and perigee (Moon closest to Earth).

[2] *Sundial Software* by Arlene Kramer (see Resources)

[3] *www.geocosmic.org*   Planetary hours currently accessed from link on the home page can't be guaranteed as permanent, but there are no plans to change it anytime soon.

# Chapter Nine

# *Experiencing Your Moon in Spiritual Ritual*

To "draw down the Moon" is to invoke her energy, her flow and her magical power within. In this final chapter I want to share with you my experience of the Moon in spiritual ritual. Although, as I have told you earlier, I practice as a Wiccan priestess, the rituals within this book are not specifically Wiccan. Though they could also be used within Wiccan rituals, they can easily be used with no connection to Wicca at all, for they are the type of "self-help" exercises with affirmations that are also called by labels like experiential astrology or creative visualization or active meditation. If you invoke a deity within the rituals, then they can become a form of active prayer.

## Experiential Astrology: A Valuable Way to Learn!

For those readers who are accustomed to meditation and ritual, this chapter needs no introductory commentary, and may actually be your favorite part of the book. For readers who have done little or no work in astrological ritual, I think there are things that need to be said, so I'll begin with some background. From my long association with astrologers, I can expect that quite a number of readers, who may be interested in the theory and examples I've presented on the Moon and her phases, have not worked with experiential astrology and in fact, may feel uncomfortable with it. The experiential track at the typical astrology conference often draws an enthusiastic roomful, but compared to the conference as a whole, the entire track attracts a small percentage of total conference attendees. I can understand that. Part of the resistance stems from discomfort with being exposed within group movement and exercises that may feel silly or childish.

Another reason for non-participation in experiential work may be the thought that such things don't fit within a preferred business-professional approach to astrology. Then, some people may feel uncomfortable with a spiritual practice that feels possibly contrary to their own. Many astrologers practice a mainstream religion, and feeling already pressured to reconcile astrology with others of their faith who frown on it, would prefer not to compound the problem by mixing it with alternative spiritualities.

Finally, some reluctance toward experiential astrology may be an assumption that it's a waste of time, when there is more to be learned from attending a lecture. That assumption would be the recognition that astrology is, more than anything other topic of the "new age" genre, a left-brain discipline. In order to become adept at it, one has to learn a great deal of technique.

Now that I've enumerated the excuses, I'll admit that the "waste of time" attitude above would best describe my own concerns in my early years of studying astrology, even though I'd been introduced to it through what can only be described as psychic experience. But, once I'd been "hooked," there was so much to learn that I deliberately avoided opportunities to participate in psychic development activities. Though I sponsored them (in a metaphysical shop I had in the 70s), I was still somewhat afraid of being too influenced by them. I'd fallen back on the attitudes of my childhood, that success depended on left-brain learning, and I was fiercely determined to learn my astrological technique and earn my professional certificates. So, prior to my move to California (at a time when I'd been a practicing professional astrologer for more than a decade), I would always have chosen the lectures on technique, too.

So, what can you learn by doing ritual? I discovered, with some surprise, that I could learn a great deal—much more than I expected—but I only discovered that after I began working regularly with ritual in California. I should preface that by saying that I did have some prior background with meditation, a practice very basic to ritual that is also good for your health and ability to handle stress. So, I strongly recommend you begin with meditation, and I will include some meditation techniques in the rituals to follow.

## Learn Astrology Intuitively with Active Meditation

Ritual could be described as active meditation, the experience of which is individual and inner, such that I can't say exactly what it will do for you, but only what happened for me. It restored some of the intuitive flow that I'd suppressed through all the years of studying technique. I discovered the richness within the simplest of astrological themes, and learned that a ritual based on, for example, just one sign polarity of a Full Moon could touch people in a way that they would often tell me later was just what they needed at that time. It had nothing apparent to do with whether the sign theme was prominent in their own charts. Most any astrological theme on which a ritual was based would somehow speak to a mixed group of people each in his or her own special way, and I learned that the experience of enacting the themes had the power to answer inner questions, to calm, to guide and to heal. Perhaps this phenomenon has to do with what could be called the "astrological weather." My rituals have almost always been based on current patterns of the planets, so perhaps this is evidence that all of us do respond to the sign of transiting Moon in some small way, even if her passage through the signs moves so quickly we seldom consciously realize that we are responding.

On some occasions, in recent years, I've included little rituals within lectures based on transits of that exact time—Moon sign and phase, planetary hour and aspects among the planets. For some of those, the configurations were of the type considered so challenging that some astrologers would take one look and ask to be scheduled to speak at a better time. But with ritual, the "bad" aspects became dramatic fodder for good ritual, and that was the result—good!

## Don't Fret About Your Transits—Set Positive Intent with Ritual!

Ritual is an excellent way to turn the energy of your transits into the best possible manifestation of their themes, and every transit, without exception, has an "upside." It's far better to set the intent within your subconscious mind to do them well, than to fret about what will happen during them. I've heard the analogy that looking ahead astrologically to prepare for upcoming transits is like looking at a weather report to decide if you'll need to take an umbrella. That works, but it has just a tinge of the pessimistic about it—"It might rain, I'll need to protect myself somehow." How about this analogy instead: "Rain is coming! I'll take off my shoes, dance in the rain, and maybe even draw on the energy of the lightning bolts and direct them to charge my will to do  (fill in the blank here with a current goal). Like the wet grass beneath my feet, I'm growing!" That would be an attitude of ritual, and now that I've written it, I like it! This "rain dance" could work within a great solitary ritual, maybe for a Moon in a water sign or for a First Quarter theme. Remember that little chant I mentioned in the last chapter under Balsamic? *Right brain, free rein*…hey, you could use it here! Or make up one of your own. Though ritual like this can be healing, it can also be fun.

## Ritual for Creative Change

What ritual did for me, and can do for you, is directly related to Moon, so that is why this book is incomplete, and I believe your understanding of Moon in your life is incomplete, without the **experience** of her in spiritual ritual.  As I've said previously, the subconscious mind, the realm of Moon, is very powerful. Without her cooperation, the decisions and choices of your conscious mind have much less chance of success, and in fact, may be completely sabotaged. Your subconscious is loaded with feelings and experiences that you no longer consciously remember. Out of these stem fears, attitudes, habits, assumptions and prejudices that can exert major influence on what you think and do, even when you are not aware this is happening. In order for you to fulfill your goals, the subconscious must be brought into alignment with conscious choice, for if it is not, the choice can fizzle into one of those good intents that gets nowhere.

Let me give you a simple example that may sound silly, but I daresay will strike chords with some of you: Conscious choice: "I really ought to lose 20 pounds. I'll go on a diet." Subconscious: "If I don't clean my plate, I'll not be allowed to leave the table." Or maybe from an even earlier past-life memory: "I'd better eat this now because in this horrible famine, it may be a long time before I'll have another chance." Or (and this is one real life example from someone I know well): "The last time I lost weight, it turned out I was seriously ill. Thin = illness. Nope, no diet for me." Or, try this one: "When I'm hungry, I'm sad. Food is comforting. Food is love. I don't want to feel sad." Obviously, these are all opinions of a subconscious plotting serious sabotage. The problem is that while the conscious mind can give a dozen good reasons why it would be a good idea to lose weight, the subconscious doesn't listen to reason, nor does she learn that way. Subconscious is instinctive and intuitive. She learns from sensual experience—from sight, sound, touch, taste and smell, and from all the feelings such experiences conjure. To convince your subconscious, your Moon self, that she is safe and secure and will really like the results of her support for your conscious choice, you have to appeal to her in her own way. So, read your books and lectures on technique, but for your Moon's sake, do ritual, too!

The rituals in this book are designed with inner change as the intent and goal, and with the expectation that you will be doing them alone, although some of them may be adaptable for groups, if you choose. Other than ritual for pure spiritual attunement, inner change is the safest and most ethical type of ritual to do. It is the most essential type of ritual, as well, to bring about what one wants for oneself without interfering with the free will of anyone else. I do not consider it ethical to focus a ritual on another person, not even a healing, without that person's full knowledge and permission in advance, and if possible, active or at least passive participation. Even in healing circles, the instruction is to not send direct healing energy into a person who has not specifically agreed to receive it, but instead to send a healing light nearby so that the soul may choose, or not choose, to reach out and accept it. It is not for one person to decide what another person's soul needs. It should be that soul's choice alone. Do the rituals as you read them here only if you choose and feel they serve your needs. If there is anything about any of them that you're uncomfortable with, then use them only as a starting point from which you may be inspired to design a ritual of your own that will be more appropriate for you.

## Astrological Timing

It has been my experience that rituals of pure worship, for the sole purpose of spiritual attunement, transcend any astrological indicators, and can be successful at any time. For rituals that also include a mundane goal, timing matters. For the same reason that it can be observed that people respond to "astrological weather," it can be expected that if you choose to do a ritual at a time when your intent matches the theme of Moon sign and/or phase, you are more likely to see successful results. Think of it like flowing with the tidal pull rather than fighting against it. The rituals here are all designed to be done with Moon in a specific phase, and in some cases also a sign—the most basic timing choices.[1]

## Appeal to the Subconscious though Your Senses

You'll see that each of the ritual designs presented use one or more specific appeals to the senses. Music, the smell of incense, textures, visual images, tastes—all these help reach the subconscious and enhance intuitive flow. Affirmations are often written in the form of rhyming verses or chants. That, too, appeals to the subconscious memory, and helps pull it into alignment with your conscious intent for the ritual. Rhyme and rhythm are the reason why songs or nursery rhymes stick in your mind long after memories of many other things have faded. (I've noticed this among Alzheimer's patients who can remember very little of anything, but still sing along with "oldie" songs of their youth.) Subconscious has been called "inner child." That's because she likes to play. Cater to that, if you want her cooperation.

# Rituals for Centering

Either of the two following rituals will be good for centering yourself. Before you begin any of the rituals to follow you should take a moment to center. This creates a transition between the mundane and spiritual realms, serves the alignment of consciousness with the subconscious and higher consciousness. Centered, you are open to derive maximum benefit from the ritual.

## Drawing Down the Moon

I started this chapter with the above phrase, so I'll begin with it as a very basic ritual for solitary attunement. It's usually thought of in connection with Full Moon rite, and it is most dramatic with Full Moon visible overhead, but it can be done at any time, during any phase. For that matter, it can be easily adapted to draw the energy of any planet, such as to call the energy of Venus into yourself, as you gaze at her as that bright evening "first star I see tonight." It's definitely a more powerful form than merely "wish I may, wish I might." I suggest you do this "drawing down" ritual and/or the one that follows it first and often. If you're new to ritual and feel awkward trying it, nobody else need know or see. Just try it when you are alone in privacy, and notice your feelings as you do. Open your awareness to your feelings while drawing down the Moon, and of how they change and become more profound over time and through repetition. Again, as I've mentioned before, journaling your experience afterward is always a good idea. Memory fades, but a note can trigger remembrance.

Go where you can see the sky and the Moon, preferably outdoors and barefooted, so you can fully feel Earth beneath your feet. For the first time, it is best to try this at Full Moon or near Full, for the strong visual focus. Later you will find that you can sense the Moon and call her energy even when she's dark. Look up at the Moon, take a deep breath and stretch your arms up toward her. If you let your eyes go just slightly out of focus, you should see beams of light shining down toward you. Now bring your outstretched hands inward to loosely cup around the moon, fingers not touching—give her space. Gaze intently at her and in a moment it will seem as if there are two Moons. Cup your hands around one of them and close your eyes as you bring her down, turning your palms toward your head and slowly moving them down over each side of your body—not quite touching. Let them flow over your aura, and feel the energy move downward inside your body as your hands pass energy over your aura. Continue the flow all the way down to your feet, bending as you go, then bring the energy slowly upward within your body and your aura as you as you pass your hands back up and out again, releasing some of your energy back to the Moon while keeping what you need for yourself. Now, just stand and *be* for a moment, feeling the lunar energy, honoring her within you.

Often if the above ritual includes either a silent or spoken invocation of Moon as Goddess with openness to a message, you will receive one, perhaps an answer to a current problem. It may come to you as a feeling or the "still small voice inside" that is your intuitive connection with divine Spirit.

If you do this ritual to draw down the Sun, obviously you don't stare at him, for that can damage your eyes. Reach up with your eyes shut and just feel the warmth! Drawing down the solar energy can be an invigorating way to start your morning.

### As above, so below...

This ritual is a variation on the one above that incorporates the entire Hermetic concept I told you about in the Introduction to this book. Again, it calls for no special timing; it's good for any time, and an excellent one to do when you get up in the morning to set a tone for your day, or just before bedtime to close it peacefully.

Take a deep breath, lift your arms high to the sky, stretch and exhale, saying "*As above...*" Inhale as you move your hands down over your aura and exhale as you touch the ground. Say "*so below...*" Inhale slowly as you bring your hands up your body and with both of them touch your heart area. Exhale. Say "*as within...*" and then inhale as you slowly and gracefully stretch your arms outward to each side. Exhale. Say "*so without.*" Pivot slowly all around in place thinking of your world and how you intend to both influence and respond to it according to your highest consciousness. Back in place, thrust your arms up to the sky again, saying "*as the Universe*" and then cross arms across your chest, saying "*so the soul.*"

## Rituals for Eclipses

Many of thee rituals in this eclipse section and in the phase section to follow are either directly from or adapted from the archive of rituals I once wrote monthly for the website of my daughter Molly's metaphysical book and gift shop in San Diego.[2] In the column I've written short interpretations for the lunar phases of the current month with suggestions for what might be done within them, plus little rituals for some of them.

The first one was specifically designed for the Gemini Solar Eclipse of May 2003. Using the 19-year repetition that often happens with eclipses (this one was a repeat of one in 1984), the ritual was designed to assist in remembering the past eclipse period in order to gain insight into what personal patterns may be in play again now, for the purpose of improvement in the handling of them. This ritual would be appropriate for any Solar Eclipse in an Air sign that echoes a previous one, just as it is. After it, I'll suggest a simple variation for an eclipse in signs of the other elements.

## Experiencing a Solar Eclipse, with Variations for Each Element

**Intent:** to gain insight and understanding of what the eclipse symbolizes for you personally

**Preparation:** Scan the Table of Eclipses to see if the current eclipse repeats the same or very close to the same degree as one in the past. (Check about 19 years ago.) If this degree is strong in your birth chart, you will probably recognize that past year as especially significant. Repeated eclipses often trigger the development of similar personal issues. If you need help remembering that past time, a diary, old photo album and an internet search can help you put your life events in context. Bring an item or two of memorabilia to your ritual, along with two candles, one for Sun (gold or yellow) and one for Moon (silver, ivory or pale blue). Play meditation music. **First,** charge your ritual circle with a tool of the element associated with the sign of the eclipse. **The variation for each elemental charge follows:**

### To Charge an Eclipse in an Air sign:
Light incense of air correspondence: sage or benzoin can be used alone; benzoin and lavender buds combine well. A feather to direct the incense smoke is helpful. Face the east holding the censer and feather and invoke Air, the element of the eclipse:

> *Oh power of Air I seek to see*
> *Memories and thoughts of clarity.*
> *From past to future help me know*
> *The wisdom that will help me grow*
> *With open mind for what will be*
> *I call your winds of change to me!*

Carry the smoking incense in a clockwise circle around your altar table to clear and charge the space.

**To Charge an Eclipse in a Fire sign:**
Face south for the invocation, and carry a lighted red candle, or if they are legal in your area, a sparkler, around the circle.

> *Oh power of Fire and energy*
> *Open my heart to what will be.*
> *With will and faith I seek to know*
> *How I can change, how I can grow*
> *With courage and with spirit free,*
> *I welcome change that comes to me!*

**To Charge an Eclipse in a Water sign:**
Face west for the invocation. Mix salt with water, visualizing as you do that you are creating the oceanic womb of Mother Earth. Carry your bowl of saltwater around the circle, sprinkling it as you go.

> *Oh power of Water, I seek to see*
> *Beyond your depths of mystery.*
> *From past to future help me know*
> *The wisdom that will help me grow*
> *I wait in calm for what will be*
> *And call your tides of change to me!*

**To Charge an Eclipse in an Earth sign:**
Face north for the invocation, and carry a drum around the circle, beating it slowly in the rhythm of a heartbeat. If you have no drum, you could sprinkle flower petals to mark your circle, or carry a crystal around it.

*Oh power of Earth I seek to birth*
*Within my world new work of worth.*
*From seeds of harvest's past now show*
*How strong new healthy plans can grow*
*In trust and love for what will be*
*I call this season's change to me!*

**After charging the circle**, light the Moon Candle, saying:

*Oh Moon of deepest memory*
*Reveal to me your mystery*
*Let thoughts about my past return*
*Bring insights that will help me learn*
*What I should know, what I must see*
*For future growth, serenity.*

Light the Sun candle, saying:

*Sun of power and strongest light*
*Shine on this, my sacred rite*
*Energize my will to know*
*How to change and how to grow*
*Guide my path toward what will be*
*For highest good, so shall it be!*

Now, meditate on your memories. Open your mind to deeper insights into what happened in the past. If there are painful memories, what was your part in them? Could you have handled things better? What did you do well? What did you do badly? If so, how might you have done it better? What have you learned? Can you relate any issues from the past to what is happening currently? If so, how will you apply what you have learned to the present and the future? Write notes, if you wish. When you feel the meditation has brought you the insight that will help you move forward, give thanks to the Moon and Sun for their assistance and then snuff the candles.

## Experiencing a Lunar Eclipse

**Intent:** Insight into life purpose and direction.
Note from the eclipse tables if this eclipse is a repeat of a prior one in the same degree, or if it is close in degree (5° or less) to your prenatal eclipse points or your birth Sun or Moon.

**Preparation:** Set three candles in holders: silver or white for Moon to the left, black for Earth at center, and gold or yellow for Sun to the right. Have a green candle the same size as the black one, set aside but easily reachable. Also have ready the following: metal bowl, matches, small pieces of scrap paper, a pen, one piece of parchment paper at least 3" square in size, an incense burner with two incenses, one for exorcism (such as myrrh) and for consecration (such as frankincense). Soft meditation music in the background can assist with your meditative mood. The room should be darkened.

**Center** yourself and then sit comfortably but with straight back for ease in deep breathing. Light the Sun candle and gaze at the flame for a moment, visualizing the Sun's brightness and heat and the vitality of purpose he symbolizes in your life. Light the Moon candle and gaze at the flame for a moment, visualizing her as Full Moon in all her beauty and contemplating the deep feelings she evokes in your life. Light the Earth candle and as you do, ask Earth as Dark Mother to be your guide. Light the exorcism incense, close your eyes and breath slowly and deeply as you visualize walking in the night, gazing at the Full Moon above you in all her beauty. Open your eyes for a moment and light the Earth candle, gazing at her flame for a moment. Soon a shadow approaches, as the dark hand of Earth casts a veil over Moon's light, gradually and then completely shrouding her brightness, as you allow your eyes to close. Breathe slowly and deeply as you visualize the transition. In the light now very dim, visualize the shadow across the Moon take on the form of an old woman with very wise eyes that look at you kindly. She speaks to you:

*Child of Earth, I have cast my shadow over the Moon this night because your need is to look beyond her beauty as she reflects Sun's light, and to probe within your soul. If you are to shine like the Sun in fulfillment of your purpose in this life, you must change attitudes and habits that hold you back— banish them! Probe within, my child. The answer is within you.*

Listen to the voice within for attitudes or habits that you should banish. Then open your eyes and write them down, each on a small scrap of paper. Pass each paper through the incense smoke, and then commit to the changes you must make to release what you have written within yourself, as you light the edge of each paper from the flame of the Earth candle and then drop it inside the metal bowl to burn into ash.

Close your eyes again. Visualize the dark old woman, who says to you:

*The lessons of Earth are not always easy, my child, but you have taken a first step in your commitment to change. Now you must reach beyond what you have released toward the light of your highest purpose in this life. Meditate upon your purpose and then create a talisman of power. Be patient. Though your progress may seem slowed at times, this is only part of your growth. The tide will turn. Be ready for it! Go now, to the light!*

See the Old One raise her arms and cause the shadow to move away from the Moon. See her as bright Full Moon again and give silent thanks to Earth for the wisdom you have gained from her this night. Open your eyes. Light the incense of consecration. Create a talisman on the parchment paper by writing words and drawing symbols on it that represent your commitment to your purpose. Pass the completed paper talisman through the consecration incense as you say:

> *I consecrate the choice I make*
> *My path is clear, new light I see*
> *By Earth and Sun and Moon I swear*
> *This is my will, so shall it be!*

Give thanks for what you have learned. Then fold the talisman into a small square to keep in a special place where you can retrieve and re-read it if you need a reinforcement of your commitment.

When you have achieved the goals for which you created it, return the talisman to Spirit in a ritual fire. Things that have been created in spiritual rituals such as this must never just be thrown away. Always return them to Spirit with respect through fire or one of the other elements. This includes the ash from the papers you burned, that can be returned to Spirit by mixing it with soil or water or blowing it away into the wind.

# Rituals for the Eight Lunar Phases

## Experiencing New Moon, with Variations for Each Element

**Key:** instinctive choice and momentum for new projects or goals, either for Progressed New Moon phase, or for any monthly New Moon.

**Intent:** to aid instinct and intuition in setting goals and/or priorities

### New Moon in a Water Sign

Gather small flowers or petals as an offering and then go to a beach to do this ritual if you can, and collect your gifts from the sea at random as you walk along. Or, do the same ritual at home by creating your own sea, with small shells or stones in a large bowl of water. You also need salt. Recorded surf sounds will enhance the experience. Center yourself, then blend salt into the water. Bless the saltwater as the oceanic womb of Mother Earth.

Now, whether you are at home with a bowl, or standing barefoot by the edge of the ocean, breathe deeply and visualize the flow of cosmic energy from above and earth energy from below flowing through your body. Cast your petals onto the water, saying:

> *Womb of life, Oh Mother Sea*
> *Accept this gift of love from me*
> *Insight I seek as Moon is New*
> *Guide me toward what I must do.*

Wade in if you're at the beach, or dabble your fingers in the bowl and wash yourself with the water, touching face and body as you relax, allowing your mind to be free of all stress and open to the feel of the cleansing and life-giving cool water. Notice thoughts that come to you, as you look for small gifts of the sea. As you see a shell or stone that appeals to you, pick it up.  If a thought comes to you then, of something you'd like to try, or have tried and wish you could expand upon, then associate it with the shell or stone in your hand.  After you have collected a few (each time focusing to remember which is which!), sit and meditate on them. If one stands out strongly for you, trust that instinct. If none do, then try this: take a deep breath, silently asking spiritual guidance, then hold your hand over each object for a moment, sensing its energy. One will feel stronger, perhaps warmer, than the others. Pick it up, and holding it to your heart, thank Mother Sea for this gift of intuitive choice. Return the other gifts to the sea, and keep your gift of intuitive choice as token and talisman of your new beginning that has emerged.

## New Moon in a Fire Sign

For active brainstorming session you can do alone, either have a tape recorder handy to record your voice, or a note pad for quick notes. Brainstorming means you call out whatever pops to mind about goals to set for this month. Don't second-guess— just say it, regardless of whether it's improbable or even silly. The review process comes later. Brainstorm while in the midst of an energy-charging physical activity that allows your mind to be free— exercise, dancing, drumming, gardening—whatever works. Before you begin, take moment to breathe deeply and center, feeling the flow of cosmic and Earth energy through your body. Then chant the rhyme nine times (three times three—nine is a number of completion). Build the energy by speaking faster and a little louder with each repetition. Then immediately launch into your activity, and whenever an idea comes to you, call it out into the recorder or pause for only one quick moment to jot it down.

*By fire bright, by three times three*
*New ideas flow to me!*

Afterwards, relax and review your ideas. Most likely you'll instinctively narrow them down to just a few, if not one, that stands out as your priority.

Likely you'll also find that you've come up with some surprisingly fresh ideas, compared to what might have emerged if you'd just sat down to make a list without the energy charge of ritual. If you wind up with more than one priority, and aren't sure which is prime, write a symbol of each on a separate paper and try feeling for which has the strongest energy (as in the Water ritual above). Or do them both (fire has lots of energy!) and trust that the priority goal will instinctively emerge for you as you proceed.


## New Moon in an Earth Sign

For this variation, you'll take a Nature walk. Most anywhere outside will do, so long as you can legally pick up small stones, sticks, leaves or flowers here and there. For an offering to Earth, take a handful of garden fertilizer to spread where it's useful, or sprinkle birdseed for the wild birds, or pour an offering of water on plants. Breathe deeply and center, then make your offering, saying:

> *Oh Mother Earth on which I stand*
> *Accept this offering from my hand.*
> *Guidance I seek as Moon is New*
> *Lead me toward what I must do.*

Take your walk and when you notice a small natural object that appeals to you, name it for a thought that comes to you then about a potential goal, and focus on it, so you'll remember. After collecting a few things and naming them, meditate on them. If one stands out strongly for you, trust that instinct. If none do, then try taking a deep breath, silently asking spiritual guidance and hold your hand over each object for a moment, sensing its energy. One will feel stronger, perhaps warmer, than the others. Pick it up, and holding it to your heart, thank Mother Earth for her gift of intuitive choice.

Return the other gifts to the Earth, and keep your chosen gift as token and talisman of your new beginning that has emerged.

## New Moon in an Air Sign

This is a solo brainstorming session for Air. It's more logical than the fire variation, but still works with lunar intuition. Get a hat, a pack of 3" x 5" cards and a marking pen. Rhythmic music in the background may help charge your energy and providing a shield from background "white noises." Use Air incense such as sage. Breathe deeply and center as you feel the energy flow from Cosmos to Earth and back again. Waft the burning sage around you and your tools. Then chant the affirmation nine times and begin to brainstorm. Jot down, each on a separate card, whatever pops into your head as goals to set for this New Moon. Don't second guess. Write it, even if it seems improbable or silly. Don't dwell on any of your ideas. Just write them down quickly and go on to the next. Here's the Air chant:

> *By power of Air, by three times three*
> *New ideas flow to me!*

After you are finished, put the cards into the hat, toss it into the air above you and let the cards fall down all around. Sit down in the middle of them and pick them up randomly, one at a time. Look at each card and make a quick decision, trusting your instinct. If it's "out," put it to your left. If it's "right," put to your right. If it's "maybe," put it in front of you.

When you have all the cards lined up, toss the "outs" into a wastebasket. Pick up the "rights" and hold them in one hand while you take a second look at the "maybe" cards. Pass your free hand over each of them, saying, "If I should have called this card "right," let it feel warm." If you feel warm energy rising from any of them, add it to your "right" pile. Throw away the rejects. Line up all the cards you've kept in the order you think should be their priority. If you are not sure, try the warm hand pass again.

When the order satisfies you, use the marking pen to number the cards. Number One is your priority for New Moon action. Act on it!

## Experiencing Crescent Moon

**Key:** struggle to overcome self-doubt or lethargy so as to thrust forward within waxing light.

**Intent:** Resist pull of old habits, or the naysaying of others. To get back on track when focus and momentum have been interrupted.

## Ritual for Getting Back on Track

Face the East and call the Air:
> *Air I call for clarity, balance and focused mind that's free.*

Turn to the South and call Fire:
> *Fire I call for energy, passion, faith and spirit free.*

Turn to the West and call Water:
> *Water I call for mystery, compassion and serenity.*

Turn to the North and call Earth:
> *Earth I call my goal to see, complete and fine as it will be!*

Now, standing at center facing East again, raise hands high into the air and stretch:
> *At center I call the cosmos above…*

Kneel to touch the ground: *And Mother Earth below…*

Stand again with hands over your heart…*I call these powers within me, and knowing that as the power is within, so it expands without…*

Move hands and arms slowly outward as if to encompass the Universe and then slowly circle in place, saying.
> *And as my Universe, so is my soul!*

Now, centered and focused again, you can get back to work!

**Experiencing First Quarter Moon**

**Key:** "crisis of action" phase. Time to make things happen.

**Intent:** manage the "crisis" by clearing your space—to clear your head and create a staging area for productive work

**Clearing Space for Effective Action**

This is a variation of a little "spell" I learned in attending a business seminar on creative management. (It was an eye-opener to find out how "new age-y" such workshops have become.) My desk is a prime candidate for occasional repetitions of this ritual, and it always works to help me move forward again more effectively.

Required tools are a trash container, a stick of clearing incense, water, cleaning fluid and a sponge. Yes, incense. It and the rhyme get that "inner child" to help you. Define the space you intend to clear while chanting the rhyme:

> *Air and Fire, my desire*
> *Cleared for action, here shall be*
> *Only things that serve my goal*
> *This is my will, so must it be!*

Pick up each item of the clutter in your working area only once. Immediately decide and then act to handle it in one of these four ways (be ruthless, assertive, no exceptions!):1. Throw it in the trash. 2. Move it out of this area and take it to its proper place, immediately, no procrastination allowed. 3. Do with it —NOW—what you intended to do by having it in this place, then get rid of it (as in 1 or 2). 4. If it is here because it will remain consistently essential to your current activity, only then should you keep it here.

Once all the clutter is reduced to only those things that are constantly essential, use the water and sponge to clean the surfaces of your space and neatly organize the things you are keeping within it.  Done! Ready to move forward in your work with greater ease and new energy.

## Experiencing Gibbous Moon

**Key:** goal is clear, but not yet fulfilled. Learning and skills need further development and meet resistance.

**Intent:** to keep smiling through frustrating times as you move toward that goal.

## Mirror Meditation to Start the Day

Most of us stand before a mirror early in our day. One glimpse of ourselves frowning or looking grumpy is usually enough for us to turn on a smile or even a pleasant look to the mirror so we can face ourselves and feel better. Think about it—how do others feel when we frown or look grumpy in public? We are all mirrors for each other, and it is our choice when we encounter a "mirror" to just react, or to be an initiator and seek to improve what is reflected to us. Close your eyes, take a deep breath, stretch, exhale, relax and then look into the mirror with your most pleasant smile, and chant this charm:

> *Throughout this day to all who see*
> *A welcome mirror I pledge to be*
> *Reflecting back good energy,*
> *Of kindness, peace, serenity.*

Once again, stretch, exhale, relax and smile, resolving to not become upset by the actions or words of any tired or stressed people you encounter, but instead to reflect kindness back to them. Take the initiative to be an image for others that will raise their spirits, and surely your spirit will soar as well.

## Experiencing Full Moon, with Variations for the Elements

**Key:** culmination and fulfillment, but need for illumination and balance

**Intent:** to achieve or restore elemental balance within

**Full Moon** is an opposition of Sun and Moon. Usually they are in complementary opposite signs.

**Variations:** Choose one of the two following rituals according to the element of either the Moon sign or the Sun sign.

## Full Moon in Air/Fire

Playing with fire and air in ritual is a good way to learn, on all levels of consciousness, of the damage of conflict and the benefit of harmony. In order to connect this ritual to a conflict you'd like to resolve, you could designate Fire for one "side" and Air as the other. If you are one of the "sides" you have in mind, be especially honest about which one you are! Fire can be creative, passionate and courageous—or impulsive and hotheaded; air can be creative, intellectual, rational—or can rationalize, be air-headed and quite cool (even stand-offish). If both "sides" seem to exhibit both fire and air traits, don't designate, just observe and reflect as you work with the two elements. You'll need a candle, a lighter, a snuffer, papers and a pen, and a large metal bowl. Begin by asking for understanding and insight:

> *By Moon and Sun, I seek insight*
> *By breath of air, by fire's light*
> *Turn conflict into harmony*
> *May balance reign, so shall it be!*

Light the candle, and enjoy how the flame burns brightly upward. Blow out the flame. Too much air! Light the candle again. Now, put the snuffer over it. Out goes the flame again, this time due to not enough air. Light it again. This time blow very gently at the flame. Notice that the flame burns even more brightly, and it has direction!

Snuff the candle again. Take your paper and pen and begin to write what you've learned so far. As you do, visualize that you are in a cold room trying to work on your papers. Feel chilly air on your face and arms. You are becoming quite uncomfortable, too cold to think clearly. Now light the candle and imagine that it's fire you're building in a fireplace. Hold your hands near the flame as you visualize the fire warming the air around you. Feel yourself becoming much more comfortable. Your thoughts are clear again, ideas come. Pick up your paper. Imagine that you are so absorbed in your thoughts that you forget to tend your fire, and suddenly a spark ignites your paper. Allow the corner of your paper to ignite. Hold it, for a moment visualizing the fire burning out of control, your good thoughts vanishing as it becomes hard to breath. Drop the paper into the metal bowl as you mentally escape the fire.

Reflect on what you've learned that can assist you in turning conflict into harmony. Write it down. (A few themes: Mind (air) influences the direction of energy (fire) or squelches it. Or, mental flow directs fiery intensity, stimulating growth, assisting focus. Fiery impulsiveness out of control rattles ability to think or reason. Pure intellect is "cold" and needs adventuring spirit and energy to stimulate its purpose.)

In conclusion, speak this affirmation:

> *Moon and Sun, I do now see*
> *My path to greater harmony.*
> *I pledge myself by fire and air*
> *To seek solutions wise and fair*
> *And do my best with what will be.*
> *I thank you for new energy!*

## Full Moon in Water/Earth

Working with the balance of these two elements is most satisfying on a beach on a Full Moon night, but if that isn't possible you can simulate many of the same things by playing with water, sand, rock and soil in your yard or even within a large, plastic box in your indoor ritual circle. Begin by asking for insight:

> *By earth alive, by water's flow,*
> *By this rite, I seek to know*
> *My path to growth and harmony.*
> *May balance reign, so shall it be.*

In reality or in your thoughts, create these effects: Stand on the sand at water's edge. Water flows gently around your feet, feeling good. Now a bigger wave comes in and then recedes. What happens? The sand that felt firm now flows right out from under you and you have to dig in your toes to hold your balance. Climb up on the rocks nearby and view the scene from a different perspective. See how the water flows into pools among the rocks and hard ground that contains it, into every crevice, every opening or low point. The earth contains the water, but over time, eventually, the water will wear away the soil, and even the rocks, and new forms will be created. Look at that little clear pool of contained water. Dump some soil in it. No longer clear. But then pour in enough water and it clears again—you can see your reflection.

Continue playing with the elements and contemplate how they relate to the balance of body and soul, and to form (life structures and responsibilities for them) vs. feelings. Reflect on what you can learn and write it down. (A few themes: What seems solid in your life (sand) can dissolve in a moment when watery emotions overwhelm (the waves pulling sand from under your feet). Waters of feeling must be contained by form (the rocks), as accepting responsibility for what you have built helps you grow. Too much containment or suppression (soil dumped in closely contained water) holds back the soul…for a time. But, eventually the water will wash away the soil, and even, over time, the rocks, changing their form, for soul is eternal…)

In conclusion, speak this affirmation:

> *Moon and Sun, I do now see*
> *My path to greater harmony.*
> *I pledge myself by water and earth,*
> *To seek a life of growth and worth,*
> *And do my best with what will be.*
> *I thank you for new energy!*

## Experiencing Disseminating Moon

**Key:** sharing, demonstrating, presenting, teaching. Give from what you've learned.

**Intent:** to achieve focus and direction in how to share what you've learned with your world

**Preparation:** Assemble symbols of each of the four elements. For Air, burning incense; Fire, a red candle; Water, a chalice of water (or other beverage); Earth, food (a cookie.)

Waft incense toward the Moon and say: *Lady, I hold the Air, power of conscious thought and communication, in my hands and in my mind. How might I direct and share this power?*

As you gaze at Moon, feel her energy flow toward you and receive the answer in your soul with thanks as you waft the charged incense all around you.

Hold up the burning candle saying: *Lady, I hold the Fire, power of action, courage and initiative in my hands and in my heart. How might I rouse and share this power?*

Again, feel the energy flow of the Moon and receive her answer with thanks, as you make a full clockwise turn with your candle visualizing how you will share your energy.

Hold your chalice toward the Moon, saying: *Lady, I hold the Water, power of feeling, empathy and deep, inner knowing, in my hands and in my mind. How might I compassionately share this power?*

Feel the energy of the Moon flow down, receive her answer with thanks. Drink from the beverage that has now been infused with lunar power.

Finally, hold up your cookie saying: *Lady, I hold the Earth, power of form, manifestation and growth in my hands and in my being. In gratitude for the earthly abundance I have received, how might I most effectively share this power?*

Feel the energy of Moon's flow toward you and your cookie and then slowly eat it, savoring and assimilating it. Save the last bit, crumble it in your hand and return it to Earth with your thanks for the with thanks for the message Lady Moon has given you.

## Experiencing Last Quarter Moon

**Key:** A "crisis of consciousness" brings the urge for change.

**Intent:** To evoke the mental process of release of the old to make space for the new.

**Preparation:** paper, pen, metal bowl, matches, water and a garden trowel or spoon.

Write what you intend to release on the paper and present it to each of the four directions, as you carry out the actions given after each affirmation:

*I turn to the East and release to the winds!* (Hold list aloft; wave it.)

*I turn to the West! Wash away that which ends!*
    (Sprinkle list lightly with water.)

*I turn to the South, Spirit fires now burn!*
    (Burn list in cauldron or metal bowl.)

*I give back to the Earth and with thanks now return.*
    (Facing North. bury the ashes in soil.)

## Experiencing Balsamic Moon

**Key:** Banishing and release

**Intent:** To banish that which is finished and let go of the past

In a peaceful walk along the beach, if you are fortunate enough to be near one, you can do a banishing rite in the sand. Near the water's edge, trace out a representation—words, symbols, pictures—of whatever you wish to banish, and trace a circle around it. Then stand within the circle, meditate on letting go and wait for the waves to come and wash your tracing away beneath your bare feet. It is gone. (If you've made symbols representing multiple things you'd like to banish, it will be enlightening to reflect upon which parts the waves take away most quickly and which things stubbornly hang on the longest.)

No ocean? Create one with a little bed of sand or soil, a hose or bucket of water. Here's play that Young Self ought to love. Trace the symbols of what you want to release in the sand with a stick. Close your eyes and flow water over your bare feet a little at a time, stopping occasionally to see which what parts of your tracing have washed away.

A chant to augment the banishing energy:

> *On Earth I stand, change I seek*
> *Earth holds what is past for me*
> *Water wash away what's done.*
> *With harm to none, so shall it be.*

# Labyrinth Walk and Meditation
## *Follow the Moon to the Sun*

As a closing ritual, I'd like to share with you a special group ritual I helped lead at the Full Moon that occurred during the 2002 United Astrology Conference. It is appropriate for this book because it creates a depth experience of how your experience of your Moon can lead you to understanding of your life purpose, symbolized by your Sun. For the first time in this book, it also introduces the meanings of the other planets in our solar system that have been observed and studied for thousands of years. If you have the opportunity to walk a labyrinth—a wonderful meditative experience—you can use this them as you do. But if not, I will also show you a way you can "walk" it with your finger and experience much the same meditative effect.

First, the background: Claudia Bader, astrologer and art therapist, provided a huge, beautiful canvas painting of a seven-circuit labyrinth in swirling tones of blue reminiscent of Earth from outer space. A special room was set aside so that people seeking a meditative respite from the brain-drain of classes could come and walk the labyrinth. Claudia had encouraged me to write a ritual for the Full Moon, and I enlisted the assistance of Barbara Schermer, who is well known for her work in experiential astrology, and is the author of a good book on it, *Astrology Alive*. We planned that I, as Moon the seeker, would walk the labyrinth paths to meet Barbara, as the Sun, for a message of purpose I could then reflect back to my world as I returned to it through the labyrinth paths. With this, we could demonstrate how others might meditate as they, too, walked the labyrinth. In unexpected but perfect serendipity, I found out by accident that astrologer David Mosley, had written a song about *Following the Moon to the Sun* that was perfect within the theme and for the call to the four directions. David sang it, accompanying himself on guitar.

Though I framed the ritual in advance, Barbara and I spoke of the planets extemporaneously, as we felt appropriate at the time, so what follows is, in part, remembrance of it. If you know the planets, it is best to use your own words in meditation, rather than reading mine. Let the words of this ritual be only a guide.

## A Seven-Circuit Labyrinth

Below is a labyrinth with each path marked with its corresponding planet. If you can, do take advantage of any opportunity to walk a large labyrinth, but if you can't, it is possible to have a profound meditative experience by slowly tracing the paths with your finger while thinking about the meaning of each path. Enter the labyrinth at Mars. Each path as marked by its planet. At first glance labyrinths appear to be mazes, but they are not. So long as you follow the path, you can never get lost. You'll always find your way to the center and back out again. Finding your spiritual center is the meditative goal, and it cannot be described just how that will feel to you, other than to say the experience speaks to you intuitively.

Move into the labyrinth to find your Center. Return through the paths as you meditate on what, having found your center, you can bring back to your world.

## Labyrinth Full Moon—UAC 2002

All join hands around the labyrinth, Sun Priestess South, Moon Priestess North. Chant in the manner of Gregorian:

**Sun:** *As above*
**Moon:** *So below*
**Sun:** *As within*
**Moon:** *So without*
**Both:** *As the Universe, so the Soul!*

### Opening Dedication (Moon):

*We have gathered here to honor and study that which is above in correspondence with that which is below—Earth and Cosmos, the Universe, the whole, that we may grow in understanding and wisdom of our place within it. We gather in a circle, as all of Nature moves in cycles, never ending, wheels ever turning, the Circle of Life, death and life once again, always turning, never ending. All in Spirit, Spirit within each one that impacts the whole, and so it is that " as within, so without. "*

*Above you visualize the lights of the Cosmos sending a golden, luminous ray down toward you, entering your body through your head, flowing throughout, illuminating your heart. Now feel your feet firmly planted in the ground with root spirits going down through the floor, through the layers of earth, the waters, the rocks to the molten center, heart of the Earth Mother. Feel her strong energy flowing back up toward you like silver light rays, entering your body through your feet, flowing throughout, blending with the light of the Cosmos, illuminating your heart. Share your energy as you feel it pass from hand to hand, flowing throughout, and thus is our sacred circle formed.*

*We stand around this beautiful labyrinth, an ancient symbol with 7 circuits, each corresponding to a visible planet of the ancients. As Sun is the center of that system, so it is the center of the labyrinth, and one walks inward seeking one's center. Moon, satellite of Earth, is nearly full this night. She reflects the Sun's full light that is too bright for earthlings to directly view, and in so doing, casts that light to Earth in softer tones, helping us know and understand our purpose.*

*We call the Great Goddess in her aspects of Sun and Moon to reveal the mystery of the labyrinth—Sun as its center, Moon as the seeker of the center who when having found it, shines more brightly to her world.*

*Before we begin, I call forth the **Bard**, who will lead us in honoring the four directions of the Earth, and the four elements of life.*

### Become the Deliverer
©1994 David Moseley[3]

*The words I choose are like doors that I open*
*The pattern implicit in all that I say*

*I turn to the East for what I must show*
*I turn to the West for who I must know*
*I turn to the North to face where I'm from*
*I turn to the South for what I must do*

*To Become the Deliverer of all the promises*
*I have brought with me to share with everyone*
*I have been given this life with a purpose*
*Ever unfolding, I follow the Moon to the Sun.*

*And all the promises that seem broken*
*Were only seeds that could not find their way*

*So turn to the East for this you must show*
*Turn to the West for who you must know*
*Turn to the North to face where you're from*
*Turn to the South for what you must do*

*To Become the Deliverer of all the promises*
*You have brought with you to share with everyone*
*You have been given this life with a purpose*
*Ever unfolding, go follow the Moon to the Sun*

*And all the words that could be, will be spoken*
*And all the promises will know the day*

*And we'll turn to the East for what we must show*
*We'll turn to the West for who we must know*
*We'll turn to the North to face where we're from*
*We'll turn to the South for what we must do*

*To Become the Deliverer of all the promises*
*We have brought with us to share with everyone*
*We have been given this life with a purpose*
*Ever unfolding, we follow the Moon…*

*To the Sun!*

**Sun Priestess:**
*I call to the Sun as the Goddess of brilliant energy that warms Mother Earth so that all who come forth from her womb may have energy and purpose. Be with and within me, oh divine light, that I may shine brightly forth to all who seek to know your message.*

**Moon Priestess:**
*I call to the Moon who rises tonight in full light, and I call her as Goddess. Be with and within this seeker, as I enter the labyrinth. By seed and root, by leaf and bud, by flower and fruit, by the Moon in all her glory, I do invoke thee, to descend upon me and aid me, who am thy servant and priestess.*

**Sun** move to the center of the labyrinth. **Moon** move to the entrance of it. As **Moon** enters each path, **Sun** announces its planet and why the Seeker must experience it.

**Mars:** *This is your capacity to act—to stand up for what you believe and assert yourself…or not. Through Mars you express anger or repress it. Feel the call of Mars within you. How will you act to fulfill your purpose?*

**Jupiter:** *Through the path of Jupiter you must seek to expand wisdom and grow spiritually. Feel the call of Jupiter for understanding of your purpose.*

**Saturn:** *On the path of Saturn you will meet and must accept the responsibilities involved in achieving your purpose.*

**Earth:** *On Earth you encounter physical limitation, though this is the form through which you must grow, if your purpose be well met.*

**Mercury:** *Through the path of Mercury you must learn to think, to seek knowledge, and to communicate what you learn as you travel toward your purpose.*

**Venus:** *Through Venus you are to seek purpose through the path of love.*

**Moon:** *As the Moon you are to feel your path to your purpose through the flow of emotion and memory.*

**Moon** arrives at center; **Sun** asks: *Do you understand?*

**Moon** responds: *Yes, I believe I do.*

**Sun:** *Then go back to the world and reflect brightly and fully on the illumination you have received.*

**Both** lift arms high and rounded like Sun and Moon, bow to each other, then **Moon** turns to walk back out of the labyrinth. As **Moon** enters each path, she reflects aloud:

**Moon:** *I will reflect the phases of my soul with compassion for others and for myself.*

**Venus:** *I will strive to reflect always the quest for beauty, balance, love and peace.*

**Mercury:** *I will probe to learn and then speak my truth, with openness to learn more.*

**Earth:** *I will appreciate and honor the Earth and all she offers me.*

**Saturn:** *I accept the limitations and responsibilities of my life, and will strive to build structures of benefit to my world.*

**Jupiter:** *I will seek spiritual guidance and higher wisdom to reflect honorably.*

**Mars:** *By all this, may I ever reflect through my actions and my expression, the highest purpose that I have found in the center of my being, though following my Moon to my Sun.*

**Sun Priestess:** *Oh, bright and mighty Sun I do thank you for your presence in my body and especially in my heart, for the purpose you show me and through me, have shown to others in this rite.*

**Moon Priestess:** *Oh Lady of the Moon, Queen of night and Goddess of my soul, I do thank you for your presence within, and for your guidance to me and to all gathered here as we seek and receive a greater understanding of our purpose.*

**Closing:** Priestesses return to South and North of the circle, and all joined hands

**Moon Priestess:** *We will formally close the circle now. The hour is very late, so you will be free to leave as you wish, but the room will remain open to any who wish to walk the labyrinth. Join us now in chanting as we opened:*

**All:** *As above, so below, as within, so without, as the Universe, so the soul.*

## Endotes

[1] For more advanced timing techniques that are accessible to beginners (planetary hours and how to use an astrological calendar) see my book, *A Time for Magick*.

[2] Since first publication of this book, Molly sold her Starcrafts store. My monthly column, now called *Magical Moon*, appears on my own website, the address for which is *www.starcraftspublishing.com*. Click on the *Magical Moon* bar on the home page. With the caveat that no guarantee can ever be given in regard to references to website addresses within a printed book, I expect my site to remain accessible by that URL, and also by *starcraftseast.com*. The new owners of Starcrafts

in San Diego also intend to continue linking to my column from the store URL: *www.starcraftsob.com*

[3] Used with permission of the author. Contact info for those who would like the music that goes with these words—a very pretty and singable tune—or other information is David Mosley, PO Box 219, Kaaawa, HI 96730-0219. Email: david@ZodiacArts.com

**Earth Mother**
pen & ink drawing by Maria Kay Simms

# Chapter 10

# *Concluding Reflections*

Up until this final chapter, the primary changes for this Second Edition of *Moon Tides, Soul Passages* are in the art. Because of the switch from print-on-demand to a big press, it was necessary to group the color paintings into one signature. That was a little disappointing to me at first, but happily it has meant I could add a few more paintings! Then, rather than have blank pages at the end of chapters, I decided to add some black and white drawings, too, and the sample report pages. Other than a few minor updates, the text is much the same as it was in the First Edition. Now, though, I've come to my "concluding reflections" and realize that, at least to some extent, they've changed—no surprise, really. After all, change is constant.

What I was thinking and feeling during the fall of 2004, as I finished the first edition of this book, was a stage in my process. Now, nearly a year and a half later, I still find validity in what I was feeling then. I'll begin as I did before, but then add my current thoughts—one more year into the cycle.

Writing this book brought home to me just how much living with the Moon and learning from her phases is a continual, never-ending process. Writing it, alone, it extended over several phases. After prior articles, I began a book in 1993, when I was head of Astro Communications Services in San Diego. Then, when Demetra George submitted her *Finding Our Way Through the Dark* to us, all finished and very good, I made the only decision a sensible publisher could. We published hers and I tabled mine in favor of alternative projects. That was my progressed Gibbous Phase—just one of the challenges I encountered then, and a relatively minor one at that. I'm glad now that I was derailed, because living longer has deepened my experience of the phases.

By 2002, then fully settled into my new life following my 1998 sale of ACS, subsequent remarriage and move to New Hampshire, plus most of my first term as NCGR Chair, I finally returned to my Moon book project. I first engaged Rique Pottenger to design software for me that would do the lifetime lunar phases previously only available in easy to access format from ACS' chart services system. It was the right time for this book, for the words flowed. I enjoyed writing it more than any of my previous books. It was time, as my Progressed Disseminating Phase suggested, to teach what I had learned, and so I did—poured it out, from both extensive study and observation of others, and from memories and reflections on my own soul passages. I submitted a book proposal and was contracted in early 2003, with a deadline and a projected publication date of fall 2004.

I turned in my manuscript right on time, but then nine months later, almost precisely as my Progressed Last Quarter phase began, I heard from my publisher that they wanted the book, but one-third shorter! It was a business decision, to get a desired price point, and with my background as both publisher and writer, I understood that, but...one THIRD?!

Feeling as protective of my precious words as the most naive of any new author I'd ever encountered, my "crisis of consciousness" was launched. The words weren't the only things I had to confront letting go of, but they became symbolic of a process I'd thought I'd learned enough about to be prepared to handle well and even anticipate with some degree of welcome.

After a lifetime of priority focus on responsibilities toward others, I'd imagined I'd at last do what I'd been threatening to do for many years of always juggling too many things at once. I'd let go of much of the "Mother" role I've always found myself taking on (responsibilities for businesses and organizations, in addition to family), and truly embrace my time as Crone— the elder, wise woman who has time to contemplate while working, or just resting, in my stone circle garden.  I would do my creative work however the spirit moved me, rather than because I must do it, on a deadline. Well, I still visualize that future potential, but meanwhile, those words…

The process of drastically cutting my words, painful at first, became therapeutic as I went back over every line I'd written, thinking about it all over again. "Though undoubtedly this is a good Last Quarter exercise," I told myself, "my guess is that on a scale of one to ten this will be only about a two, in terms of changes I'll face or precipitate over the next few years." Little did I know then how quickly the next mandate for change would come! Well, let's call it a "test." I like that better.

I turned in my one-third shorter version of this book on schedule, after grudgingly admitting to myself that tightening it up had been good for both the book and for my own process. But, there was more to come, nine more months past the time when I'd been given the directive to cut. I can now reflect with some amusement that the "baby" we birth is often not quite what we imagined.

Changes in my publisher's all-over plans for its astrology line, plus the all-important numbers on what was selling best, precipitated another request for me to rewrite. This time I was asked to change the book to straight astrological theory—a "how-to" pointed toward forecasting. All the Goddess mythology was to be cut, along with all references to the Wheel of the Year (too Pagan) and the entire chapter on experiential astrology. This was just too much. I was being asked to cut what I consider to be the most creative parts of the book, the parts of it that I like best! Besides, to point it toward forecasting was just not the way I felt knowledge of lunar phases would be of most benefit to my readers.

To me the techniques in this book are about process, about personal and spiritual development, not forecasting. While studying and using them can give insight into what the future might hold, that is only a minor part of how they are best used. The power and magic of your Moon comes through your increased self-awareness and faith in yourself, including the courage and the ability to make choices that will create a better future.

In meditation, I listened to the flow I've learned to trust, and knew what I had to do. I asked for release from my contract and self-published this book as I wanted it to be, albeit realizing that I'd be unlikely to reach anywhere near the size of audience I'd have reached through the publisher. I feel at peace with that decision, and in part that has to do with my experiences of my previous cycle thirty years ago. Now, in further reflection, I can also see parallels with my first progressed Last Quarter Phase in early childhood.

So, what was really going on here? And what were the parallels? As the process of personal reflection continues, more layers peel away, and I understand even more about what I've written! This is the value of self-examination and journaling, to get beneath the surface happenings of life for a better understanding of what I have called "soul passages." In the many examples I've given you of what was happening to others during various phases, we can only speculate what they were feeling inside, and what that meant to them going forward. So, in part to model the way I hope you will use this book for your own personal reflections, I'll tell you a little more about my own thoughts and perceptions that have come to the surface in the year since first publication of this book. My current Last Quarter Phase makes a good example of how differently a phase can manifest in early childhood, in one's 30s and in one's 60s, and yet still have a similar, though evolutionary, core theme.

My first Last Quarter phase began soon after my 4th birthday and lasted until I was 7-1/2. There was no kindergarten in the small town where I grew up, so I started 1st grade when I was five. I don't remember much detail about when I was that young, but there are a few very vivid flash pictures that stick in my mind. The first one, and probably the earliest, was surely traumatic. I see myself falling through very dark blue-green water, my mouth wide open screaming. Then, my Dad grabbed me and I have a vague memory of being on shore coughing up water. I'd been riding piggyback as he swam across a canal and I somehow let go of him and slipped off. In another picture I'm standing very quietly, feeling puzzled and left out, as I watched my mother nursing my newborn baby brother. In another memory my first grade teacher is scolding me because I had forgotten to bring a paper to school. I'm feeling absolutely mortified, and this is the only thing I remember clearly about my entire first grade experience. One more flash picture is of running toward my house, crying with blood streaming down my face. A little friend and I had found two hatchets and decided it would be fun to chop hay in the barn. I bent over as she chopped. Fortunately, it wasn't as bad as it looked then, and my hair covers any scar. If in retrospect, these memories were all within my first encounter with the progressed Last Quarter "crisis of consciousness," then what was it all about? What can I learn from it about this phase in general, and specifically, what has it to do with my soul passages?

My second progressed Last Quarter phase began in May of 1974, the month before my then husband, two small daughters and I moved away from San Francisco. My paintings were in three galleries and selling well. I had moved away from my preferred earlier style with which I'd won juried shows, but seldom sold, to a more salable style of painting, so that I could make a needed contribution to family income. I also free-lanced as a commercial artist, and I'd begun studying astrology. Now, though, we were moving east so that my husband, an opera singer, could re-center his expanding career out of New York City. I know in retrospect that my marriage was already in trouble, but then, I was in denial. We settled in Connecticut, where he could easily commute to New York. For me, though, living away from the city with two small children made reestablishing my art career far more difficult. He was on the road more than he was home, and by mid 1975, marriage problems clearly surfaced. We cooperatively filed for divorce.

The divorce process went quite smoothly and I thought I was handling it all very well—until a February week about two months after the divorce was final. That is when the "crisis of consciousness" welled up within me full blast, and I'll never forget the experience. In the months prior, everyone—my ex, my parents—assumed that surely I'd go back to teaching art again, as I had for five years after college, because this would be the best way to secure a dependable income. I got my provisional certificate for Connecticut, and began looking for a position, but I absolutely hated the idea. All of a sudden it fully hit me that I was actually divorced! I'd married the summer I graduated from college, so this was the first time in my life I'd been on my own. I had the children to care for, no job and nobody else with whom I was obliged to consult on my decisions. I got sick, literally sick with the flu, and for more than a week I could hardly pull myself out of bed. I'd had a preliminary interview for a high school teaching job that looked very promising, but the application had been sitting in my typewriter for nearly two weeks now, and I couldn't bear to fill it out. I just did not want to go back into teaching again. It felt like giving up, backtracking. There had to be something more, something I could feel enthusiastic about, something that I wanted to do instead of just "should do." Somehow, I got myself up out of bed, deciding, "Dammit! I've spent 35 years trying to measure up to what I've thought was expected of me—to be the perfect daughter, perfect wife, perfect mother—but I'm not perfect. I don't want to be perfect. I don't even know who I am other than what I'm expected to be!" I remember this time as the single most disillusioning of my life, because it was the first time of such a fully conscious realization.

A few other times since then have been as traumatic in their way, but I was better able to handle them. It was that particular time in early 1976 that I consciously learned, for the first time, that no matter what happened, I would get through it. I would survive. I went into New York City one day soon after my inner crisis, for a class in astrology I'd been taking with Charles Emerson, and I asked him to look at my chart. He said, "You have a good chart for business. Why don't you start a little metaphysical shop in Connecticut and then you can start an NCGR Chapter." "But, Charles, I have no money." "Find a place to live that's zoned for business," he suggested, "then maybe I can help you get some books."

That suggestion of Charles' led to my first experience as a businesswoman, Mystic Arts, begun later in 1976, as I was entering the final year of my progressed Last Quarter. My father loaned me $2000, half of which I used to lease an old colonial house off the corner of a business street in New Milford, CT. My daughters and I lived in an apartment upstairs and I took a half-day position teaching high school art, while fixing up the downstairs of the house into a consignment arts and crafts gallery. True to his word, Charles helped me put together an astrology conference in the area. He came himself to speak and brought several prominent New York astrologers with him. He also arranged for a big book table with the plan that I would be able to keep the books that didn't sell on consignment as an opening inventory for a bookshop within my building. The conference was a success, and so was my little business (although not without a few traumas along the way, one of which I used as an example on page 91). And, I did start that NCGR chapter. By the close of Balsamic Phase, it was increasingly evident that astrology would become my new career focus.

So, what is the common theme underlying my three experiences of Last Quarter Phase by progression? Each involved a "crisis of consciousness" when I had to experience loss of a prior sense of security and confront the scary realization of being alone. Then, somehow, I found a way to deal with the loss, and in the process, I reoriented my feelings, my thinking and my activities so that I could move on and create something new. This theme is not due to Last Quarter phase, alone. It also ties in with my Aries prenatal lunar eclipse and my birth lunar phase of Full Moon. My mother wrote in my baby book that my first complete sentence was an emphatically stated, "I do it myself!" Did my soul come into this life prepared to tackle that lesson? Well, in my mind it certainly it fits the core theory. My prenatal solar eclipse is in Libra and my comfort mode has been —and still is—to relate, cooperate and compromise. But, my soul lesson, symbolized by Aries, would challenge me to learn to stand alone. In my Full Moon illuminations, too, I've come to realize that, regardless of any of the difficulties I've experienced in relationships there were also many benefits. All in all, I do very much prefer being in partnership—sharing my personal life in marriage, and my professional life through working with others. But, by having learned that I can also find happiness and personal fulfillment in the times when I've been on my own, I've also become far more conscious of my own responsibility in maintaining the balance necessary within good relationships. I know now that nobody else can be for me what I cannot find within myself. The only true sense of completion is that which we can find within, just as Goddess and God are within, two who are One—wholeness in Spirit.

My current "crisis of consciousness" has one more year to go, as of this writing. As a little girl in the 1940s, I chose approval as the path of safety. As a divorcee at age 35, whose primary form of expression, art, had been compromised for the sake of sales and then stymied through a move, I got through my initial crisis to strike out in an unexpected direction and create something new. That new direction eventually became more than I ever could have imagined at the time. Now, in my 60s, I can look back at those two earlier Last Quarter phases and see the parallels with my decision, at the beginning of this one, to break away from what others might see as the path of safety to forge my own path. A primary realization was that I absolutely could not sacrifice this book on the altar of sales projections, as I'd once sacrificed my painting. When I paint what I feel, it feeds my soul. When I compromised my art, it lost something very important to me that I've only recently found again—the joy and intuitive flow that feeds my soul. That is the way I wrote this book—from the creative flow of soul expression—and it is why I felt that I had to insist on doing it my way, regardless of the risks involved in breaking free and "I do it myself." I trust that if it has connected with you, then you and I have a soul connection on some level, and I can only hope that something I have written will touch you in a meaningful and beneficial way.

We learn and grow from everything in life. Keep telling yourself that, whenever the process of living that you're currently going through is not to your liking, and especially when it's painful. It's those times that you often look back on later and say, "What happened then was difficult—really challenging—but it was also a good thing, a turning point that led me to something better."

Writing this book and then producing it, including the addition of paintings of my own and by my daughter, Molly Sullivan, became part of my inner process well beyond what I expected when I began. This final reflection on my own personal process is just one more example I can give you of how the seasons of life flow one into the other in a somewhat predictable pattern of change, while at the same time provide major opportunities for choice, and in the process of choice, personal and spiritual growth.

Though examples from the lives of others can aid your understanding, ultimately this book is about you. I offer it to you as a tool of your own soul process. I hope you will use the techniques, myths, rituals and example stories within it as the means to then reflect upon your own story—your own soul passages. Journal them, and learn and grow through the process.

May you become increasingly aware of Moon's passage through the skies and through your life, through her phases and signs. Join in her dance with Earth and Sun in both the constancy of change and the eternity of the ever-turning wheel. See how her cycles are revealed in your life, both mundane and spiritual…how they are echoed in the life cycles and soul of Nature, and within the depths of your soul. Through the Moon we are called to remember the past, flow more wisely in the present, and look toward the future with confidence. As we probe the mysteries of the Moon, we grow in wisdom, in soul and in Spirit.

# Appendix I

# *Getting Started with Moon Tides Software*

On the *Moon Tides* CD you will find an extensive Help section that answers even more questions than you may ever think to ask about how the software works and about the basic astrology involved. This short "getting started" instruction is to alert you to what to expect when you insert the CD into your computer.

**Compatibilities:** *Moon Tides* software has been sucessfully tested on all versions of Windows in current use (2006), including older versions back to WIN 98. Personally, I'm a dedicated Mac user, so I run my *Moon Tides* software on my G-4 Power Macintosh with Virtual PC installed. This enables my Mac to run Windows either in a corner of my screen, or full screen, if I choose, and I can also run several other popular Windows astrological calculation and report writer programs quite easily. When I began research for this book, I was using a much older Version 4 of Virtual PC with Win 98 on Mac OS 9. Then I upgraded to OSX and Virtual PC6 when I was preparing the book for first publication. Now, as I'm completing this second editon, I'm using OSX 10.3.4 and Virtual PC7 on both my desk computer and on my Powerbook laptop with which I travel. The point to be made here is: *Moon Tides* software may be programmed for Windows computers, but it can work as well on a Power Mac as it does on a PC. Check Microsoft's Mactopia at microsoft.com/mac/ for further information on Virtual PC software, and news about other new options for running Windows on Macs.

**Installation:** Insert the CD into your computer. A message box will offer you the option to download the full JPL (Jet Propulsion Laboratory) ephemeris data or leave it on the CD. If you have a fairly new computer with a lot of space, full installation should be no problem. With an older system, you might prefer to leave JPL on the CD and download *Moon Tides* without it. If you leave the CD in your computer, the *Moon Tides* software will use it; if you don't, the software will use mathematical routines and still work just fine, calculating reports sufficiently precise to satisfy all except perhaps the more "techie" of advanced astrologers. Coordinate and time changes data are essential for all astrological calculations, so the 2006 updated *ACS Atlas* software is included on your *Moon Tides* CD. If *Moon Tides* does not find *ACS Atlas* on your hard drive, it wil install it for you. If you already have *ACS Atlas* installed, *Moon Tides* will automatically locate it and link to it. If for any reason it does not automatically link, you'll find instructions for setting the path in *Moon Tides* Help.

**Install Moon Tides**.
Insert the CD into your CD drive and go! The install program will mostly install itself other than to give you options to Save or Open from the CD.

## Entering Birth Data for Your Report

Past the opening art page, you'll see a mostly white page with a small box to enter a name, and a sentence of instruction telling you how to start. It's very easy. Do enter your birth data in the order the data entry box asks, for when you do, other data, such as correct longitude and latitude and time changes will appear automatically. As soon as you've entered the data and clicked Ok, the report will appear on your screen

**Page one** of the *Moon Tides* report shows your personal astrological data— all that you need to work with this book. **Pages two and three** list transiting Moon phases for one year, plus eclipses and the dates and exact times of all eight solar-seasonal holidays. This will be for your birth location, beginning on the current day, unless you choose the options of an alternate **Start Date** and/or **Location**.

## Questions?

If at any time you have a question, **click on the question mark** on the menu bar and you'll find that **Help** answers everything—certainly everything I could think of to ask and more. Rique is very through! His help section is, in itself, like a textbook on basic astrology.

# Appendix II

# Eclipse Tables
## Solar Eclipses 1950-2030

| 1950 | Mar 18 | Pisces | 27°28 |
|---|---|---|---|
|  | Sep 12 | Virgo | 18°49 |
| 1951 | Mar 7 | Pisces | 16°29 |
|  | Sep 1 | Virgo | 8°17 |
| 1952 | Feb 25 | Pisces | 5°43 |
|  | Aug 20 | Leo | 27°31 |
| 1953 | Feb 14 | Aquarius | 25°03 |
|  | Jul 11 | Cancer | 18°30 |
|  | Aug 9 | Leo | 16°45 |
| 1954 | Jan 5 | Capricorn | 14°14 |
|  | Jun 30 | Cancer | 8°10 |
|  | Dec 25 | Capricorn | 2°59 |
| 1955 | Jun 20 | Gemini | 28°05 |
|  | Dec 14 | Sagittarius | 21°31 |
| 1956 | Jun 8 | Gemini | 18°01 |
|  | Dec 2 | Sagittarius | 10°08 |
| 1957 | Apr 30 | Taurus | 9°23 |
|  | Oct 23 | Libra | 29°31 |
| 1958 | Apr 19 | Aries | 28°34 |
|  | Oct 12 | Libra | 19°01 |
| 1959 | Apr 8 | Aries | 17°33 |
|  | Oct 2 | Libra | 8°34 |
| 1960 | Mar 27 | Aries | 6°38 |
|  | Sep 20 | Virgo | 27°58 |
| 1961 | Feb 15 | Aquarius | 26°26 |
|  | Aug 11 | Leo | 18°31 |
| 1962 | Feb 5 | Aquarius | 15°43 |
|  | Jul 31 | Leo | 7°49 |

| 1963 | Jan 25 | Aquarius | 4°52 |
|---|---|---|---|
|  | Jul 20 | Cancer | 27°24 |
| 1964 | Jan 14 | Capricorn | 23°43 |
|  | Jun 10 | Gemini | 19°19 |
|  | Jul 9 | Cancer | 17°15 |
|  | Dec 4 | Sagittarius | 11°56 |
| 1965 | May 30 | Gemini | 9°13 |
|  | Nov 23 | Sagittarius | 0°40 |
| 1966 | May 20 | Taurus | 28°55 |
|  | Nov 12 | Scorpio | 19°45 |
| 1967 | May 9 | Taurus | 18°17 |
|  | Nov 2 | Scorpio | 9°07 |
| 1968 | Mar 28 | Aries | 8°19 |
|  | Sep 22 | Virgo | 29°30 |
| 1969 | Mar 18 | Pisces | 27°25 |
|  | Sep 11 | Virgo | 18°53 |
| 1970 | Mar 7 | Pisces | 16°44 |
|  | Aug 31 | Virgo | 8°04 |
| 1971 | Feb 25 | Pisces | 6°08 |
|  | Jul 22 | Cancer | 28°56 |
|  | Aug 20 | Leo | 27°15 |
| 1972 | Jan 16 | Capricorn | 25°25 |
|  | Jul 10 | Cancer | 18°37 |
| 1973 | Jan 4 | Capricorn | 14°10 |
|  | Jun 30 | Cancer | 8°32 |
|  | Dec 24 | Capricorn | 2°40 |
| 1974 | Jun 20 | Gemini | 28°30 |
|  | Dec 13 | Sagittarius | 21°16 |

| | | | | | | | | |
|------|------|----|------------|--------|------|------|----|------------|--------|
| 1975 | May | 11 | Taurus | 20°00 | 1990 | Jan | 26 | Aquarius | 6°35 |
| | Nov | 3 | Scorpio | 10°30 | | Jul | 22 | Cancer | 29°04 |
| 1976 | Apr | 29 | Taurus | 9°13 | 1991 | Jan | 15 | Capricorn | 25°20 |
| | Oct | 23 | Libra | 29°56 | | Jul | 11 | Cancer | 18°59 |
| 1977 | Apr | 18 | Aries | 28°16 | 1992 | Jan | 4 | Capricorn | 13°51 |
| | Oct | 12 | Libra | 19°24 | | Jun | 30 | Cancer | 8°56 |
| 1978 | Apr | 7 | Aries | 17°26 | | Dec | 24 | Capricorn | 2°27 |
| | Oct | 2 | Libra | 8°43 | 1993 | May | 21 | Gemini | 0°32 |
| 1979 | Feb | 26 | Pisces | 7°30 | | Nov | 13 | Scorpio | 21°32 |
| | Aug | 22 | Leo | 29°01 | 1994 | May | 10 | Taurus | 19°49 |
| 1980 | Feb | 16 | Aquarius | 26°50 | | Nov | 3 | Scorpio | 10°54 |
| | Aug | 10 | Leo | 18°17 | 1995 | Apr | 29 | Taurus | 8°56 |
| 1981 | Feb | 4 | Aquarius | 16°01 | | Oct | 24 | Scorpio | 0°17 |
| | Jul | 31 | Leo | 7°51 | 1996 | Apr | 17 | Aries | 28°11 |
| 1982 | Jan | 25 | Aquarius | 4°53 | | Oct | 12 | Libra | 19°31 |
| | Jun | 21 | Gemini | 29°47 | 1997 | Mar | 9 | Pisces | 18°31 |
| | Jul | 20 | Cancer | 27°43 | | Sep | 2 | Virgo | 9°34 |
| | Dec | 15 | Sagittarius | 23°05 | 1998 | Feb | 26 | Pisces | 7°55 |
| 1983 | Jun | 11 | Gemini | 19°43 | | Aug | 22 | Leo | 28°48 |
| | Dec | 4 | Sagittarius | 11°47 | 1999 | Feb | 16 | Aquarius | 27°08 |
| 1984 | May | 30 | Gemini | 9°26 | | Aug | 11 | Leo | 18°21 |
| | Nov | 22 | Sagittarius | 0°50 | 2000 | Feb | 5 | Aquarius | 16°01 |
| 1985 | May | 19 | Taurus | 28°50 | | Jul | 1 | Cancer | 10°15 |
| | Nov | 12 | Scorpio | 20°08 | | Jul | 31 | Leo | 8°11 |
| 1986 | Apr | 9 | Aries | 19°07 | | Dec | 25 | Capricorn | 4°15 |
| | Oct | 3 | Libra | 10°16 | 2001 | Jun | 21 | Cancer | 0°11 |
| 1987 | Mar | 29 | Aries | 8°18 | | Dec | 14 | Sagittarius | 22°56 |
| | Sep | 23 | Virgo | 29°34 | 2002 | Jun | 10 | Gemini | 19°54 |
| 1988 | Mar | 18 | Pisces | 27°42 | | Dec | 4 | Sagittarius | 11°58 |
| | Sep | 11 | Virgo | 18°40 | 2003 | May | 31 | Gemini | 9°19 |
| 1989 | Mar | 7 | Pisces | 17°09 | | Nov | 23 | Sagittarius | 1°14 |
| | Aug | 31 | Virgo | 7°48 | 2004 | Apr | 19 | Aries | 29°50 |
| | | | | | | Oct | 14 | Libra | 21°06 |

| 2005 | Apr | 8 | Aries | 19°06 |
| | Oct | 3 | Libra | 10°19 |
| 2006 | Mar | 29 | Aries | 8°35 |
| | Sep | 22 | Virgo | 29°20 |
| 2007 | Mar | 19 | Pisces | 28°07 |
| | Sep | 11 | Virgo | 18°24 |
| 2008 | Feb | 7 | Aquarius | 17°45 |
| | Aug | 1 | Leo | 9°32 |
| 2009 | Jan | 26 | Aquarius | 6°30 |
| | Jul | 22 | Cancer | 29°27 |
| 2010 | Jan | 15 | Capricorn | 25°01 |
| | Jul | 11 | Cancer | 19°24 |
| 2011 | Jan | 4 | Capricorn | 13°38 |
| | Jun | 1 | Gemini | 11°02 |
| | Jul | 1 | Cancer | 9°12 |
| | Nov | 25 | Sagittarius | 2°37 |
| 2012 | May | 20 | Gemini | 0°21 |
| | Nov | 13 | Scorpio | 21°57 |
| 2013 | May | 10 | Taurus | 19°31 |
| | Nov | 3 | Scorpio | 11°16 |
| 2014 | Apr | 29 | Taurus | 8°51 |
| | Oct | 23 | Scorpio | 0°24 |
| 2015 | Mar | 20 | Pisces | 29°28 |
| | Sep | 13 | Virgo | 20°11 |
| 2016 | Mar | 9 | Pisces | 18°56 |
| | Sep | 1 | Virgo | 9°21 |
| 2017 | Feb | 26 | Pisces | 8°12 |
| | Aug | 21 | Leo | 28°53 |
| 2018 | Feb | 15 | Aquarius | 27°07 |
| | Jul | 13 | Cancer | 20°42 |
| | Aug | 11 | Leo | 18°41 |

| 2019 | Jan | 6 | Capricorn | 15°26 |
| | Jul | 2 | Cancer | 10°38 |
| | Dec | 26 | Capricorn | 4°07 |
| 2020 | Jun | 21 | Cancer | 0°21 |
| | Dec | 14 | Sagittarius | 23°08 |
| 2021 | Jun | 10 | Gemini | 19°47 |
| | Dec | 4 | Sagittarius | 12°22 |
| 2022 | Apr | 30 | Taurus | 10°29 |
| | Oct | 25 | Scorpio | 2°01 |
| 2023 | Apr | 20 | Aries | 29°50 |
| | Oct | 14 | Libra | 21°08 |
| 2024 | Apr | 8 | Aries | 19°24 |
| | Oct | 2 | Libra | 10°04 |
| 2025 | Mar | 29 | Aries | 9°00 |
| | Sep | 21 | Virgo | 29°05 |
| 2026 | Feb | 17 | Aquarius | 28°50 |
| | Aug | 12 | Leo | 20°02 |
| 2027 | Feb | 6 | Aquarius | 17°38 |
| | Aug | 2 | Leo | 9°55 |
| 2028 | Jan | 26 | Aquarius | 6°11 |
| | Jul | 22 | Cancer | 29°50 |
| 2029 | Jan | 14 | Capricorn | 24°50 |
| | Jun | 12 | Gemini | 21°30 |
| | Jul | 11 | Cancer | 19°37 |
| | Dec | 5 | Sagittarius | 13°46 |
| 2030 | Jun | 1 | Gemini | 10°50 |
| | Nov | 25 | Sagittarius | 3°02 |

# Lunar Eclipses 1950-2030

| | | | | | | | | |
|---|---|---|---|---|---|---|---|---|
| 1950 | Apr 2 | Libra | 12°29 | 1963 | Jan 9 | Cancer | 19°04 |
| | Sep 26 | Aries | 2°28 | | Jul 6 | Capricorn | 14°09 |
| | | | | | Dec 30 | Cancer | 8°03 |
| 1951 | Mar 23 | Libra | 1°52 | | | | |
| | Aug 17 | Aquarius | 23°33 | 1964 | Jun 25 | Capricorn | 3 |
| | Sep 15 | Pisces | 21°45 | | Dec 19 | Gemini | 27°11 |
| 1952 | Feb 11 | Leo | 21°19 | 1965 | Jun 14 | Sagittarius | 22°43 |
| | Aug 5 | Aquarius | 13°22 | | Dec 8 | Gemini | 16°18 |
| 1953 | Jan 29 | Leo | 9°49 | 1966 | May 4 | Scorpio | 14°02 |
| | Jul 26 | Aquarius | 3°12 | | Oct 29 | Taurus | 5°38 |
| 1954 | Jan 19 | Cancer | 28°27 | 1967 | Apr 24 | Scorpio | 3°39 |
| | Jul 16 | Capricorn | 22°52 | | Oct 18 | Aries | 24°22 |
| 1955 | Jan 8 | Cancer | 17°21 | 1968 | Apr 13 | Libra | 23°17 |
| | Jun 5 | Sagittarius | 14°15 | | Oct 6 | Aries | 13°14 |
| | Nov 29 | Gemini | 6°47 | | | | |
| | | | | 1969 | Apr 2 | Libra | 12°43 |
| 1956 | May 24 | Sagittarius | 3°27 | | Aug 27 | Pisces | 4°07 |
| | Nov 18 | Taurus | 25°56 | | Sep 25 | Aries | 2°28 |
| 1957 | May 13 | Scorpio | 22°50 | 1970 | Feb 21 | Virgo | 2°23 |
| | Nov 7 | Taurus | 14°53 | | Aug 17 | Aquarius | 23°53 |
| 1958 | Apr 4 | Libra | 14°02 | 1971 | Feb 10 | Leo | 20°56 |
| | May 3 | Scorpio | 12°27 | | Aug 6 | Aquarius | 13°41 |
| | Oct 27 | Taurus | 3°36 | | | | |
| | | | | 1972 | Jan 30 | Leo | 9°36 |
| 1959 | Mar 24 | Libra | 3°31 | | Jul 26 | Aquarius | 3°19 |
| | Sep 17 | Pisces | 23°29 | | | | |
| | | | | 1973 | Jan 18 | Cancer | 28°33 |
| 1960 | Mar 13 | Virgo | 22°47 | | Jun 15 | Sagittarius | 24°42 |
| | Sep 5 | Pisces | 12°54 | | Jul 15 | Capricorn | 22°42 |
| | | | | | Dec 10 | Gemini | 17°57 |
| 1961 | Mar 2 | Virgo | 11°41 | | | | |
| | Aug 26 | Pisces | 2°35 | 1974 | Jun 4 | Sagittarius | 13°57 |
| | | | | | Nov 29 | Gemini | 7°03 |
| 1962 | Feb 19 | Virgo | 0°18 | | | | |
| | Jul 17 | Capricorn | 24°32 | 1975 | May 25 | Sagittarius | 3°23 |
| | Aug 15 | Aquarius | 22°22 | | Nov 18 | Taurus | 25°55 |

| | | | | | | | |
|---|---|---|---|---|---|---|---|
| 1976 | May 13 | Scorpio | 23°03 | 1990 | Feb 9 | Leo | 20°44 |
| | Nov 6 | Taurus | 14°34 | | Aug 6 | Aquarius | 13°48 |
| 1977 | Apr 4 | Libra | 14°22 | 1991 | Jan 30 | Leo | 9°43 |
| | Sep 27 | Aries | 4°13 | | Jun 27 | Capricorn | 5°07 |
| | | | | | Jul 26 | Aquarius | 3°08 |
| 1978 | Mar 24 | Libra | 3°41 | | Dec 21 | Gemini | 29°08 |
| | Sep 16 | Pisces | 23°35 | | | | |
| | | | | 1992 | Jun 15 | Sagittarius | 24°23 |
| 1979 | Mar 13 | Virgo | 22°38 | | Dec 9 | Gemini | 18°12 |
| | Sep 6 | Pisces | 13°12 | | | | |
| | | | | 1993 | Jun 4 | Sagittarius | 13°53 |
| 1980 | Mar 1 | Virgo | 11°19 | | Nov 29 | Gemini | 7°00 |
| | Jul 27 | Aquarius | 5°00 | | | | |
| | Aug 26 | Pisces | 2°56 | 1994 | May 25 | Sagittarius | 3°37 |
| | | | | | Nov 18 | Taurus | 25°35 |
| 1981 | Jan 20 | Leo | 0°16 | | | | |
| | Jul 17 | Capricorn | 24°35 | 1995 | Apr 15 | Libra | 25°09 |
| | | | | | Oct 8 | Aries | 15°00 |
| 1982 | Jan 9 | Cancer | 19°16 | | | | |
| | Jul 6 | Capricorn | 13°54 | 1996 | Apr 4 | Libra | 14°32 |
| | Dec 30 | Cancer | 8°24 | | Sep 27 | Aries | 4°18 |
| 1983 | Jun 25 | Capricorn | 3°09 | 1997 | Mar 24 | Libra | 3°32 |
| | Dec 20 | Gemini | 27°29 | | Sep 16 | Pisces | 23°53 |
| 1984 | May 15 | Scorpio | 24°38 | 1998 | Mar 13 | Virgo | 22°16 |
| | Jun 13 | Sagittarius | 22°35 | | Aug 8 | Aquarius | 15°29 |
| | Nov 8 | Taurus | 16°36 | | Sep 6 | Pisces | 13°33 |
| 1985 | May 4 | Scorpio | 14°19 | 1999 | Jan 31 | Leo | 11°25 |
| | Oct 28 | Taurus | 5°17 | | Jul 28 | Aquarius | 5°02 |
| 1986 | Apr 24 | Scorpio | 4°00 | 2000 | Jan 21 | Leo | 0°27 |
| | Oct 17 | Aries | 24°05 | | Jul 16 | Capricorn | 24°19 |
| 1987 | Apr 14 | Libra | 23°30 | 2001 | Jan 9 | Cancer | 19° |
| | Oct 7 | Aries | 13°15 | | Jul 5 | Capricorn | 13°34 |
| | | | | | Dec 30 | Cancer | 8°41 |
| 1988 | Mar 3 | Virgo | 13°23 | | | | |
| | Aug 27 | Pisces | 4°28 | 2002 | May 26 | Sagittarius | 5°10 |
| | | | | | Jun 24 | Capricorn | 3°02 |
| 1989 | Feb 20 | Virgo | 2°00 | | Nov 20 | Taurus | 27°39 |
| | Aug 17 | Aquarius | 24°12 | | | | |

| 2003 | May 16 | Scorpio | 24°55 |
| | Nov 9 | Taurus | 16°15 |
| 2004 | May 4 | Scorpio | 14°39 |
| | Oct 28 | Taurus | 5°00 |
| 2005 | Apr 24 | Scorpio | 4°12 |
| | Oct 17 | Aries | 24°07 |
| 2006 | Mar 14 | Virgo | 24°20 |
| | Sep 7 | Pisces | 15°05 |
| 2007 | Mar 3 | Virgo | 13°01 |
| | Aug 28 | Pisces | 4°46 |
| 2008 | Feb 21 | Virgo | 1°50 |
| | Aug 16 | Aquarius | 24°17 |
| 2009 | Feb 9 | Leo | 20°52 |
| | Jul 7 | Capricorn | 15°32 |
| | Aug 6 | Aquarius | 13°35 |
| | Dec 31 | Cancer | 10°20 |
| 2010 | Jun 26 | Capricorn | 4°50 |
| | Dec 21 | Gemini | 29°22 |
| 2011 | Jun 15 | Sagittarius | 24°22 |
| | Dec 10 | Gemini | 18°08 |
| 2012 | Jun 4 | Sagittarius | 14°08 |
| | Nov 28 | Gemini | 6°40 |
| 2013 | Apr 25 | Scorpio | 5°51 |
| | May 25 | Sagittarius | 3°58 |
| | Oct 18 | Aries | 25°51 |
| 2014 | Apr 15 | Libra | 25°17 |
| | Oct 8 | Aries | 15°07 |
| 2015 | Apr 4 | Libra | 14°21 |
| | Sep 28 | Aries | 4°38 |
| 2016 | Mar 23 | Libra | 3°10 |
| | Sep 16 | Pisces | 24°13 |
| 2017 | Feb 11 | Leo | 22°34 |
| | Aug 7 | Aquarius | 15°30 |
| 2018 | Jan 31 | Leo | 11°38 |
| | Jul 27 | Aquarius | 4°45 |
| 2019 | Jan 21 | Leo | 0°49 |
| | Jul 16 | Capricorn | 24°00 |
| 2020 | Jan 10 | Cancer | 19°53 |
| | Jun 5 | Sagittarius | 15°41 |
| | Jul 5 | Capricorn | 13°29 |
| | Nov 30 | Gemini | 8°44 |
| 2021 | May 26 | Sagittarius | 5°28 |
| | Nov 19 | Taurus | 27°17 |
| 2022 | May 16 | Scorpio | 25°16 |
| | Nov 8 | Taurus | 15°59 |
| 2023 | May 5 | Scorpio | 14°51 |
| | Oct 28 | Taurus | 5°03 |
| 2024 | Mar 25 | Libra | 5°13 |
| | Sep 18 | Pisces | 25°46 |
| 2025 | Mar 14 | Virgo | 23°58 |
| | Sep 7 | Pisces | 15°24 |
| 2026 | Mar 3 | Virgo | 12°51 |
| | Aug 28 | Pisces | 4°51 |
| 2027 | Feb 20 | Virgo | 1°58 |
| | Jul 18 | Capricorn | 25°57 |
| | Aug 17 | Aquarius | 24°04 |
| 2028 | Jan 12 | Cancer | 21°33 |
| | Jul 6 | Capricorn | 15°15 |
| | Dec 31 | Cancer | 10°34 |
| 2029 | Jun 26 | Capricorn | 4°49 |
| | Dec 20 | Gemini | 29°18 |
| 2030 | Jun 15 | Sagittarius | 24°38 |
| | Dec 9 | Gemini | 17°47 |

# Appendix III

# Public Figures Cited
## in *Moon Tides* Examples

All of the birthdata used for public figures in this book were verified with *AstroDatabank* software, an extremely valuable reference and research tool that no serious astrologer should be without. Lois Rodden, whose devotion to accuracy in data collection led to the development of *AstroDatabank*, sadly passed away in 2003. She left a tremendous legacy in her collection of data, and her rating system has become so widely recognized within the "astrological community" that virtually all of us know what it means. For those who may be new to this system, a brief explanation: AA means data verified by birth records. A means the data was quoted to Lois by the person or a close relative or associate. B means the data comes from a published biography. C means caution, the source not verified. DD means there are two or more conflicting sources, therefore undependable. X means no time of birth can be verified. XX means that even the date of birth cannot be confirmed for certain. Mark McDonough, who in partnership with Lois, created the technology that has made her valuable research accessible and easy to utilize, designed *AstroDatabank* software. See *Bibliography and Resources* for contact information.

*Moon Tides* report does not absolutely require accurate birth time for most of the astrological information included on it. The natal phase and dates of phase changes will vary little if the time is off. Still, I prefer using accurate data whenever possible, so you will note that most of the people I've used for examples are rated AA or A, with a few Bs. In a very, very few instances I have used unverifiable data for people prominent in the current news, if after checking against published events, their progressed phases seemed to fit well. This does illustrate my point that one can derive quite a lot of information from this report, even if exact birth time is not known. I have not used as examples for sign or house of Moon anyone whose data I could not confirm as accurate. You will note that I have given only birth dates here. It would be an infringement of copyright to cite a list such as this with full birth data derived from *AstroDatabank*. You'll find free full charts for some public figures cited in this book if you check *www.astrodatabank. com*. The home page always has a good list of current newsmakers with accompanying charts. Although I could cite some birth times from several other published sources, I thought it best to be consistent in presentation of this list.

Beyond my choice, for the most part, of using AA or A data, my selection of people for this study is random, with no claim of being anything other than anecdotal research. At first, I just looked through my own mundane chart files, and then through *AstroDatabank's* biographical info section for people who interested me, whose names I thought would be easily recognizable to various potential readers (acknowledging recognition variances of age group and/or interests). Beyond that my criteria of choice was from among those people for whom a good deal of biographical information with dates of occurrence was either given in *AstroDatabank* or could be easily obtained elsewhere, and who would represent a diversity of careers and reasons for renown. Eventually, as I collected people, I would find "holes"—not enough of this phase or that Moon sign or house, or not enough variety in occupation, or I'd think I needed someone that the younger or older generation would think interesting. Then, I'd go back and search again for more interesting people to fill in my gaps. As the book developed, I added a few extra people when they became prominent in the news, such as John Kerry and John Edwards when they became the Democratic candidates for election 2004.

Following is a complete list of the public figures used as examples in this book, with birthday and Rodden rating. Birthdates are given in the common USA format of month-day-year.

It should be noted that in writing the interpretive text and some of the examples I also relied heavily on information derived from *Moon Tides* reports I ran for a large number of relatives, friends, colleagues, students and clients whose data I cannot give, but whose stories heavily influenced my interpretations. Only those individuals whose data is published and clearly filtered in *AstroDatabank* as "public figure" are included on this list.

| | | | | | |
|---|---|---|---|---|---|
| Adler, Margot | 4/16/1946 | AA | Ebertin, Reinhold | 2/16/1901 | A |
| Alcott, Louisa May | 11/29/1832 | AA | Eddy, Mary Baker | 7/16/1821 | B |
| Aldrin, Buzz | 1/20/1930 | AA | Edwards, John | 6/10/1953 | A |
| Ali, Muhammad | 1/17/1942 | AA | Einstein, Albert | 3/4/1879 | AA |
| Allen, Woody | 12/1/1935 | AA | Elizabeth II, Queen | 4/21/1926 | AA |
| Angelou, Maya | 4/4/1928 | AA | Emerson, Charles | 7/26/1923 | A |
| Bakker, Jim | 1/2/1940 | AA | Emerson, Ralph Waldo | 5/25/1803 | AA |
| Bakker, Tammy | 3/7/1942 | AA | Fonda, Jane | 12/21/1937 | AA |
| Ball, Lucille | 8/6/1911 | AA | Freud, Sigmund | 5/6/1856 | AA |
| Barton, Clara | 12/25/1821 | B | Friedan, Betty | 2/4/1921 | AA |
| Besant, Annie | 10/1/1847 | A | Gandhi, Indira | 11/19/1917 | A |
| Black, Shirley Temple | 4/23/1928 | AA | Gandhi, Mohandas | 10/2/1869 | C |
| Blair, Tony | 5/6/1953 | AA | Gates, Bill | 10/28/1955 | B |
| Brando, Marlon | 4/3/1924 | AA | George, Demetra | 7/25/1946 | A |
| Brown, Helen Gurley | 2/18/1922 | AA | Glenn, John | 7/18/1921 | AA |
| Browning, Eliz. Barrett | 3/6/1806 | B | Goethe, Johann Von | 8/28/1749 | B |
| Bush, George H.W. | 6/12/1924 | A | Gore, Al | 3/31/1948 | AA |
| Bush, George W. | 7/6/1946 | AA | Hamill, Dorothy | 7/26/1956 | AA |
| Callas, Maria | 12/2/1923 | A | Hand, Rob | 12/5/1942 | A |
| Chanel, Coco | 8/19/1883 | AA | Hearst, Patty | 2/20/1954 | AA |
| Charles, Prince | 11/14/1948 | A | Hepburn, Katharine | 5/12/1907 | AA |
| Cheney, Dick | 1/30/1941 | AA | Heston, Charlton | 10/4/1923 | AA |
| Cher | 5/20/1946 | AA | Hope, Bob | 5/29/1903 | C |
| Cline, Patsy | 9/8/1932 | AA | Hitler, Adolph | 4/20/1889 | AA |
| Clinton, Bill | 8/19/1946 | A | Hoffa, Jimmy | 2/14/1913 | AA |
| Clinton, Hillary | 10/26/1947 | DD | Hussein, Saddam | 4/28/1937 | XX |
| Connery, Sean | 8/25/1930 | AA | Jackson, Michael | 8/29/1958 | X |
| Crowley, Aleister | 10/12/1875 | B | Jagger, Mick | 7/26/1943 | A |
| Dalai Lama | 7/6/1935 | A | John Paul II | 5/18/1920 | A |
| Davis, Angela | 1/26/1944 | AA | Johnson, Lyndon | 8/271908 | A |
| De Kooning, Willem | 4/24/1904 | AA | Jones, Marc Edmund | 10/1/1888 | A |
| Diana, Princess | 7/1/1961 | A | Jung, Karl Gustav | 7/26/1875 | AA |
| Disney, Walt | 12/5/1901 | A | Kennedy, John F. | 5/29/1917 | A |
| Dobyns, Zipporah | 8/26/1921 | A | Kerry, John | 12/11/1943 | A |
| Doherty, Shannen | 4/12/1971 | AA | Krishnamurti, Jeddu | 5/12/1895 | B |
| Douglas, Kirk | 12/9/1916 | AA | Kubler-Ross, Elizabeth | 7/8/1926 | A |
| Duncan, Isadora | 5/26/1877 | A | Leary, Timothy | 10/22/1920 | AA |
| Eastwood, Clint | 5/31/1930 | AA | Leek, Sybil | 2/22/1917 | A |

| | | | | | |
|---|---|---|---|---|---|
| Lennon, John | 10/9/1940 | A | Reagan, Ronald | 2/6/1911 | AA |
| Liberace | 5/16/1919 | AA | Roosevelt, Eleanor | 10/11/1884 | AA |
| Lincoln, Abraham | 2/12/1809 | B | Roosevelt, Franklin D. | 1/30/1882 | B |
| MacLaine, Shirley | 4/24/1934 | AA | Rudhyar, Dane | 3/23/1895 | A |
| Madonna | 8/16/1958 | AA | Sarandon, Susan | 10/4/1946 | A |
| March, Marion | 2/10/1923 | A | Schweitzer, Albert | 1/14/1875 | AA |
| Marx, Karl | 5/5/1818 | AA | Simpson, O. J. | 7/9/1947 | AA |
| McCain, John | 8/29/1936 | A | Springsteen, Bruce | 9/23/1949 | AA |
| Michelangelo | 3/15/1475 | B | Star, Gloria | 9/6/1948 | AA |
| Michelsen, Neil F. | 5/11/1931 | A | Starr, Ringo | 7/7/1940 | A |
| Monroe, Marilyn | 6/1/1926 | AA | Steinem, Gloria | 3/25/1934 | AA |
| Montessori, Maria | 8/31/1870 | AA | Steiner, Rudolph | 2/25/1861 | AA |
| Nicoholson, Jack | 4/22/1937 | A | Stewart, Martha | 8/3/1941 | AA |
| North, Oliver | 10/7/1943 | AA | Taylor, Elizabeth | 2/27/1932 | B |
| Omarr, Syndney | 8/5/1926 | A | Thatcher, Margaret | 10/13/1925 | A |
| Onassis, Jacqueline K. | 7/28/1929 | A | Travolta, John | 2/18/1954 | AA |
| Ono, Yoko | 2/18/1933 | A | Tyson, Mike | 6/30/1966 | X |
| Pavarotti, Luciano | 10/12/1935 | AA | Van Gogh, Vincent | 3/30/1853 | AA |
| Picasso, Pablo | 10/25/1881 | AA | Washington, George | 2/22/1732 | AA |
| Pottenger, Maritha | 5/21/1952 | A | Weschcke, Carl L. | 9/10/1930 | AA |
| Presley, Elvis | 1/8/1935 | AA | Winfrey, Oprah | 1/29/1954 | A |
| Puccini, Giacomo | 12/22/1858 | AA | Witte, Alfred | 3/2/1878 | A |
| Reagan, Nancy | 7/6/1921 | B | Zeta-Jones, Catherine | 9/25/1969 | A |

# Bibliography and Resources

*American Heritage Dictionary, The*, Fourth Edition, Boston: Houghton Mifflin, 2001.

Bartlett, John, *Bartlett's Familiar Quotations*, 16ᵗʰ Edition, Boston: Little, Brown and Company, 1992.

Bolen, M.D., Jean Shinoda, *Goddesses in Everywoman*, San Francisco, CA: Harper & Row, 1984.

Cain, Kathleen, *Luna Myth & Mystery*, Boulder, CO: Johnson Printing, 1991.

Darion, Joe and Mitch Leigh, "The Impossible Dream" from *Man of la Mancha,* Andrew Scott, Inc. and Helena Music Corp. 1965.

Eisler, Riane, *The Chalice & the Blade*, San Francisco, CA: Harper & Row, 1988.

Farrar, Janet & Stewart, *The Witches' Goddess*, Custer, WA.: Phoenix Publishing, 1987.

Frazer, Sir James George, *The Golden Bough*, New York: Collier Books, 1922.

Gadon, Elinor W., *The Once & Future Goddess*, San Francisco, CA: Harper & Row, 1989.

George, Demetra, *Finding Our Way Through the Dark*, San Diego: ACS Publications, 1994.

George, Demetra, *Mysteries of the Dark Moon*, San Francisco, CA: Harper & Row, 1992.

Gerhardt, Dana, "Moonwatching," *The Mountain Astrologer*, Cedar Ridge, CA., series of nine articles: Oct./Nov. 2001 through Feb./Mar. 2003, issues 99 through 107.

Graves, Robert, *The White Goddess*, New York: Farrar, Straus and Giroux, 1944.

Grimassi, Raven, *Encyclopedia of Wicca & Witchcraft*, St. Paul, MN: Llewellyn Publications, 2000.

Jansky, Robert, *Interpreting the Eclipses*, San Diego, CA: ACS Publications, 1979.

Harvey, Andrew & Anne Baring, *The Divine Feminine*, Berkeley, CA: Conari Press, 1996.

Hines, Welch and Bacon, *Our Latin Heritage*, New York: Harcourt, Brace, Jovanovich, 1966.

McKennitt, Loreena, *The Mask and Mirror*, Quinlan Road, Warner Music, 1994.

Mercer, Johnny and Henry Mancini, *Moon River,* New York: Famous Music Co., 1961

Michelsen, Neil F., with revisions by Rique Pottenger, *The American Ephemeris for the 21st Century*, San Diego: ACS Publications, 1982.

Michelsen, Neil F., *Tables of Planetary Phenomena*, article by Maria Kay Simms, "The Lunar Cycle: An 8-Fold Cycle of Transformation," San Diego: ACS Publications, 1990.

Monoghan, Patricia, *The New Book of Goddesses & Heroines*, St. Paul, MN: Llewellyn Publications, 2001, 1997.

Moore, Marcia and Mark Douglas, *Astrology, the Divine Science*, York Harbor, ME: Arcane Publications, MCMLXXI.

Patterson, Helena, *The Celtic Lunar Zodiac*, Boston, MA: Charles E. Tuttle Co, Inc., 1992.

Poe, Edgar Allan, with notes by Arthur Holson Quinn and Edward O'Neill, *The Complete Tales and Poems of Edgar Allan Poe*, New York: Dorsett Press: 1989.

Pottenger, Maritha, *Easy Astrology Guide*, San Diego, CA: ACS Publications, 1996.

Pottenger,Maritha with Zipporah Dobyns, Ph.D., *Unveiling Your Future*, San Diego: ACS Publications, 1998.

Regula, DeTraci, *The Mysteries of Isis*, St. Paul, MN: Llewellyn Publications, 2001.

Robertson, Marc, *Not a Sign in the Sky but a Living Person*, Tempe, AZ: American Federation of Astrologers, Inc, 1975.

Reif, Jennifer, *Mysteries of Demeter*, York Beach, ME: Samuel Weiser, Inc., 1999.

River, Lindsay and Sally Gillespie, *The Knot of Time*, New York: Harper & Row, 1987.

Rudhyar, Dane, *The Lunation Cycle*, Santa Fe, NM: Aurora Press, 1967.

Schutte, Dan, S.J., *Glory and Praise*, Phoenix, AZ: North American Liturgy Resources, 1982.

Simms, Maria Kay, *Your Magical Child*, San Diego, CA: ACS Publications, 1994.

Simms, Maria Kay, *A Time for Magick*, St. Paul, MN: Llewellyn Publications, 2001.

Simms, Maria Kay, *Future Signs*, San Diego, CA: ACS Publications, 1994.

Simms, Maria Kay, *The Witch's Circle*, St. Paul, MN: Llewellyn Publications, 1996.

Sjoo, Monica & Barbara Mor, *The Great Cosmic Mother*, San Francisco, CA: Harper & Row, 1987.

Star, Gloria, *Astrology: Woman to Woman*, St. Paul, MN: Llewellyn Publications, 1999.

Stone, Merlin, *When God Was A Woman*, San Diego, CA: Harcourt Brace Jovanovich, 1976.

Walker, Barbara, *The Woman's Dictionary of Symbols & Sacred Objects*, San Francisco, CA: Harper & Row, 1988.

Walker, Barbara, *The Woman's Encyclopedia of Myths and Secrets*, San Francisco, CA: Harper & Row, 1983.

Welsh, Lorraine, Ed., with Alphee Lavoie, *Essentials of Intermediate Astrology*, Essay by Maria Kay Simms, "The Eight Lunar Phases," Brewster, MA: National Council for Geocosmic Research, Inc., 1995.

Wood, Juliette, *The Celtic Book of Living and Dying*, San Francisco: Chronical Books, 2000.

**Internet Sources**

Most of the internet material cited in this book stemmed from Google search: www.google.com. Cited by words entered into Search. No guarantee can be given that the cited URLs are still valid.

Fellowship of ISIS *www.fellowshipofisis.com*

Dark Night of the Soul: *www.xs4all.nl/~josvg/cits/lm/stjohn01.html*

Eleanor Roosevelt: *www.pbs.org, www.whitehouse.gov/history/firstladies*

Brighid Kildare: *www.ordbrighideach.org/links.html*

Full Moon associated with volcanic activity: article by Brian Handwerk, "Are Volcanic Eruptions Tied to Lunar Cycle." My husband pointed this out to me while he was exploring *www.news.nationalgeographic.com*

Planetary Hours, daily: *www.geocosmic.org*

Moon column featuring transiting lunar phases with ritual ideas: *www. starcraftsob.com*

**Software Cited Chapter 8:**

*WinHours,* Sundial Software, Windows software for planetary hours and minutes by Arlene A. Kramer, 22410-1 Victory Blvd., Woodland Hills, CA 91367, 818-999-2389.

**Software: Especially Recommended for Beginners in Astrology:**

Pottenger, Rique, *The Electronic Astrologer Reveals Your Horoscope*, text by Maritha Pottenger, San Diego: ACS Publications.

Pottenger, Rique, *The Electronic Astrologer Reveals Your Future*, transit text by Maria Kay Simms, progressed text by Maritha Pottenger and Zipporah Dobyns, Ph.D., San Diego: ACS Publications.

Pottenger, Rique, *The Electronic Astrologer Reveals Your Love Life*, text by Maritha Pottenger, San Diego: ACS Publications.

The above three Windows programs are "electronic books" in that they contain comprehensive help sections on basic astrology, as well as extensive interpretive text from which personalized reports are compiled. Exceptionally easy data entry. Charts are interactive—a mouse click on anything within the chart causes the interpretive text to pop up. Personalized reports can be printed, with flexibility in choice of format. *www.astrocom.com*

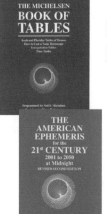

# Index